The Jaguar and the Priest

The Linda Schele Series in Maya and Pre-Columbian Studies

This series was made possible through the generosity of William C. Nowlin, Jr., and Bettye H. Nowlin, the National Endowment for the Humanities, and various individual donors.

The Jaguar and the Priest

An Ethnography of Tzeltal Souls

PEDRO PITARCH

FOREWORD BY ROY WAGNER

University of Texas Press 🢗🢖 *Austin*

Ch'ulel: Una etnografía de las almas tzeltales by Pedro Pitarch Ramón
D.R. © (1996) FONDO DE CULTURA ECONÓMICA
Carretera Picacho-Ajusco 227, C.P. 14738, México, D.F.
Esta edición consta de 1,500 ejemplares
English translation copyright © 2010 by the University of Texas Press
First edition, 2010

Requests for permission to reproduce material from this work should be sent to:

Permissions
University of Texas Press
P.O. Box 7819
Austin, TX 78713-7819
utpress.utexas.edu/index.php/rp-form

Library of Congress Cataloging-in-Publication Data

Pitarch Ramón, Pedro.
  [Ch'ulel. English]
  The jaguar and the priest : an ethnography of Tzeltal souls / Pedro Pitarch. —
1st ed.
    p. cm. — (The Linda Schele series in Maya and pre-Columbian studies)
  Includes bibliographical references and index.
  ISBN 978-0-292-72331-3 (cloth)
  ISBN 978-0-292-73747-1 (paper)
  1. Tzeltal Indians—Rites and ceremonies. 2. Tzeltal Indians—Religion.
3. Shamanism—Mexico—Cancuc. 4. Cancuc (Mexico)—Social life and
customs.
  F1221.T8P5713 2010
  305.897'428072—dc22
                                                              2010023644

To my mother and to the memory of my father

And there is as much difference between us and ourselves as between us and others.
MICHEL DE MONTAIGNE, *ESSAYS*

Contents

Foreword

ROY WAGNER

For most peoples, everything that matters—the character of a person that we often confuse with personality, the anticipatory intelligence that is necessary for all meaningful forms of innovation, the energies that bind us to the people and places we love—is joined together in this word that we call the "soul." It is the soul that gets to decide whether there is a God or not, and generally, like all things in this mirror-reflection universe, this is reciprocated. More than that, for the Tzeltal people of Cancuc, it gets to decide just *how* this happens and *why*. Perhaps these otherwise obscure people of the Mexican highlands have just *remembered* something that the Old World peoples have long forgotten, which is that without the *drama*, the acute holographic *intensity*, that unfolds around every significant lesson, the lesson itself is worthless. This is a book of just such significant lessons and the drama that follows upon them as the thunder encompasses the lightning, without which it would have no voice.

An astonishing number of correspondences exist between Mexican ideas of the soul and the ones found among the peoples of interior New Guinea and Aboriginal Australia. According to Jeffrey Clark, the Wiru people of the Southern Highlands Province of Papua New Guinea speak of the *physical* body of a person as the "picture-soul" of that person. This is an exact figure-ground reversal of the way in which European peoples have traditionally approached the relation between volition and physicality, though it does resemble Plato's "cave" analogy. It inverts the sense and imagery of *being* itself.

But of what is the "picture-soul" itself a picture? The Wiru were ancient enemies and trading partners of the Daribi, with whom I had worked, and Clark intended his study as a comparison with Daribi concepts. One evening in June 2000, I was crossing the airstrip at Karimuri with a group of small Daribi boys. They appeared startled, and then amused, by the long shadows cast across the cleared area by the setting sun. "Wow!" they said. "Souls!" and then they giggled. The next day I approached the village magistrate, a man known for his articulative skills (good *tonal*, Carlos Castaneda would say). "Why is it that you people regard the shadow of a person, or his name, reflection, or picture, as evidence of the soul that animates us?" "Well, Roy," he said, "stand over there in the bright sunlight and stare at your black shadow on the ground, and then look up at the bright blue sky and tell me what you see." I did as it was told, and when I looked up at the sky, I saw the silhouette-like afterimage of my shadow glowing against the blue—like the "luminous body" described by Castaneda. "But this is a well-known optical effect," I protested, "caused by the rods and cones in the eye; how can you pretend it is evidence of the principle that animates us?" "Well," said the magistrate dryly, "it just *animated* you, did it not?"

As Professor Pitarch tells us in his introduction, "An Indian soul is first and foremost an 'other.'" But it is a strange sort of otherness indeed, one that is almost too *familiar* for most people to stand. Elsewhere (Wagner 2001) I have written of "the One you see in the mirror, who steals your act of looking, but only to see *itself*." It borrows your own eyes, but then turns them against you, to see a kind of human imago that could never exist on this earth. Perhaps the magistrate would want to tell both Pedro Pitarch and myself that "it is only because your souls have been wrenched free of the conventional and turned inside out by the trials of fieldwork that you are *allowed* to be anthropologist." A South Angan speaker from Papua New Guinea once told me (in Aix en Provence, France) that "when you look into a pool of water or a mirror, the one you see there is not you, and *it is not human*."

In an excellent poem called "Ballad for Gloom," the American poet Ezra Pound writes:

> For God, our God is a gallant foe
> that playeth behind the veil.
> Whom God deigns not to overthrow
> hath need of triple mail.

But of what is that picture of God itself a picture? Castaneda uses the term *nagual* (a Nahuatl term borrowed from the Toltec; the Mayan equivalent would be *ue*) for what amounts to *the exact opposite of all phenomenal being*, or what we might call "the absurdly innate"—that which is so immanent in existence itself that it will never appear on anyone's register. It is not merely passive but *impassive*, and so completely impassive that it is the root of all *happening*. As the Japanese sage Dogen Zenji put it: "What is happening here and now is obstructed by happening itself; it has sprung free from the brains of happening." The nagual is that part of being that is by definition the whole of being, and only "obstructed," as Dogen would have it, by the futile human habit of dividing things into parts. Its strengths are beyond comparison; it is the *one* thing that has no limitations of any kind. But what of its *weaknesses?* Here too it has us at a disadvantage, and one that seems to have brought about the ruin of Castaneda's Don Juan. As Ian Fleming tells us in *Diamonds Are Forever*, humility is the worst possible form of conceit. Without supreme confidence and pride in its accomplishment, even a small bug will not last long, but nagual is "that part of us that is never born and will never die." It was there watching when it was conceived by your parents, and also when *they* were conceived, and so back to the conception of conception itself:

> Your death was hiding in that jolt of sperm,
> your life is hiding on the day you die—
> the tenure in between without a term;
> before and after, everything is NOW,
> the THEN goes out like starlight in the sky,
> and when you reach its concourse, take a bow.

Like a matador in his suit of lights, *death honors us in our reception of it, just as in its reception of us*. Or like Professor Pitarch's magnificent confrère, the shaman Xun P'in. What we see outlined as the story of his life would appear to many to be an all-too-familiar tragedy, a poor Indian worn to the bone by factional infighting and the almost obscene tedium of everyday domestic life. But to the Lord Hummingbird or to Balam, the Jaguar, it would be the exact opposite of tragedy: the moment of truth, when world-in-the-person and person-in-the-world execute a complete flipover, *the classic shamanic death, known to peoples all over the world*. Of course, Xun P'in is not the only shaman in this book, for its author, the one who brought you the story of the story, belongs to an even more esoteric form of shamanism, one that Don Juan, in *The Power of Silence*, calls the *sorcerer storyteller*, "who attains his whole perfection simply through the telling of stories." For every shamanic death in his text, such a sorcerer dies a thousand times.

That one could have a *lab*, a *species miniature* that resides in the interior of one's being but also manifests on the outside as a living animal, is a form of prescience that would be dismissed in Europe as a superstition at best, but embraced in Aboriginal Australia as evidence that someone had finally gotten the Dreaming (e.g., evolution) right. It is actually the "tip of the iceberg" of something that is very ancient in the human race, more esoteric than shamanism. It is a form of perspectivism that Eduardo Viveiros de Castro and his colleagues have found "all over the Amazon," and that Feld and Schieffelin have described in New Guinea: "When a pig looks at a pig it sees a human being, but when it looks at a human being it sees another pig." This is mute testimony to the basic holography of animate being, which Goethe and Heinrich de Lambert had tried to incorporate into the natural sciences, and which, taken at its full compass, would render the concept of natural selection unnecessary. *Animals exist as parts of the human soul, just as we ourselves exist as part of theirs.*

Julian Pitt-Rivers was one of my teachers, and perhaps the best of my teachers. His comment that for the peoples of Chiapas "the man and his animal are the same person" echoes a comment made to the pioneer ethnographers Baldwin Spencer and Frank J. Gillen by an Aboriginal Australian. They had taken a photograph of the man and shown him the photograph, the like of which he had never seen before, and asked him whether it was anything like him. "Yes," he replied, "that one is just like me, and it is like me in exactly the same way as a kangaroo is like me." The kangaroo, perhaps, was what Professor Pitarch calls "the European within." I, for example, have made many attempts to discover the true identity of my *lab*; various candidates, including grizzly bear, deer, hummingbird, and wolverine, have presented themselves in visions, but without my ability to ascertain which of them was my true *lab*. I strongly suspect that this is because my household is controlled by cats, and cats are very difficult creatures to figure out (e.g., *they* figure *you* out before you even get the chance). The *lab*, of course, *cannot* be anything that has you figured out, precisely because it has you already figured *in*. I am still looking for what my true *lab* might be.

No one ever said it was easy to be a *lab*, or a shaman, or an Indian, or a first-rate ethnographer like Pedro Pitarch. The easy ones are all dead, and first-rate ethnographers have become exceedingly rare in what we like to call our modern world. Someday it will be discovered that real ethnography was the only thing anthropology had to offer, but by that time, all our books will be dust.

"Closely related to the loss of sense (sleep or drunkenness) is the loss of bodily uprightness, a factor distinctive enough to merit consideration as the second axis around which the exposure of the content of the heart occurs." *Do not tell this to Lord Hummingbird;* he already knows. He is the god of equilibrium, and therefore also of upright posture (the distinctive mark and flight pattern of the human race), and therefore of the wheel principle that the Mayans never invented, but only because *it* had invented *them.* Do not take my word for this; instead take a deep draught of the decocted juice of dried morning-glory seeds (the "Mayan fix"), as I did on July 7, 1995. Then *he* will come and tell you (as he did me) that he has his origin in the solar eclipse, the rarest and most beautiful of all phenomena on the face of this earth. (I swear I do not know where these lines are coming from, even at the moment of this writing; sometimes even staid academics go into possession trances, and this is an example of what Don Juan calls "stopping the world.") Besides that, watch your back; this is the most ruthless warrior-god in the annals of human history, lord of the electron, the vortex, the tornado, and the hydrogen bomb.

"In this way the sun first made its appearance, and that is also the origin of the animals, or perhaps the *lab* animals." Compare this with the opening lines of the *Tao Te Ching*: "The *named* is the mother of the myriad creatures," and you will get a good idea of what Don Juan means by "silent knowledge, knowledge without words." We do not get to know what the animals really are, except for the names we give them and the stories we tell about them (or they about us), and we do not know what people really are either, for all of the stories they tell about themselves. Similarities are easy; our work on this earth is not really one of finding resemblances or relations between things, but of finding out how to *differentiate* them from one another, and from ourselves, and from our very knowing of this fact. We need to *quarantine* ourselves from our words. In a book called *Coyote Anthropology* (another of my foiled attempts to find out who my *lab* really is), I have written that the oldest story on record goes like this: "Back in the beginning, *stories* sat around the campfire telling *people* to one another." Character for character, that is, how could you or I ever tell the difference, and why should we even bother to try?

Ritual! Ritual is what a riddle would be like if the words that make it up solved the human being, rather than the human being solving the riddle. "One characteristic shared by all these public ceremonies is more intriguing: they are bereft of any meaning." So, one might add, is the public and domestic life of the shaman Xun P'in. Elsewhere I have called this effect *obviation*, and it is the natural destiny of all symbolic representations. Think of it, if you will, as the epistemological consequence of the discovery of the zero. During the great Pueblo Revolt in Nuevo Mexico in 1680, the rebel warriors surrounded the surviving settlers, who had taken refuge in the Governor's Palace in Santa Fe, and chanted to them the Roman Catholic Mass, in *Latin! Obviation* comes from the Latin phrase *ob via*, and its dictionary definition is "to anticipate and dispose of."

The mirror in the saints. I was once told by the daughter of a Kali worshipper from Calcutta, India, that the priests there use a mirror to demonstrate the perceptual powers of the goddess, as though to point out the immanent veracity of figure-ground reversal, the single principle that controls our perception (or anything) to such a degree that were one able to master it, take control of it for oneself, one would attain all the powers of the goddess. (This is probably Hummingbird's secret as well, since the solar eclipse is the actual figure-ground reversal of the Mayan *k'in*, or diurnal sun cycle.) Tempting as that prospect may be, however, it is not what the priests are after; they are after something called the *darsan*, or "sight of the goddess," a kind of holographic bivisual in which the worshipper and the goddess each play the role of "the One in the mirror who steals your act of looking but only to see itself" with respect to the other. Neither, of course, sees an image that they will ever see unaided, directly with their own eyes, for, as Gregory Bateson pointed out, what you are looking at in the mirror is the *back* of an image—the right and left sides of your body reversed—so that you two are not twins at all, but *anti-twins.*

This is a technique described by Castaneda in *The Power of Silence* (1987), whereby a *bruja* in Mexico City used the shamanic representation of an ancient Aztec warrior to bring the concerted *intent* of her audience (like a sleight-of-hand magician) to a sharp focus and manipulate it to effect a cure (what actually happened, said Don Juan, is indescribable in empirical "first-attention" terms). Here, as in India, the "mirror in the saint" (or other divine impersonation) is a figure-ground reversal fulcrum, using the curer's mediation to merge the "autoimmune systems" of a large group of people and concentrate them on the perceived disorders of the patient.

"A person is a fold, or an imprint, of the outside. On being born, the future human being folds in on him- or herself, capturing fragments of the Other World and the presolar past—that is, souls. . . ." The embryo is the "mirror in the person" or, in Castaneda's terms, the "luminous being" of the individual, one for which the "passage of time" or the narrative sequence of a text or an explanation represents a kind of hypnotic trance state according to which we are obliged to live out our lives in the shape of a secular or scientific reality. The soul is the *real*, or self-completing, aspect of the person—the true measure of their worth. Hence we come to the most wonderful of all Pitarch's sentences: "The fold, as an internalized part of the outside, also drags history into the person." Here we touch upon "personal history" and *memory*, and the exercise of purposive *recapitulation* (reflecting the internal mirror as it reflects upon itself) that plays as definitive a role in the Buddhism of the Far East as it does in the "warriors of the third attention" movement described by Castaneda. Think of the embryo as a tiny penitent within the recapitulation chamber of the living body, turning the tarnished reflection of its worldly experiences into a pure light of the void. World-in-the-person and person-in-the-world become one and the same thing.

This book gives new meaning to Oswald Spengler's observation that the ancient cultures of Mexico, like our own with its quantum physics and fractal mathematics, were among the most esoteric on this earth. Like moths to the flames, we do not merely speculate upon or experiment with *that which we pretend not to understand*, but *absolutely fall in love with it*. With the skill and daring of a Mayan mirror-shaman, Pedro Pitarch has brought our own experiences to witness within us—through our own experiences of his—the self-perfection of the Tzeltal soul in a transformation that is literally "out of this world." *You* are now as *they*.

Preface

This book is an ethnography of Cancuc, a Tzeltal-language indigenous village situated in the mountainous region of the Chiapas highlands in southern Mexico. It focuses on the Tzeltal concept of the person from the perspective of indigenous ideas about souls. Seen from this approach, the topic may seem too limited in scope and possibly somewhat banal. But, as I will attempt to show in these pages, souls and, in a more general way, the category of the person—as elaborated in shamanism, illness, dreams, the exploration of personal character, etc.—represent one of the most strategic avenues leading to an understanding of Tzeltal ideas about society and history.

If this is so, it is because the Tzeltal culture itself insists on it. In indigenous terms, discourse on the self provides a privileged language through which to express and handle social, political, and religious relationships, especially issues related to conflict and social change. If modern Western civilization grants areas of knowledge such as political economics, history, sociology, and even anthropology—disciplines we would consider objectivist—the status of core values, indigenous culture, in contrast, grants this condition to knowledge about what a human being is and what each human being is like. Those who have worked in this ethnographic region will be well aware that each time one returns and asks one's Indian friends what has happened during one's absence, what follows is a lengthy list of illnesses that both the speaker and others have suffered, right down to the last detail. But it is clear that from the Indian perspective, what could be interpreted as an explanation of a medical nature is also considered to be a social and political profile.

Therefore, a Tzeltal anthropology, taking the word in its etymological sense, rapidly transcends the domain of representation of the person to penetrate other aspects of the culture. In this study, the description and interpretation of souls make up a common thread for exploring both the Indian concept of self and the role this plays in their conception of culture and community, their notions of identity and alterity, and their interpretation of interethnic relations and types of historical memory.

This book is a revised version of my book *Ch'ulel: Una etnografía de las almas tzeltales*, published in Mexico in 1996. A large proportion of the ethnographic data, together with an initial attempt at interpretation, was presented as a doctoral thesis in 1993 at the State University of New York in Albany.

Only after the original publication of the book did I become aware of the contributions made by anthropologists working in other parts of the world, particularly Melanesia and Amazonia—anthropologists whose studies problematized, from an ethnographic viewpoint, the category of the person and its implications for understanding native culture. Particularly relevant to the argument of this book is the theory of Roy Wagner (1981) on the inversion, with respect to Western rationalism, of the place assigned to the innate and the artificial in tribal and peasant cultures. However, I have to admit that the current version of the book barely integrates or seriously addresses these contributions, which would have given it a more precise language, and also, in all likelihood, clearer concepts. At least I am able to find some consolation in the idea that a very conceptually defined language carries with it the risk of excessive inflexibility, and in this sense—to make a virtue out of necessity—I hope that the imprecision that to a certain extent characterizes the text prevents it from congealing, so to speak, thereby thwarting alternative interpretations of the data it contains.

The ethnographic data the book is based on are the result of field research carried out between 1989 and 1994, including a period of continuous residence between August 1989 and December 1990, and several subsequent shorter stays. I have carried on working in Chiapas ever since, often on topics related to the questions raised in this book. For the last eight years, for example, I have been working on an extensive corpus of healing chants, which have required me to go into questions of shamanism, cosmology, and the idea of self in greater depth. Nevertheless, at the risk of appearing presumptuous, I feel I should mention that the book has worked well as a basis for my later work, and that, even after all this time, I still agree with the fundamental elements regarding both the ethnographic material presented and the interpretation proposed. Rather than a need for rectification, what I am now aware of is that certain topics are either absent altogether or were not sufficiently elaborated or subtle enough. Without doubt, the main source of neglect in this respect has been the scant attention paid to the description and discussion of the body. It is only with time that I have come to realize the enormous complexity of Tzeltal ideas about the human body—about what a body actually is—to the point where, in a recent article, I postulated that the Indians do not distinguish one body but two (Pitarch 2009). I also failed to develop the relationship between body and language: the role of language in triggering illnesses and its relationship with problems of corporality, orality, and the written word (Pitarch 2000). Thirdly, the book does not explore the very close relationship between the conversion of Indians to evangelical groups or Catholicism—or political organizations—and their preoccupation with the proper formation and control of the body, in contrast with their disinterest in doctrinal issues and salvation of the soul (Pitarch 2004). With respect to the souls, despite the accumulation of new data (I must confess I am still curious and amazed by what I continue to learn), the layout of the book still seems satisfactory to me.

I have received help from a great many people, both during my fieldwork in Chiapas and in the preparation and editing of this book. Mentioning each one by name would be impossible, but I wish to mention at least some of the teachers, colleagues, and friends who, through conversations, critiques, suggestions, and other forms of assistance, made an active contribution to the development of this work. My heartfelt gratitude and affection go to the following: in Spain, to Manuel Gutiérrez Estévez, whose scholarly input has been invaluable throughout the writing of the book, and also to Julián López García and Francisco Ferrandiz; in the United States, to Gary Gossen, Robert Carmack, Lyle Campbell, Bill Hanks, John S. Justeson, Jorge Klor de Alva, June Nash, and Evon Vogt; in Mexico, to Dolores Aramoni, María Elena Fernández Galán, Mario H. Ruz, Juan Pedro Viqueira, and Jan de Vos. I owe a great debt of gratitude to Gary Gossen for his efforts and endless patience over the two years he dedicated to teaching me the Tzotzil language; without this background, it would have been extremely difficult to conduct fieldwork with the Tzeltal. Since the beginning of my fieldwork in Chiapas, I have been affiliated with the Instituto de Estudios Indígenas at the Autonomous University of Chiapas, where the researchers have been a continuous source of support. Modifications to the current English version have benefited from ideas put forward by Jérôme Baschet, Stanley Brandes, Roger Magazine, Jan Rus, David Stoll, Alexandre

Surrallés, and Eduardo Viveiros de Castro. I am extremely grateful to Ted Fischer and Christine Eber, who read through the entire English manuscript and offered excellent suggestions for improvement. Also, I take this opportunity to thank Theresa May of the University of Texas Press for her extraordinarily long and patient support, and Nancy Warrington for her editorial wisdom.

That Professor Roy Wagner—whose intellectual project is among the most important and original in anthropology, and whose relevance for the development of Mesoamerican ethnography seems to me now indubitable—agreed to write the foreword to the English version of this book is for me an honor beyond anything I can acknowledge.

This book is the fruit of my relationship with some dear friends in Cancuc. I am deeply grateful to Esteban Santis (mamal Xun P'in), who died in 1997; Marian Santis Terát (mamal Tukut); María Ruiz Pérez (me'el Xmal Oxom), who died in 2002; Sebastián Sánchez (mamal Sebastian K'aal); Lorenzo Pérez López (mamal Lorentso Lol); Juan Domínguez (mamal Xun Lul), who died in 2001; Mario Sánchez; Antonia Hernández (me'el Antonia Ts'iib); Miguel Gómez Gómez; and Diego Domínguez (mamal Tyak Wol). During his teachings, Xun P'in used to ask me, jokingly, although with an element of seriousness, when his explanations to me would "stay in a book." Well, here it is, to the best of my ability; it is because of you.

December 2008

The Jaguar and the Priest

CHAPTER 1

Introduction

What Are the Souls?

The Tzeltal people of Chiapas, Mexico, claim that human beings hold a heterogeneous combination of souls in the heart, from a minimum of four to a maximum of sixteen. One of these souls, known as *ch'ulel*, takes the form of a human body; it resides in the heart and, as a double, also lives inside a mountain where, together with the rest of the souls from the same lineage, it forms a society parallel to that of humans. In contrast, other souls called *lab* have a nonhuman form. They may be animals of any species, such as hummingbirds, butterflies, jaguars, rodents, or creatures of the river, or atmospheric phenomena like lightning bolts, winds, or rainbows; others are spirits of European appearance, such as Catholic priests, Castilian scribes, schoolteachers, or evangelical musicians. Human beings may have up to thirteen of these beings.

Nevertheless, although in appearance these souls embody beings that for the most part may be found in the ordinary natural world, in reality they are other beings; they are not of this world but come from the "other side." Some come from heaven and enter the embryo at the moment of conception; others are transmitted to the fetus by a relative from the generation of the grandparents at the time of their death—in other words, they come from death. This "other side" represents an existence that is different from that of our ordinary world. We could call this state "sacred," as understood to mean that which is "the other." In the Tzeltal language, this state is known as *ch'ul* or *ch'ulel*, the same words that are used to designate the souls, a state that is the opposite of the *jamalal* state, the everyday plane of existence. The Tzeltal cosmos can be divided into these two realms. However, the difference between one and the other is not so much physical or geographical but ontological.

The *jamalal*, or ordinary state, is fundamentally the world of the sun. Gary Gossen (1974) demonstrates at length how, from the Indian perspective, the present-day world is a product of the appearance of the sun. Its heat and light gave rise to the coordinates of time and space, and with these the fundamental discriminations governing society. In this solar world, living things and objects formed from solid opaque matter have a stable identity regardless of circumstances. By contrast, beings and things are permanently unstable in the sacred *ch'ul* state, where boundaries and categories are not clearly distinguished, and where anything is liable to change into something else. It is not so much that the categories that bestow order on the ordinary world become muddled here as that identities fluctuate and beings can either be themselves or their opposites.

The state of *ch'ul* is equivalent to what the Barasana people of the Vaupés rainforest in Amazonian Colombia call the *He*. According to the excellent synthesis by Stephen Hugh-Jones (1979), *He*, in its broad sense, refers to a state of being that predates present-day society but continues to exist as another dimension of everyday life. In the beginning, everything was *He*, and the human-animal characters that appear in myths are prehuman beings in which the present humans have been transformed. Life existed in an undifferentiated state of *He* in the form of a primordial sun, located out of this world or the "cosmic house." *He* people and the state of *He* are situated in a distant past, but at the same time they form part of an unchangeable present that exists as another reality parallel to this world. The Barasana enter into controlled contact with the *He* state through ritual, but they also experience it during dreams, illness, childbirth, and the death of others.

Returning to the Tzeltal of Chiapas, what is essential, nonetheless, is that this sacred state is found not only "outside" but also *inside* every human being in the shape of what are conventionally known as "souls." Souls are no more than fragments of the sacred state encapsulated in the body. This circumstance of the sacred being contained within the body—in the heart—can be described by the figure of the fold. While the fetus remains in the maternal womb—in a situation of transition between the sacred and ordinary states—its body is turned inside out on itself: what will be inside it after birth—the souls—are still "outside," in contact with the placenta. At the moment of birth, the body folds in on itself to capture inside it the souls that will form part of that person for the rest of his or her individual life, until death—the moment of unfolding—when, with the end of the body, these fragments are restored to the sacred state.[1]

As a consequence of this folding, we human beings carry the other world within us. But this other world is also an "other" world. This is the starting point of the argument of this book: an Indian soul is first and foremost an "other." The souls of the Tzeltal are made up of beings that personify the antithesis of their native selves. Instead of expressing cultural identity and continuity with their own past, souls represent, in their maximum expression, that which is alien: not a pole of identity but of alterity.

At this point, my interpretation differs fundamentally from the common perspective of Mesoamerican anthropology, where the description of souls has tended to be formulated in the language of collective identity and personal socialization. In this view, the soul represents the core of social morality. The quintessence of Indianness would be deposited in the soul.[2] The key issue, however, is that in the indigenous anthropology, the positions held by body and soul differ from those of the European. In the former, the body is thought of as belonging to the realm of the "cultural," of what human beings can and should morally do, and thus to be fabricated through human intervention, while the soul belongs to the realm of the "sacred," and comes to this world as something already given.

In *The Invention of Culture* (1981), Roy Wagner has shown how most non-Western cultures (par excellence, tribal peoples and peasants) distribute the content of what is perceived as "innate" and what is perceived as the realm of human responsibility ("the artificial") in a way that is essentially the reverse of the Western rationalist tradition. If for "us," *convention* ("the rules, laws, traditions, and other conventional regularities of society" [Wagner 1978, 27]) pertains to the artificial domain of the universe, for "them," in this case Mesoamerican Indians, convention is considered to be what is innate and belonging to the immanent principles of the universe. And conversely, *invention*, which for us pertains to the innate, for them is part of the artificial dimension. In other words, that which is perceived as innate and that which is considered artificial switch positions. Thus, the body becomes the variable element of existence, the responsibility of human action, while the soul or *spiritual* principle becomes the invariable element, that which is not susceptible to being substantially modified by human action—the innate, and thus "given."

Eduardo Viveiros de Castro (1998) deals with the question of the naturalization of culture and the culturalization of nature in a particularly lucid contribution to the field of Amerindian studies. If the Europeans, observes Viveiros de Castro, have a multiculturalist cosmology based on the concept of the unity of nature and the plurality of cultures, the Amerindians, in contrast, have "multinaturalist" cosmologies based on the idea of spiritual unity and bodily diversity. The first "postulates a physical continuity and a metaphysical discontinuity" between humans and all other living beings: the body integrates natural beings into one category; the soul or the spirit (or the mind) is what differentiates us from other living beings. On the other hand, Amerindian cosmology "postulates a metaphysical continuity and a physical continuity between the beings of the cosmos. . . . The spirit or soul integrates while the body differentiates" (1998, 479). As a consequence, in Indian terms, the body has to be fabricated because, contrary to European common sense, it is not conceived as something innate or inherited biologically but as a social object belonging to the domain of invention and the artificial.

In short, if we *are* the body and *do* the soul, indigenous peoples *are* the soul and *do* the body. As Wagner (1981, 98) remarks: "Whereas error and excess are expectable tendencies of an individual self, to be 'corrected' by discipline and education, the soul, as a comparatively 'passive' quality of discernment, can only be 'lost.' And when the soul is lost, the only recourse is to *restore* it, to 'find' it, rather in the way that a perspective or insight is 'found,' and not to constrain or educate it. A soul is not disciplined." In effect, Tzeltal souls are not susceptible to transformation or domestication; they are a requirement for the process of personal socialization, but they themselves cannot be instructed in cultural conventions. In fact, as we shall see, this idea is actually expressed by the Tzeltal in one of the names they give to the group of souls: *jtaleltik*. Formed from the verb *tal*, meaning "to come," its literal meaning is "what is already given to us," that is, the part of us that, unlike the body, is inherited.

Mesoamerican ethnography has nevertheless tended to place the soul in a position similar to the one it occupies in Christian anthropology. From the Christian point of view, the aspect in a person that must be molded and disciplined in order to attain an appropriately moral condition is the soul, which is where ethical substance resides. The "path to perfection" is of the soul, and although the body doubtless intervenes, it does so only to the extent that it enhances or hinders what is par excellence the Christian telos: salvation of the soul. Moreover, in the Christian view, the soul represents the essence of individual identity; the flesh will disappear after death, but the "self" will remain in a vertiginous vision, whether it be hell or everlasting glory.

In Indian terms, however, morality is in the body, and to the extent that we may speak of a main personal identity, this is the body; in normal conditions, the "I" is the body. Perhaps because of its volatile nature and because it is placed within the human body, the Indian soul has tended to be defined in Mesoamerican studies as an "essence" or a "co-essence" to the extent that it is shared with other beings. But it is not difficult to slot the Christian idea into this first sense, the idea of the soul as the essence of the self, defined as what is permanent and necessary in the person, the principle of identity, that is, essence as opposed to appearance (Gutiérrez Estévez 2002). From the Indian viewpoint, however, appearance is the locus of personal identity and morality. One is what one shows to others. The birth of the body is what initiates the process of differentiation, that is, humanization and, ultimately, Indianization. The body gradually takes its shape through nurture and the development of bodily *gestus*. If the Christian moral imperative is cultivation of the soul, then the indigenous imperative is cultivation of the body.

The Self as European

The internal distinction to the person between the artificial and the innate, between body and soul, translates into a self/other polarity. The indigenous self is permanently subject to this complementary dialectic, which, to take Paul Ricoeur's (1990) formula, may be expressed as the tension between *the self as oneself* and *the self as "other."* This internal dialectic has two major implications for the way the Tzeltal think of the person, which represent the main aspects of the argument of this book.

In the first place, if, as I have suggested, an Indian soul is an "other," what sort of "other" is it? Basically, it is that of a European. It is true that souls form a heterogeneous collection of beings, like animals of all species and atmospheric and other phenomena. We should focus, however, on the fact that in reality we are not dealing with these beings as such, but with their "other" sacred side. A soul that is a jaguar is not an ordinary jaguar but the *ch'ul* version of this animal, its reverse. And it is precisely this other side of existence that is characterized by having a European culture. To the extent that they are found in the realm of the sacred, these animals that are Indian souls form collectivities with

European characteristics in which members behave like Europeans—in a similar vein to what happens to the Indians when they show their "other side" (for example, when they get drunk) and adopt European or Mexican attitudes. There are cases of certain souls, such as those of Catholic priests or schoolteachers, for which European identity is very evident; they are European figures both in a physical and qualitative sense. However, as we shall see, this happens with both the ant and the jaguar, lightning bolts and rainbows, sheep and mermaids.

In other words, Indian/European polarity is the privileged figure of difference. Animals, spirits, the dead, and other forms of "otherness" that make up the array of Indian souls are subsumed in a more fundamental plane of difference related to interethnic relations. What is more, the distinction between body and souls reproduces the contrast between the Indian and the European: if the body, which is outermost, public, and ordinary, is culturally Amerindian, the hearts (and souls), which are its antithesis, are distinguished by their European qualities.

At this point, I should specify that by "European" I am translating the Tzeltal term *kaxlan*. In all probability, it is a loan word from the Nahuatl *castilian* (Castilian), the term by which the Nahua named the Spaniards in the sixteenth century. Nowadays, both in Tzeltal and in other Mayan languages, *kaxlan* has a wide semantic range that describes the Spanish-speaking population in the Indian regions and, in more general terms, Mexicans, Guatemalans, and people of European origin, as well as products considered to be exotic, such as plants, livestock, and objects of urban or industrial origin. It also means "strength" as understood by brute force or uncontrolled sentiments. Thus, *kaxlan* may be summarized in the abstract as "stranger" or "non-Indian." The stranger is the European, and the European is, par excellence, the "other."[3]

Returning to our argument, the second implication of this dialectic within the person is that if the Indians have the European inside them, they also contain the history of their relationship with Europeans. The fragments of the sacred state that, as a consequence of the folding of birth, are internalized in the heart, not only have a European character but also reproduce the Indian colonial past. As we shall see, included among Indian souls are Catholic priests, scribes of the Crown of Castile, schoolteachers, Mexican cattle ranchers, metallic instruments, goats, sheep, and chickens, as well as other beings pertaining to the Old World. The Indian heart contains, all in the form of souls, the history of the relationship between Indians and Europeans from the beginning of the Spanish Conquest to the present. In reality, we could imagine

Tzeltal souls not so much as "beings" in themselves but as events, experiences, institutional processes, financial practices, categorical definitions of reality. They are rather like a *representation* of the power relations of European origin to which the indigenous people were once subjected—relations that, in the form of ghosts now, give no peace to Indian bodies.

The Tzeltal carry their *history* inside them, and this is surely at its most evident in the Indian experience of illness. To a large extent, illness is a consequence of the European past, and shamanic treatment of the same essentially consists of working with history. In the shamanic songs of healing rituals, the European world is omnipresent. The spirits that inflict illness or steal one of the souls are also Indian souls: Dominican friars singing morbid liturgical songs, Jesuits uttering lethal sermons, the king's scribes noting down the names of their Indian victims, and so on. It is not just the diseases that are closely associated with the European past and culture, but the shaman, too, as well as his medicinal substances and supernatural helpers. Each time an Indian patient is subjected to a shamanic healing ritual, he actively gets involved in an exercise in historical memory.

This quality, whereby souls are able to function as social memory internalized in the self, seems to me to be a good example of the Indian inclination to express in the language of the body and the person those narratives that, like history, have an external character, so to speak, in the Western tradition. From this point of view, an ethnography of Tzeltal souls should also be a study on native *historicity*.

It is well known that this field has attracted much attention over the last few decades, partly as a result of the development of "postcolonial studies." In these, there has been an attempt to both redefine the idea of writing and at the same time blur the frontiers between this and the oral tradition, giving priority to the study of nonwritten forms of social memory in an effort to counteract the conventional perspective that was obscuring the very essence of Indian history. In general terms, this has focused on what we might call the relatively "objective" aspects of history—objective in the sense that they are outside the person: oral narrative, public ritual, sacred geography, and so on. However, consideration of the past as subjectivization, as the past incorporated in the self (as what is properly "memory"), is an avenue that has not yet been fully explored.[4]

It is very likely that this subjectivization of the past is the most characteristic indigenous way of recording and examining history, that is, the past and present of *their* relationship with the European world. Viveiros de Castro (2002b) observes that if Western modernity favors an objectivist type of epistemology, in which knowing is the equivalent of objectivizing (or de-subjectivizing), then the ideal in Amerindian knowledge, especially if this is shamanistic, consists of exactly the opposite. Knowing is based on subjectivizing, converting a "something" into a "somebody," because this is what makes it possible to adopt the point of view of that which has to be known. This is precisely what Tzeltal memory consists of: *personifying* the history of relations with the European world. If the forces of colonial and contemporary society in Chiapas are to be comprehended and handled, they must first be subjectivized into a "somebody" from whom a point of view can be adopted. Those "somebodies" are the souls.

The book is divided into nine chapters, including this introduction and a conclusion. Chapter 2 is a description of the Tzeltal soul entities and forms the basis of the book. It is predominantly ethnographic in character, and in it I attempt to keep my interpretations to a minimum. Although I rarely cite individual names and only occasionally transcribe comments from conversations, in numerous instances in this chapter I have endeavored to reflect the concrete way things about the souls are said.

Chapter 3 is in some ways an extension of the preceding one, although with a distinct emphasis. My interest here is in the locations, circumstances, and favorable contexts in which knowledge of souls is developed, including the domestic sphere, interpretation of dreams, the subject of gossip, and the scrutiny of personal details in which signs of a specific soul's presence are sought according to how they manifest in the body and the person's character. (The other major area where knowledge of souls is elaborated upon—shamanic rituals and healing chants—is addressed in Chapter 8.)

The subsequent chapters are, generally speaking, of a more interpretative character. Chapter 4 explores the distinction between the body as the indigenous pole of the person and the soul as the pole of European culture, an antithesis that finds particularly strong expression in the dual notion of face and heart. Among other aspects, it deals with how the *ch'iibal*, the mountain of souls, is represented as a modern Mexican or European city where the Indians live a bourgeois lifestyle, and how the autonomy of the souls associated with the loss of bodily control—with drunkenness, for example—leads to the adoption of European ways of behavior.

Chapter 5 aims to show how the field of beliefs that revolves around souls constitutes a broad means of recording and passing on the historical experience associated with European domination. In it, I attempt to make visible the connections between certain types of souls and the history of relations between Indians and Europeans in the Chiapas highlands, and to highlight the possible reasons why set events, institutions, and forces have become incarnate in the soul repertoire of the Tzeltal.

Chapter 6 is largely concerned with narrative and public festivals in Cancuc. Here I show that, on the one hand, oral narrative is somewhat underdeveloped, and on the other hand, public ritual, although very elaborate, holds little significance for the Tzeltal. This circumstance is linked to the native attitude of silence with regard to two areas (narrative and public ritual) historically considered essential by the colonial Spanish authorities in their policy of Christianization.

Chapter 7 examines the nature of the saints found inside the church in Cancuc. What kind of beings are they? My argument is that the saints, like any other spirit that appears in the ordinary world, are only partially folded, in such a way that they show, again partially, what for human beings is hidden in the heart—in other words, souls. Examining the saints therefore makes it possible to recognize souls (and, more generally, the sacred) in the way they go around in the ordinary state.

Historical awareness and experience of illness are intimately connected spheres in Tzeltal. In some respects, shamanic treatment of illness produces reasoning power about history: long-term memory—that which exceeds the individual memory of those who were witnesses to events, and that which fundamentally concerns the historical relations between natives and Europeans—is stored and functions in the healing chants that the shamans recite in the presence of patients during therapeutic rituals. Chapter 8 presents one of these healing texts, preceded by a description of the ceremony in which it was delivered, and followed by a commentary on the text. My intention here is that the reading of a healing text will shed light on the apparent correlation between illness, experience of alterity, and historical awareness.

Conversations about Souls

At the outset of my research, the issue of "souls" was not among my main concerns. I had decided to study indigenous religion, so in those early stages I devoted all my attention to public ceremonies and formal narratives. But after the first months of fieldwork, as I listened to conversations about sundry events, details, and fragments regarding various incidents that seemed to have some bearing on views of the soul, I began to develop a true curiosity about these, which in subsequent months grew into an obsession.

I began living in Cancuc one December, which marks the beginning of the period in the annual cycle in which the majority of public ritual activity in the principal hamlets is concentrated. Between preparations and performances from then until May, the most important public festivals in the ceremonial calendar—Christmas, Carnival, Easter, San Juan (the patron saint of Cancuc)—take place. Meanwhile, markets become the bustling stage for all kinds of exchanges that bring together the inhabitants of the different hamlets belonging to the *municipio*. Afterward, from April to August, time is mainly filled with agricultural tasks requiring the most effort: first, the slash and burn of any vegetation in the fields, sowing before the arrival of the annual rains in May, then two or three sessions of weeding together with other necessary tasks until the end of August, when the corn is ready for harvest in the valley's temperate strips of land. Around the month of September, there is a dramatic reduction in the workload, and public rituals in the center of town come to a virtual standstill. The days become shorter as the brief, heavy downpours of summer storms give way to more regular and persistent rainfall; rivers and streams swell in volume, and paths turn into mud-filled channels. Families withdraw into their homes, sprinkled over the hilly landscape, and turn inward to tasks of home maintenance. It is also the time when relatives from other villages take advantage of the lull in activity to visit for a few days.

It is during this period of domestic introversion, from September to December, that the Tzeltal pay most attention to their souls. The most prestigious shamans accumulate the most work at this time. They are the specialists who deal with the three main categories of medical work: *pik'abal*, diagnostician; *poxtaywanej*, one learned in medicines; and *ch'abajom*, recoverer of souls. In August, I began to work as an informal apprentice to one of these specialists, Xun P'in. Once I could understand the Tzeltal language and speak it to an acceptable degree, I was able to attend the healing ceremonies, record the songs, make some attempt to comprehend the distinctions made in the course of diagnoses, and recognize both what part of the body was damaged and the source of the affliction. What I was learning in the healing sessions, along with other details I heard in other contexts, rapidly began to reveal to me a dense cultural domain.

But perhaps there was a deeper reason for the gradual shift in my ethnographic focus. I was initially interested in public ceremonies and formal narrative. However, from the very start, I also intended to lend an ear to the opinions of the people about their own cultural practices, instead of striving to work out a personal interpretation or formalization of them. Little by little, I became increasingly convinced that neither public ceremonies nor narrative—in other words, public ritual and mythology—were activities that the Tzeltal had much to say about; nor, I believe, do these activities have in themselves much to tell us about the Tzeltal.

As for the former, the fiestas or religious festivals, it is easy to obtain detailed descriptions of them, above all from people who have participated in them as performers, as well as from certain ritual specialists who monitor the performances. In fact, I ended up with several notebooks and many cassettes recording the most meticulous descriptions of movements, episodes, ritual objects, offices, and so forth, dictated to me by specialists. As a matter of fact, for reasons that will later become clearer, the Tzeltal take it for granted that the *kaxlanetik*, the "Castilians," have an intrinsic interest in these fiestas. But as ethnographers who have worked among the communities of the region know, the fiestas do not inspire any interpretation or exegesis of their meaning on the part of the Indian participants. The answer to many of my questions about the meaning of ceremonies was almost always of the same tenor: *ja' yuun te jijch jajchem te nail me'el mamaletike*, "because that is how the first mothers-fathers began doing it," or more succinctly, *ma jna'tik, melel ja te kostúmbre*, "we don't know, it's the custom." We shall have to return later to that last word, which, although it is obviously a loan word from Spanish (*costumbre*) suggesting the notion of "custom" or "tradition," is used to convey an association with the Castilian world.

With respect to conventional types of narrative (tales, myths, legends, etc.), the opposite occurs, but the consequences are similar. Generally speaking, few tales are known. From time to time, a young person would accompany me on a visit to some elderly person who might live in some secluded place and perhaps know "stories" (because of his age, as well as his isolation, for story-telling, tale-telling, entails little social prestige). On these occasions, I always had to bring a gift, most often in the form of liquor, because that is the only way "the embarrassment of telling stories is lost." Yet, however interesting the interviews might be from other points of view, it was fairly common for us to leave without having heard a single tale. The Tzeltal also have the overall impression that they know few narratives. In virtually all cases, they give a similar reason: "we are only concerned with day-to-day activities, with work, with survival; furthermore, unlike the 'Castilians,' we have no writing system and have been unable to record anything that happened in the past."

Instead, the replies to many of my queries referred vaguely but insistently to soul elements and the world surrounding them: medical knowledge, curing rituals, dream interpretation, exploration of personal character, testing for physical peculiarities, and other cultural techniques that will make their appearance in what follows. Often the answer to my questions took the form of the recitation of a fragment of a shamanic healing prayer or the recounting of some happening (an event that happened to someone or to oneself) in which "something" abnormal played a role.

Indeed, souls absorb a good deal of the Tzeltal curiosity, restlessness, and reflection. Undoubtedly, there are many social and personal relationships at stake whose threads openly or surreptitiously interweave this knowledge, making it a subject of intense attraction. Yet for that very reason, it is not an easy topic to address. However sure-footedly the shamans may be believed to operate within it, it does not constitute a strictly esoteric body of knowledge. Rather, it is a sort of public secret, shared collectively; everyone knows it, and knows that everyone else knows it, yet they all must act as if they do not. The utmost discretion is required when tackling these matters, and it must be done indirectly and implicitly. In fact, whenever there is talk of souls, the entire rich repertoire of grammatical particles and rhetorical resources with which the Tzeltal language can soften a statement's force or a question's violence springs into action. This may be characterized as a vagueness that is enhanced by Tzeltal's polysemousness and further complicated by the natives' regular use of euphemisms to denote the different soul elements.

There is, of course, no canonical body of Tzeltal knowledge that defines what a soul is. For this reason, my inquiry lacked any precise method. As the kind of ethnographic testimony that I adduce in these pages will show, what I managed to learn is the result of many informal chats that normally took place under perfectly ordinary circumstances, preserving an attitude, so to speak, of "going with the flow." I also believe that the nature of knowledge about souls has tinged the overall tone of this study, which explains why its scheme is not wholly articulated and why not all the data are developed in narrative form. Akin to what the Tzeltal find interesting in a person, what I do is not so much supply a finished profile (an individual), but to underscore pieces that may be compared with other fragments and to sketch points of agreement and analogy.

Nevertheless, I was able to pursue a more systematic exploration of the field of soul elements by means of numerous recorded one-on-one talks with three people: Xun P'in, Alonso K'aal, and Lorenzo Lot. On the one hand, this procedure not only gave me deeper insight but also allowed me to identify what might be called a lowest common denominator of basic concepts. This served as a kind of sieve for capturing and sifting through the bits of data that I had been recording and that otherwise would have finally come to rest in that limbo of ethnographic data with no fixed abode. This is the minimal framework I abide by in the following chapter on ethnographic description.

On the other hand, as I was a stranger to the network of local interpersonal relations and ignorant of the proper way to broach these matters, it seemed permissible for us to discuss souls more freely. As it happens, the three individuals mentioned above were not informants in the conventional sense of the term. The interviews—usually conducted in their homes, in private, and with a lot of time on our hands—became rare opportunities for us to talk, to open up, to ponder a cultural domain about which they felt genuine curiosity, but which they would have been unable to deal with explicitly under any other circumstances.

The outcome was a series of single-subject conversations that created, to a certain extent, a novel result. There is no need, then, to insist that the elemental scheme that I follow in the next chapter does not exist as such. It is, rather, a virtual script, a compromise solution between, on the one hand, my need to find sufficiently firm ground to maintain a level of understanding, and on the other, what the three people with whom I sustained discussions were prepared, to differing degrees, to sacrifice for the sake of simplification. Without their highly valuable collaboration, I would have been unable to carry out an ethnography of souls; needless to say, I am fully responsible for the resulting ethnography.

Xun P'in, the shaman (*ch'abajom*) I worked with, was over fifty years old. As a young man, he had lived for a year or two in an Instituto Nacional Indigenista boarding school for Indians in San Cristóbal de las Casas (the main Spanish-speaking city in the Chiapas highlands region, sixty kilometers from Cancuc as the crow flies, and about a nine-hour walk from there), where he picked up a smattering of Spanish and also managed, apparently, to learn to read. He remembered having once been taken to Salina Cruz, in the neighboring state of Oaxaca, so that he might see the ocean, although he was most impressed by the railway there. Once back in Cancuc, he held some political post until, due to a bout of factional infighting that he preferred not to discuss (at one point, he was even jailed in Ocosingo), he had to renounce his political aspirations. Some years later, and after several crises, including separations from two wives, he had a dream during the illness of one of his daughters and thus discovered that his true vocation was to be a shaman. His former contact with the Mexican world imbued him with an aura of eccentricity (further enhanced by my close collaboration with him) that he himself cultivated with care, for example, in the way he dressed: he wore the traditional Indian knee-length white cotton tunic, embroidered with red wool yarn, but on top he used to sport a threadbare waist-length jacket; also, unlike most men in the community, he favored a mustache and beard. He was a taciturn character, and spent almost all his time in healing activities, for which his patients payed him with corn, money, or labor. He died in 1997.

The second person is Alonso K'aal. He must have been somewhere between forty or fifty, and he possessed the title *kawilto*, which is to say, *cabildo*, or head elder, a rank reserved for those who have carried out a certain series of religious offices, above all that of *mayordomo* to one of the saints in Cancuc's church, and other posts of a political-ceremonial character. Like Xun P'in, he, too, was "master of his house," for, in accordance with the ideal norm, he lived in the same residential complex as his male offspring, their wives, and children. This high status allowed him to talk to me about souls without too much fear. He, too, had grown, although with some difficulty, a bit of a mustache and beard. Over his white cotton tunic, he sometimes wore a long black woollen jacket, a garment regarded as an exclusive prerogative of *principales* (community leaders) like himself. He had never been to school and, when sober, did not speak a word of Spanish.

The third person was Lorenzo Lot. Roughly thirty years old, he lived in his parents' home with his wife and four children. For all practical purposes, he had never occupied any post, apart from a minor role in the celebration of Carnival, and another of quite a different kind in a new honey producers' cooperative. At that time, he was mulling over the possibility of affiliating himself with the Catholics or with one of the evangelical groups that had begun to spring up in the Cancuc Valley some decades earlier. That would have saved him from having to continue to take part in the fiestas around Carnival and the collateral liquor intoxication. He had completed his primary school studies in Cancuc and spoke and wrote a little Spanish. From my very first months in Cancuc, he was my Tzeltal teacher in exchange for writing lessons in Spanish. Unlike P'in or K'aal, Lorenzo Lot had scarcely any authority with which to speak of souls. I remember him glancing nervously around us from time to time, afraid that someone or something might be listening to our conversation; yet he was one of the people with whom I could speak most freely about that world, due in part to the fact that, from early on, I felt comfortable when raising my personal doubts and conjectures over method with him. One of his major contributions may be considered the very form in which our conversations developed.

For the truth is that conventional forms of Tzeltal conversation are among the principal impediments for an outsider to understand the domain of souls and self. Rarely are such opinions expressed in terms of opposition, and there is no such thing as a discussion constructed on the basis of linked, mutually opposing arguments—nothing that bears any resemblance to any kind of dialectic argument. Typically, it is the person with the most authority who does most of the speaking and answering, while the others present largely take turns backing up the opinion expressed, at most adding a finishing touch or some interesting detail, even though the corroborating evidence occasionally seems to be saying quite the contrary. Much to my despair, my questions almost never received a straight answer, a difficulty that also plagued my conversations with Xun P'in and Alonso K'aal. More often than not, I was regaled with a long account of some event, described in minute detail, at the end of which I was left baffled as to its relevance to my initial question. (It turns out these stories of events usually do contain small details that operate as clues; but for anyone with difficulties in understanding Tzeltal and ignorant of its idiomatic resources, finding them is like looking for a needle in a haystack.) In contrast, Lorenzo Lot had learned to sustain an "accumulative conversation," and he always made a great effort to elaborate on what he was explaining to me.

The Town of Cancuc

Cancuc is a municipality or local administrative district with roughly 22,000 inhabitants (in 1990), all speakers of Tzeltal Mayan, a language that at present has around 350,000 speakers throughout the region. It is, consequently, an Indian community (there is no Spanish-speaking population) and exceedingly conservative culturally, even by Chiapas highlands standards. Its territory crosses a tract of a long, deep valley, running east–west, and the slopes of another valley that runs parallel. It is a cramped area, 18 kilometers by 12 kilometers, with staggering differences in altitude, ranging from the strip of "cold land," covered with pines and oaks, that rises to 2,200 meters, to the valley bottom and the Tanateel River at 600 meters, where, despite intensive deforestation, some patches of tropical forest still remain.

San Juan Cancuc is the local administrative center for the municipality and a distant heir to the "Christian" township where the Cancuqueros' forebears were congregated by Dominican friars in the sixteenth century. Founded on a narrow promontory 1,500 meters high that offers a view of the whole valley, it is composed of a square framed by the church, the governmental town hall opposite the church, and other less important administrative buildings. Beyond this plaza, and scattered very thinly, are the homes of the township's five thousand inhabitants, built on artificial terraces where the ground slopes. The remainder of Cancuc's population inhabits thirty-two hamlets that emigrants from San Juan have gradually established since 1918; the farthest one is a nine-hour walk from the center.

Economy

Crop growing is the chief occupation. Apart from the small number of bilingual teachers who receive a Mexican government salary, all families grow corn and beans using the traditional slash-and-burn system of clearing and sowing a plot of brushland. They must live for the whole year off the harvest of corn and beans, which are prepared and combined in a multitude of ways to form the staple of their diet. As a complement, different kinds of chili peppers are grown on the riverbanks, along with a little sugarcane to produce cooked sugar, and some cotton to weave clothing on the backstrap loom. Around the houses there are hens and turkeys, an occasional pig, and fruit trees. Coffee has been grown for roughly three decades with the help of Mexican government agencies, which provide the young plants and some technical assistance, and buy up the harvest. Some families also produce honey for sale.

The soil of Cancuc is fertile, especially in the milder zones of the valley, where they manage to obtain two corn harvests a year, which has meant that since the 1930s, far fewer Cancuqueros have found themselves forced to work as laborers on the estates of the commercial plantations along the Pacific Coast or in the lowlands to the north of the state, unlike Indians from neighboring municipalities with poorer lands. Even now, when the sharp rise in population is making itself felt with a vengeance on available lands—mostly because the forest cleared for sowing and fertilized by the ashes resulting from burning brush does not have adequate fallow time to replenish itself—the Cancuqueros prefer to move their families to live in the lands farther north rather than to seek work as seasonal laborers on *fincas* and plantations.

The other essentials are bought in the open-air market, held once a week in a field where goods are laid out on the ground. These include handmade items sold by Indians from other nearby Tzeltal and Tzotzil towns, such as pottery from Tenango, musical instruments from Mitontic, ladies' belts from Tenejapa; industrial products sold by Indians from Oxchuc (through which a highway passes); or salted fish and vegetables sold by Spanish-speaking peddlers, who buy poultry, chili, and occasionally coffee. Also sold there are skeins of cotton, colored thread, and woolen yarn to decorate clothing; needles; *machetes* and other metal tools; flashlights; batteries; bottled drinks; hand cream; and aspirin and other medicine, mostly vitamins.

Kinship

The Cancuc kinship system is of the Omaha type (Guiteras 1947; Siverts 1969; Haehl 1980). The Cancuqueros are divided into three major exogamous patrilineal lineages, or "phratries"—named *ijk'a*, *chejeb*, and *chijk'*—which are subdivided into ninety-four "clans": 31 *ijk'a*, 30 *chejeb*, and 33 *chijk'*. Each clan has a name, which is the surname of each Indian in that clan, for example, *wol*, *oxom*, *lul*, *p'in*, etc. The Tzeltal word that denotes the lineage unit in the abstract is *chajp-pal-chajp*, "groups that form a bunch" (and its members are called *chajpomal* or *stijinalpal*), and the clan unit is simply known as *chajp*, "group" (and its members as *tajunab*, "uncles," who enjoy an equal reciprocal relationship among themselves). These are not corporate units. Neither lineage nor clan is limited by territory: each hamlet has members of all three lineages, and the clans are all represented in the municipal center; however, in the smallest hamlets, there may only be members of five or ten clans. They do not own land in common or bear mutual obligations, nor do the members of each group even meet formally or informally under any pretext. In contrast, greeting each other properly is of extraordinary importance, even if merely bumping into someone on a path, when the speaker must state which lineage he belongs to.

Lesser units include the *jun te kuil-mamil* ("one single grandmother-grandfather"), or "sublineages," a group of agnates who descend from one acknowledged "grandfather" (*mam*), generally two or three generations back. The various domestic groups that compose a lineage (in reality, its male heads) do not have to be physically close to each other or even in the same hamlet, but they do share the same lands or group of allotments (*jun lum k'inaltik*) that have been inherited from the "grandfather." Most of the time, land is not divided up, so each domestic group works it according to its needs and capacity—an arrangement that is a never-ending source of antagonism between heads of family. "Uncles" with the most sons prefer that the land remain undivided, while those with fewer sons would rather it were carved up; and in the case of such a division (the definitive settlement of boundaries can give rise to feuds that can last for generations), the allotment's subsequent sale to any other Cancuquero becomes possible. There are times when a father, getting on in years and unhappy with his offspring's attitude, simply sells the land for money or a continuous supply of corn and beans for the remainder of his life.

On the day One *pom*, when offerings are made to the dead, most of the members of a *kuil mamil* gather before the tomb of their common ancestor, where other members of the group may also be buried occasionally, to offer candles and food as tokens of gratitude for the land that has been passed on to them. At this time, the women (though they cannot inherit either land or any other chattel, apart from certain weaving tools) leave their husbands to make offerings alongside their brothers.

Government

The public government of Cancuc is shared between two groups of authorities. The first, a successor in many ways to the political posts of the colonial period and known in Chiapas as "traditional authorities," is a group of about one hundred and twenty-five old men called *cabildos* or *principales* who live in the municipal center and the hamlets. The *principales* choose from among themselves two "senior *cabildos*" (*baj kawilto*) to preside over the group for a four-year period. Each of them lives in one of the municipal center's halves, upper and lower, into which an imaginary line crossing the center from east to west divides the territory of Cancuc. The duties of *principales* are primarily ritual in nature. For example, they conduct the ceremonies of offerings to the Mountain Lords in order to obtain good harvests, or they say prayers to prevent epidemics from breaking out in Cancuc.

Principales also dream. A considerable part of the Sunday meetings that are held beside the market is taken up with long interpretations of the dreams each of them has had during the week, especially the senior *cabildos*. At one of the sessions I attended, it was necessary to examine what must have been a recurring dream that one of the two senior *cabildos* had been having for some weeks before, on account of which around fifty *principales* from the head town and villages assembled together. His dream was about two horses (almost no one had a horse in Cancuc), one of them emaciated, the other very fat. The former was very weak and unable to stand up, while the latter, although strong, went into a sudden decline. Several *cabildos*, above all the oldest, offered interpretations that the dream had to do with war, sickness, or hunger; by the end of the morning, it was agreed that the lean horse portended a poor harvest of corn in Cancuc, while the fat horse meant that some Cancuqueros would have to leave the community to plant crops elsewhere, and on the way back, they would be held up, robbed of their harvest, and perhaps even killed. The meeting took place in May at a time when the rainy season was late in coming; but also some *principales* expressed their concern over the fact that certain families were devoting too much time and effort to coffee growing, to the detriment of corn and beans, which they bought from those families that produced a surplus of them. In the end, it was decided to make an especially lavish offering to the soil, for which, later, a house-to-house collection was arranged.

Access to the group of *principales*—whose terms are for life—is open to those Cancuqueros who have previously held other offices, first of all in the service of one of the saints in the church, and who then have subsequently held one of the following six *chakel* posts: first *alcalde* of San Juan, first *alcalde* of San Lorenzo, second *alcalde* of San Juan, second *alcalde* of San Lorenzo, first *regidor*, and second *regidor*. Selected and trained annually by the *principales*, Cancuqueros generally accept these posts grudgingly (if they are accepted at all) because the duties involved—also of a ceremonial nature—require time and money, not to mention ongoing bodily restraint.

The second group of authorities are the so-called constitutional ones, and since 1989, the year Cancuc regained its municipality status, they are the posts found in any Mexican *municipio*: municipal president, judge, councilmember, and so forth. These positions are mainly filled by schoolteachers able to speak and write Spanish and therefore in a position to deal with legal paperwork; they also manage the federal budgets allocated to the *municipio*. As an adjunct to the town hall, there is a local committee of the government party, the PRI (Institutional Revolutionary Party), which obtained all available votes in the 1990 elections held in Cancuc, and the Committee of Agrarian Reform, which oversees the demarcation of municipal land and on rare occasions settles disputes over property. Before 1989, Cancuc was considered an *agencia municipal* of Ocosingo, and official posts were filled in the same way with Spanish-speaking Cancuqueros, called by the rest, today as then, "scribes." Some of them came to accrue great power in Cancuc and were known then as *tatil lum*, "father of the town," or were simply referred to with the Spanish word *cacique*. In fact, these Indian *caciques* made the most of the political backing lent to them by the Mexican federal government in the wake of the 1910 Mexican Revolution, with the probable intention of breaking up the political hegemony of conservative landowners in the highlands region. But these *caciques* in turn became too powerful, and since the 1960s, the Mexican government has focused on training bilingual Indian schoolteachers, by means of the Instituto Nacional Indigenista (INI), capable of standing their ground before the *caciques*—a policy that has been successful to date. In 1991, a proposal was made to incorporate the *principales* into the town hall as an "advisory council."[5]

Religion

According to the 1990 General Census of the Nation (Chiapas 1991), the following categories may be distinguished among the population over the age of five:

Roman Catholic: 5,218

Protestant or evangelical: 3,847

Jewish: 16

Other: 154

None: 7,311

Unspecified: 303

Nominally speaking, the Cancuqueros converted to Christianity in the sixteenth century, but after the nineteenth century, when the friars abandoned the place, the Indians ceased celebrating all the sacraments, although they preserved other Christian practices, including public ceremonies. This is the large sector hiding beneath the umbrella category of "None." Catholics and evangelicals came onto the scene as groups in the 1960s and soon experienced rapid growth, which now seems to have come to a halt. Both groups are referred to in Tzeltal as "the ones with religion," while the rest of the population are called "the ones without religion" (*mayuk religion*).

In addition to the brief descriptions of scientific travelers who passed through the region (following the old Camino Real, or royal road, of the Spanish Crown that once linked Chiapas to the state of Tabasco) at the beginning of the twentieth century, the most valuable account on Cancuc is the ethnographic report produced by Calixta Guiteras after a stay of several weeks in 1944 (Guiteras 1946, 1992). Henning Siverts (1965) also conducted fieldwork in Cancuc for a few days. This relative paucity of fieldwork in Cancuc, in contrast to other neighboring areas in Chiapas, may be attributed in part to a general mistrust of outsiders, particularly foreigners. However, by the time I arrived, toward the end of 1989, opposition to the admittance of foreigners had largely abated. This was due in no small measure to the fact that some months before, on August 17, the recently installed president of Mexico, Salinas de Gortari, had come to Cancuc in a helicopter to restore the *municipio* status that had been lost in 1922. There, surrounded by Cancuqueros, the president gave a speech on what his Indian policy would be during his six-year term and promised general financial aid for the *municipio* (because it was "one of those that had been most overlooked in the Republic"), which, by 1992, had translated into the construction of several new buildings and the rebuilding of several existing ones in the center, as well as the laying out of an unpaved road for vehicles.

CHAPTER 2

The Ethnography of Souls

We should start with a discussion of certain basic terms. In Cancuc, a person is composed of a body (*bak'etal*), made up of flesh and blood, and a group of "souls" (*ch'ulel;* plural *ch'uleltik*) residing within the heart of each individual. The term *soul* is used here for the sake of convenience. The conventional translation of the word's root (*ch'ul*) in both Tzeltal and Tzotzil is "holy" or "sacred." However, in a strict sense, *ch'ul* denotes a thing's radical "other." Thus, it is a purely relative concept, and when applied to the notion of personhood, *ch'ulel* may be defined as "the body's other."

This "body's other" (*ch'ulel*) is, in turn, composed of three classes of beings. The first is a tiny bird, often referred to as the "Bird of the Heart." The second *ch'ulel* is a being usually called *bats'il ch'ulel*, the "genuine *ch'ulel*," to distinguish it from the more inclusive term. Finally, the third sort of soul is called the *lab*, a complex of many kinds of beings.

The Bird of Our Heart

In the heart of each person nests a *mutil o'tan*, literally "bird-heart" (more often than not, the plural form is used: *mutil ko'tantik*, "the bird in our hearts"). It is a tiny creature that is usually imagined as a hen in women and a rooster in men, like the ones bred and eaten in homes. On some occasions, it was described to me as a pigeon (*palóma-mut*), and once as a grackle (*sanáte*). This bird is regarded as absolutely essential to life and cannot and must not leave the heart, because once it does, the body immediately falls ill and dies soon after.[1]

Nevertheless, it is a highly prized trophy for a certain type of being (the *pále*, a species of *lab*, in other words, another soul entity for the people of Cancuc, as we shall see later), which contrives to extract the bird and eat it up. The people offered the most graphic descriptions of the *pále* and sometimes repeated them almost word for word. These beings sing or whistle a tune near their victim, and the Bird of the Heart, captivated by the song, escapes through the victim's mouth or, in other versions, through the crown of the head. Once outside the body, it is trapped by a demon, who tosses it into the air four times until it becomes the normal size of a hen or a rooster. Hiding it beneath his clothes, he makes off with it to the lair he shares with his fellow beings, in the depths of the forest or in some cave, where they make preparations to cook it. There are tables and chairs there. Then, in some versions, they pluck the bird and place it in a metal pot with boiling water, serving it on a plate when cooked. In other versions, water from a porcelain bowl is sprinkled directly on the bird. Up to that moment, the person from whom the bird has been taken is not yet dead, although by then he is very ill and feels intense pain in his chest, and "he feels that he is going to die soon, grows sad, begins to bid farewell to his wife and children." At the very moment the demons in the cave add salt to the bird, the person passes away.

Even for the best shaman, it is very hard to recover the stolen Bird of the Heart, in part because they barely have time to act, in part because the *pále* usually reject real birds from the yard offered in exchange. For some unknown reason, they prefer to eat the Bird of the Heart. The victim may only save himself if he has a *lab* capable of defeating the *pále* and returning the bird to him; even then, it is a difficult process. In those rare cases (usually coinciding with sudden, rapidly debilitating illnesses or mortal blows) in which the shaman diagnoses "loss of bird," the prognosis is almost always death.

Apart from being an indispensable life spirit, the Bird of the Heart does not seem to be attributed any other direct role in each individual's character, sensibility, or conscience. The creature responsible for the heart's palpitations is jumpy and skittish, and when confronted with danger or bodily exertion, becomes agitated and flutters. Outside the body, it is completely defenseless. The body is born with it, but no one knows where it might come from. When the body perishes, the bird is released into the world, where it will end up being devoured by demons or some wild animal.

One event concerning the Bird of the Heart (the only one that I heard about) was told to me by Alonso K'aal, whose mother told him the story when he was a child. She had heard it because the main characters were more or less close neighbors of hers. Two brothers had a sister who lived in a different house with her husband. He was a heavy drinker and mistreated her, so the brothers decided to step in and teach him a lesson. By means of their *lab* (some extraordinary powers), they extracted the bird from their sister's body, making sure to keep it carefully in a small wooden box, so that the other *lab* could not devour it. The sister fell ill at once and had to go lie down. When her husband sobered up, he demanded lunch, but his wife was unable to even sit up in bed. The husband began to bemoan his lot and went to the house of his brothers-in-law. Pretending not to know anything, they agreed to help cure their sister. They diagnosed the loss of her Bird of the Heart on account of the blows she had suffered at the hands of her husband (untrue), and, in exchange for curing her, they demanded ten liters of liquor and the promise that he would treat her well in the future. The brothers returned home, where they had the bird hidden away, and they tucked it up carefully in their clothing. The nearer they came to their sister's house, the better she began to feel, and she gradually became able to speak. They placed the bird upon the crown of her head, and it found its own way back down into her heart. In the twinkling of an eye, the woman recovered completely and set about preparing lunch.

The *ch'ulel*

The second kind of soul, the *ch'ulel*, also lodges in the heart and is needed to continue living; but in addition, it plays a role in shaping each person's individual character. The *ch'ulel* is the seat of memory, feelings, and emotions; it is responsible for dreams; and it is the source of language. The different nature of each *ch'ulel* is, in a nutshell, what gives each human being a unique "temperament." Those who have described its appearance agree that in profile it is similar to a human body (occasionally it is specified that its silhouette is the same as its bearer's body) but "without flesh"—a dark smudge, a thick shadow.

The *ch'ulel* in *ch'iibal* Mountain

The *ch'ulel* exists in a double form. It lives in the human heart and, at the same time, inside a mountain.[2] When a baby is born, its soul appears simultaneously in the mountain. Each of the four main lineages possesses one of these mountains, called *ch'iibal*, "place of growth," where all the souls of the lineage, presently numbering about seven thousand per mountain, live in common.[3] The inside of the mountain has thirteen stories, one on top of the other in a pyramid shape, and these in turn are divided into numerous compartments with doors and windows, which include lounges, chambers, anterooms, studies, corridors, vaults, stairs, and storerooms. All the rooms are magnificently appointed, with huge tables, armchairs and benches, and beds or bunks in the bedrooms. The color of the furniture, like practically everything found here, is bright red, yellow, or green. The whole edifice is pervaded by fragrance from bunches of flowers everywhere; these are the "candles" that the shamans offer in their ceremonies from the ordinary world, but what are seen as candles in the ordinary world are smelled as flowers in the mountain. There are also ornamental gardens, fountains, and orchards.[4]

However, everything existing in the mountain has an *imaginal* nature; it has no matter but consists of *slok'omba* (images), which are things "imagined" by the souls. Although there are cornfields, they are not cultivated because they are only images of cornfields. The souls themselves, despite their characteristically human figure, do not have a body made of flesh and blood. On the thirteenth and top floor of the mountain live the souls who are over forty years old, the "mothers-fathers"; on the twelfth floor are the souls between twenty and forty, and on the eleventh live the "big-small ones" who have not yet reached twenty.[5] The lower levels, which are not permanently inhabited, are used for such things as storerooms and garages for the cars. Each mountain has a lineage council, complete with civil servants, that is elected every four years from among the most capable souls. There are also embassies of souls from other towns and countries. "They have a president, a mayor, trustees, councilors, police officers, and police chiefs—everything; it is they who govern the lineage. This is why we also have to pray to them, send them gifts and liquor, and always speak to them with respect; it is in order to keep them happy so they will look after our soul and treat it well in the *ch'iibal*."

A sizable portion of what is known about the *ch'iibal* is derived from protection or healing chants that the shamans address to those places. There can be no doubt that that is the explanation for the identical or nearly identical repetition within the different descriptions. What follows is a collection of excerpts from one such prayer, *smajtan me'il tatil* (offering for the mothers-fathers), that I recorded at the healing ceremony conducted by Xun P'in for a four-year-old boy.

. . . sacred mountains with life
revered mountains with life
where you are gathered
where all of you are
sacred mothers
sacred fathers
in great house
in great abode
on your chairs [*xila*, Spanish "*silla*"]
on your stools [*tawareta*, Spanish "*taburete*"]
on your chairs from Castile
on your great benches
with yellow-feathered chickens
with yellow-coated dogs
with yellow chairs
with yellow stools
how many houses-on-the-earth
how many *ch'iibal*
how many *kolibal*
until the elders
until the youngsters where they are embraced
where they are weighed down
their genuine *ch'ulel*
their genuine *ánjel* ["angel," Spanish "*ángel*"]
I come with my humble word
I come with my humble heart
I send two eggs
I send two hens
white hens
white pigeons
two sacred flowers
two sacred lilies
[may they arrive] making your eyes shine
making your feet shine
esteemed mothers
esteemed fathers
before your faces
before your bodies
what a lot there are of those who solve disputes
those who solve problems

you are orderly in the great house
you are lined up in the great abode
senyora mother of the *chijk'* lineage
senyora father of the *chijk'* group
this will quench your thirst
this will satisfy your heart
a bottle [of liquor]
maybe the accuser has passed
maybe the liar has passed
¡mother-presidents!
¡father-presidents!
you live in the old rooms
you live in the old chambers
they passed to give you gifts
I ask you not to accept them
accept my gift for your feet
accept my gift for your hands
your pampered little girl
your pampered little boy
once you suckled him
once you breast-fed him
hold him tight
carry him carefully
in the great house
in the great abode
don't let his shit make you sick
don't let his piss make you sick
your pampered little girl
your pampered little boy . . .

In any description of the *ch'iibal*, two aspects of the nature of the mountain stand out: It is a kindergarten where the souls of the children of each
lineage are raised, and it is also the souls' lineage council and court.

As far as the first aspect is concerned, it is said that the *ch'ulel* soul
descends to earth from the highest point in heaven, its thirteenth level,
rotating clockwise. Once there, it penetrates the maternal womb and
lodges in the fetus's body. One version of the soul stays in the heart
and another remains in the *ch'iibal*, but the latter will not appear until the child is born. From then on, the health of the child in the ordinary world will depend on how its soul in the mountain is treated.

To this end, ceremonies are held to ask that it be treated fairly, during which substances such as liquor, candles, and incense are offered and appreciation is expressed. Until the Great Mother of the mountain is satisfied with the gifts received in the ceremonies, the carnal mother will not begin to produce milk. The root *ch'i* of the word *ch'iibal* means "to grow," but the verb is only applied to the growth of plants, either cultivated plants or plants such as tobacco and medicinal herbs, which, though they grow in the wild, are tended to a certain extent by the Indians. Like the European term *kindergarten*, or "children's garden," the mountain evokes a botanical image. It is a sort of greenhouse of souls. In ritual language, its synonym is *kolibal*, meaning "healthy," something that fattens, in the sense that the health of the members of the lineage depends on the mountain.[6]

In accordance with the kindergarten nature of the lineage, the mountain is organized in a particular way. On the top floor is the Great Mother, who is chosen every four years from among the older mothers, who are more responsible as far as childcare is concerned. This job is superior to any of the positions held by males; in fact, women here—at least in the role of caregivers—are considered more important than men. On the next level, are the "mothers-sisters," middle-aged women who look after the children. The eleventh floor is occupied by those under twenty years old, the "big-small ones," and this is where all the young children live together. They are looked after and taken out by their caregivers, the older children. The Great Mother suckles the children in turns ("it isn't complete milk, only the soul of the milk"), and when they have finished, she returns them to the "mothers-sisters," who, after bathing and dressing them, hand them over to the "big-small ones," whose job it is to take them out and keep them occupied.

Descriptions of life in the mountain are imbued with language that, while maternal, is complex in its sentiments. Since each mountain only contains the souls of one lineage, and wives continue to belong to the paternal lineage, the mothers' souls do not live in the same mountain as those of their children. Infant souls are the responsibility of the husband's "sisters," meaning that the women of the mountain are not the real "mothers" of the babies, which obviously creates a delicate situation. However much rhetoric is reiterated on the commitment and dedication of these women, it is clear to everyone that one of the basic problems for survival of the child-souls is maternal inconstancy. In the ordinary world, children easily succumb to illness, they cry without apparent cause, and infant mortality is high. Accidents inevitably happen. It may happen that the Great Mother dies and while a successor is being chosen, the babies are effectively left orphaned and untended as their "mothers" are unsupervised (in a sense, the Great Mother acts like a mother-in-law). Sometimes, they are not properly cleaned or fed. A caregiver may even get drunk and drop a baby on the floor (there are a few shaman chants demanding responsibility for the death of a child). In certain cases, the caregivers may be suspected of acting with evil intent and causing willful harm, although this is rarely acknowledged openly.

Underlying all of this is the idea that these women are not the true mothers because their real children live in the mountain of another lineage, with other women in charge who are not their real mothers either. The very title given to them, *me'el-wixil* (mother-sister), in which *wix* means "older sister," and, by extension, the titles given to all the older women of the lineage, denotes an ambiguity in their position. As far as I know, this title is never used in the ordinary world. To tell the truth, the role of this group of souls is odd in itself: They are women who are not wives or, strictly speaking, mothers, thus suppressing the very meaning of what being an adult woman is. In the ordinary world, a situation like this only occurs during the observance of the Day of the Dead, when wives are separated from their children while they give offerings in the company of their brothers and sisters.

The second aspect of the *ch'iibal* emphasizes its role as lineage council. Every four years, the *ch'ulel* elect from among themselves their political officers: *alcaldes, regidores, escribanos,* and policemen (*chajpanwanetik,* "guardians of the kin group"), who are all subordinates of the Great Mother.[7] They meet in the upper chambers, where, seated on large benches, they hold audience and deliberate. Apparently, from time to time, they sit around a large rectangular table, where they write in their record books. There, decisions are made regarding lineage matters, except for difficult cases that are discussed with the authorities of the other three *ch'iibal,* with whom communication is established "as if by telegraph," for the *ch'ulel* cannot leave the mountain. In many ways, *ch'iibal* organization is analogous to the town council (*cabildo*) of Cancuc, but the *ch'ulel* who fill the positions of authority in the *ch'iibal* are not necessarily the same as the office holders of Cancuc. Their true identities are unknown even to themselves (despite claims of knowledge by some when they are drunk); common sense tells us that if they ever did find out, they would still keep their identities a secret to avoid potential vengeance seeking in Cancuc.

The council also acts as a court for the souls. One soul accuses another before the authorities, a trial is held, and, if declared guilty, the soul is sentenced to a certain length of time in jail in the mountain. What is on trial is the behavior of the souls in the mountain, not in the ordinary world. In the absence of a carnal body, souls cannot suffer any corporal damage, so to speak, but the body experiences the imprisonment of the soul as if it were an illness, and this may cause its death, in which case the soul disappears from the mountain. In the same way as the *ch'ulel* soul appears in the mountain with birth, it disappears with the death of its body. It merges with its double in the ordinary world, which resides in the heart of the body, and is exiled to the world of the dead. It seems the authorities in the mountain are aware that a harsh sentence effectively means condemning a soul to death. It is said that in such cases, agreement on the court ruling is required between four authorities from different lineages.

Descriptions of trials in the mountain can run into quite a bit of detail, especially those of the shamans. The soul denouncing the offense appears before the members of the council, who are elderly men with white hair and long white beards. They sit at a big table on wooden chairs with armrests in a large hall with a vaulted ceiling. On the table there are numerous books and notebooks, and the walls are covered with cupboards where case files from previous trials are kept. The accuser puts his case before the court: He may complain that such-and-such a soul does not speak to him with respect, or that he is vain or critical or pokes fun at him. Accusations are generally related to verbal offenses and lack of respect, but they sometimes involve physical assault; someone may complain of having been struck a blow, or a woman may claim she has been raped. Before leaving, the accuser hands over gifts to members of the court: liquor, beer, or tamales filled with meat or vegetables.

The court will deliberate for some time and whatever is said will be written down in the minute book by a scribe or typed on a typewriter or computer. Almost spontaneously, some members of the court will be inclined to believe the accuser and others will try and defend the accused, either noting that they are dealing with an adult person who is respectful, speaks correctly, and is "no longer a child," or else maintaining that he is vain, disrespectful, presumptuous, and disdainful. In some cases, witnesses are called or written evidence is presented. If no agreement is reached, the councillors of the other three lineages in the mountains are consulted by phone. Finally, if there is a guilty verdict, the soul is removed by the police and taken to jail, but if a serious crime has been committed, the soul is handed over to certain spirits as their prisoner.

The mountain is permeated by hostility, grudges, and vanity, and this makes it a permanent source of illness. Order is not incompatible with conflict; in fact, the former appears to lead inevitably to the latter. Nobody seems to believe that *ch'iibal* souls are kindhearted beings: "They might appear to be good people with kindness in their hearts, but they aren't really; they're sons of bitches and they use bad language. The young ones in the *ch'iibal* are often mean-minded; all they want is for us to give them food and drink."

It should be emphasized that the *ch'iibal* mountains of the Cancuc lineages are to be found far beyond the community's territory, although not as far as might be desired. The *ch'iibal* must be physically distant, because if not, there would be too many quarrels; if they were nearby, it would be far too easy for the *ch'ulel* to head off for the *ch'iibal*, and the number of complaints and punishments would build up and make life impossible.

In exchange, Cancuc land hosts the *ch'iibal* of other towns. Beside Alonso K'aal's house, there is a fissure in the ground, the bottom of which cannot be seen and which is by all accounts the *ch'iibal* of the people of Tila, a town located a good two days' walk away toward the northeast. In Tila, the residents speak Chol, a Mayan language related to Tzeltal, but barely intelligible to the Cancuqueros apart from a few words. Once, K'aal tossed a rotting turkey into the crack and dreamed that night that the *ch'ulel* of the people from Tila were bawling him out for the stench the bird gave off. However, no harm is to be expected from other people's *ch'iibal*. In like manner, other hills around Cancuc are suggested as being the *ch'iibal* of other peoples—always Indian groups that are not Tzeltal speaking. The Zinacantecos, Tzotzil speakers, best known as salt vendors, have their *ch'iibal* in a hill where there is a small, depleted salt mine. The *ch'iibal* of the people from Tumbalá, another Chol-speaking town, is found beneath a rocky outcrop near the river, and when you pass by in the middle of the day or night, you can hear the faint crying of the children.

It is not universally clear whether there is a *ch'iibal* for non-Indian peoples. Xun P'in, for instance, showed an interest in knowing how many *ch'iibal* formed Spain, what they were like inside, and what kind of ties there were between them and the German ones (his curiosity was kindled by recollection of the finca owners of German origin on the Pacific coast) and the inhabitants of Mexico City. With regard to the *ch'iibal* of the Spanish-speaking population of other Chiapas highland regions, he guessed that the children grew up in comfort there, because they are treated kindly, their every whim indulged. This would be in sharp contrast to the situation of their counterparts in Cancuc, where, in the *ch'iibal*, jealousies and rivalries hold sway (it is also, in my opinion, stricter), which explains in part the difference in the rates of illness between the two ethnic groups. Someone else suggested the interesting possibility that the Cancuqueros might go to live among Castilians, if that was what they wanted, which would involve transplanting their *ch'ulel* to the latter's *ch'iibal*. But this was a rather exceptional opinion, prompted perhaps by the need to explain the apparently complete integration of some emigrant Cancuqueros in the Spanish-speaking world. The most common opinion seems to be that the *ch'ulel*, regardless of where and among which people the body happens to be, remains steadfastly in the place corresponding to it by birth—that is, wherever it has been "planted."[8]

The *ch'ulel* inside the Heart

Let's leave the inside of the *ch'iibal* mountain to return to Cancuc, that is, to *jamalal*, "the unsheltered or open place," in contrast to the enclosed space of the *ch'iibal*. For the kind of *ch'ulel* that dwells here, in the heart, the situation is rather different. It so happens that this *ch'ulel* is able to leave the body without any difficulty and to wander through space, traveling the world and exposing itself to its dangers. It is normal for the *ch'ulel* to absent itself of its own accord while the body sleeps. But it may also escape in a state of wakefulness, thanks to a sudden fright, a fit of rage, some great physical effort or excitement, or even, capricious as it is, because it just feels like it. It is especially common for this to happen among young children, to whose bodies the *ch'ulel* has not yet fully adapted itself (or perhaps it is the other way around), and where it is particularly sensitive to any show of irritation on the part of the parents toward the child. However, the *ch'ulel* is not the being that suffers on account of the separation, for it is immune to any physical deterioration or harm and only sustains "emotional damage"; rather, it is the body that is made to pay. The prolonged absence of the *ch'ulel* leads to a "dispiritedness" of the affected person that increases with the length of separation, and the intensity of which depends on the body's own strength; energy and appetite are lost, "blood is watered down," and the body ends up dying in the end. This state of deterioration may go on for several months, and in some exceptional cases has lasted for up to one or two years.

On those occasions when the *ch'ulel* steals away, either because it does not feel at home in the body or because it is not able to find its way back, the solution is simply to persuade it to return and to show it the way. Once, the elder brother of a baby that was not yet one year old hit it out of jealousy. That same afternoon, its mother noticed that the baby was less perky than usual, and its grandfather began to suspect that its *ch'ulel* was on the loose. The situation was not dangerous, because the *ch'ulel* could not have gone very far away, so it was not necessary to go see a healer. The grandfather himself wafted smoking incense around the child and his mother, opened the top panel of the front door, hung out the cloth in which the mother carried the baby on her back (the *pak'*), and said softly (and it will be noted that the *ch'ulel* has the same name as the body it lived in):

> come back *tyak* [personal name]
> come back now
> return to your clothing
> return to your *pak'*
> don't be scared
> don't be scared of the birds in the yard
> don't be scared of the animals
> don't be scared of the cows
> don't be scared of the horses
> return to your clothing
> return to your *pak'*
> return to your home
> come back with the humans
> come back to eat
> come back to drink
> don't be scared of the animals
> don't be scared of the houses
> don't be scared of the paths
> you mustn't go away
> come back . . .

But the situation becomes more serious if the *ch'ulel* is detained or "imprisoned" somewhere or other. Of the forty-three kinds of prayers that compose the part of Xun P'in's repertoire that specifically deals with *ch'ulel* disorders, six are addressed to the *ch'iibal* mountain, while the rest aim at recovering the version of the *ch'ulel* from *jamalal*, in other words, the ordinary state. Of these kinds of prayers, thirty-four are for dealing with kidnappings staged by the *lab* (the third kind of soul for the Tzeltal), and three refer to the domains of the Mountain Lords.

The *lab* capture the *ch'ulel* when it is wandering outside the body, or they devise a way of tricking it into coming out. They say, for instance, "We're off to a fiesta somewhere—there'll be music and liquor . . ." (for the most part, Spanish-speaking towns or fiestas serve as bait, with their music, their food, and their multicolored garland decorations); and once out, they trap it. Their reasons for doing so depend on what kind of *lab* they are. There are times when their objective is to punish the *ch'ulel* for disturbing them as it passed by; sometimes they hope to obtain something in exchange for its liberation (basically incense, liquor, tobacco, and flattering words of recognition that the shaman serves up through the cross on the household altar); and at other times—these are the worst and most difficult cases to resolve—they aim to ensure the body's death and obtain the deceased's Bird of the Heart in advance.

The titles of some of those prayers belonging to the *chukel*, or "jail" group, give us an idea of the strange, out-of-the-way places where the *ch'ulel* is held prisoner by its *lab* enemies, for example:

yut lumil chukel: inside the earth

oxyoket chukel: in the largest of the three stones that make up the domestic hearth

chukel ta ni'te': in the tender shoots at the tops of trees (probably pines)

chukel ta kamolch'en: inside a fragment of rock that has broken off from the entrance to a cave

chukel ta nej ajawchan: in one of the rattles of the rattlesnake's tail

chukel ta kurus: inside a wooden cross

ts'unuba chukel: in the hole dug for corn kernels in a newly sown field

chukel ta yolbej: in the middle of a path

chukel ta jol sna riox: in the top niche of the façade of Cancuc's church or the church of other villages

chukel ta yan mexa manojel: inside the chest that houses the image for the Good Friday procession (Santo Entierro) inside the church

Some of these jails are hot and others cold, which gives rise in the body to fevers or chills, respectively, although it is not uncommon for the *lab* to transfer the *ch'ulel* from place to place to hamper the shaman's understanding of the symptoms.

The second dangerous passage the *ch'ulel* souls have to make is through the domains of the Mountain Lords. Within every mountain of any significance (not to be confused with the *ch'iibal* mountains) lives a powerful owner, an *ajaw* (or *yajwal witz*, "Mountain Lord," or *ánjel*, a clear borrowing from Spanish), that usually takes on a human appearance. *Ajaw* could be old, with long silvery beards, or they could look like fat ranchers with a sombrero and a big cigar. Others resemble Lacandon Indians (who live in the jungle lowlands of Chiapas and are regarded as being only semihuman), and still others are European-looking women with blond hair and wearing pants. There are other versions as well. Various tales are told about these beings. They are known, for example, to hoard great treasures; to visit one another by means of the many underground passageways that are connected to the mountains; to help, fall out with, and fall in love with one another. When a female and a male mountain marry (a female mountain is identified by her smoother contours), the land in between becomes fertile; if they separate, it falls barren. To be able to plant and grow crops with some guarantee of success, it is essential to be on good terms with these lords—which depends on the gifts that Cancuc's *principales* periodically offer up to them.

Openings in the earth's surface (springs, lakes, or caves) communicate the world aboveground with this other world below it, and the *ch'ulel* can easily get stuck in them, due simply to the magnetic force they exert over it (especially the surface of water). In such cases, it should not be difficult to get it back.

But the possibility exists of the *ch'ulel* being sold (*chonel*) to the Mountain Lord by some flesh-and-blood Tzeltal in exchange for some riches or to get revenge. The victim's body dies in the end, and the *ch'ulel* is sold. If the victim is a woman, she will be forced to work around the house for the "owner"; a man might be forced to work as a *mozo* ("servant") looking after his cattle, also inside the earth. The exact procedure followed in the selling ceremony is a secret. The interested party has to dig a hole in the ground beside a spring and put into it a bottle of a soft drink (Coca-Cola or Pepsi), a packet of cigarettes (Montana or Marlboro), a box of matches, a round bunch of differently colored candles, some drops of his own blood (collected by rubbing his tongue or thighs with a piece of string with sharp bits of glass inserted between the strands), and the victim's name, preferably written on a piece of paper. In cases such as this, long ceremonies are required to recover the *ch'ulel*; but this is possible, provided there is no great delay.

Dreams

The events and scenes in dreams are nothing more than the recollection of the *ch'ulel*'s experiences: what it sees and hears on its nocturnal excursions, or what happens to it in *ch'iibal* (apparently, it is not easy to tell the two places apart).

A man who lived for several months far away from Cancuc remembered one night visiting (actually, his *ch'ulel* was visiting) his home in Cancuc. There he saw his parents and his brothers, but all from a certain height, because the *ch'ulel* travels suspended one or two meters above the ground. He could not communicate with them. Such a trip takes place when the *ch'ulel* feels homesick for the places and beings it is used to. There can be no doubt that it moves in space, but the distances and time involved seem to depend on the *ch'ulel*, not the other way around. That explains why, for example, from time to time it may run into the *ch'ulel* of people it has known, but who have already passed away. However, it cannot see and talk to the *ch'ulel* of the dead, but it is capable of traveling through the time and space of its own life. This should come as no surprise, since the *ch'ulel* is the repository of an individual's memory; in a way, it actually *is* memory.

Asleep or while drunk, when the body is motionless and the senses, which do not depend on the *ch'ulel* but rather on the body, are drowsy, the *ch'ulel*, without even having to leave the heart, is able to perceive and see things beyond the ken of wakefulness. It is also susceptible to sleepwalking: a bad dream or a nightmare is *net'el ta ch'ulelal*, "smash the *ch'ulel*," and is often related to the appearance—in reality, the sighting—of hostile *lab*.

Around the month of May, when the unpaved road leading to the center of Cancuc had been completed and trucks loaded with building materials were going up and down it, Xun P'in dreamed that passing by his house were cars, trucks driven by priests, and trains driven by bishops. All of them passed in front of his house, going round and round, making a terrible noise, and then heading off for the main road. Also appearing in his dream were horses that tried to bite him and bulls that wanted to gore him. His neighbors were also dreaming a lot in that period: They heard the thunder of vehicles; music from the radio; the sound of harps, guitars, and violins. His wife dreamed the sound of shoes treading on the patio of the house, and in her own dream asked, "Can it be Petul (I) who has returned?" before thinking, also in the dream, "No, he left a good time before, so it had to be one of those *lab* who also go around in shoes" (the sound of steps is usually considered a bad omen). Then she awoke and felt she had to get up and check that the door was shut tight. The reason for all this "noise" was not discovered until a few days later. It turns out that in a nearby house, an old lady was dying, and the *lab* had shown up in their impatience to get hold of her Bird of the Heart. As soon as she died, the noise ceased. This, then, is the kind of world—a world with some oneiric features, but which is at the same time completely real—that the *ch'ulel* perceives and where it goes about its business.

Some kind of relationship also exists between the *ch'ulel* and shadows. The shadow cast by human beings is given the specific name of *noketal* (the root, *nok*, denotes something flat or smooth), while the names *keaw* and *yaxinal* are applied interchangeably to the shadows of other beings or objects (animals, trees, stones, or houses). Naturally, *noketal* is the shadow of the body thrown by the sun, moon, or some other source of light, but it appears that this is not so much a projection of the body as of the *ch'ulel* lodged inside the heart. This accounts for the belief that when a corpse is about to be buried, it lacks any sort of shadow, for its shadow disappears at the precise moment the *ch'ulel* leaves the body for the last time. Perhaps something similar happens during sleep. It was suggested to me that the absence of the shadow is a sign that the *ch'ulel* has been mislaid, maybe because most of the time its separation from the heart requires the adoption of a prone position. However, Xun P'in ascribes no diagnostic value to this possibility.

In any case, as long as there is light, it is not easy to lose one's shadow. It may occur when swimming in the river that while one's body remains on the surface of the water, the shadow moves away to walk on the river bottom. When this happens, there is a risk of the shadow being seized by some type of being (that is also *lab*) belonging to the group that inhabits the deepest pools; the body is unable to leave the water and ends up drowning. Rattlesnakes first bite the walker's shadow, thereby leaving the body paralyzed and easier to bite moments later. Nevertheless, despite these details, the shadow is hardly an object of great concern, as it does not form a self-contained entity or fit exactly into the *ch'ul* category. Rather, it lacks a will of its own: "It's outside the body, not in the heart"; it is nothing more or less than something—the manifestation of the *ch'ulel*'s substance—that is projected out from within the heart whenever there is light, as if the body were not completely opaque.

Death and the *ch'ulel*

The answers to the questions of where the *ch'ulel* comes from and where it goes once the body has died are far from certain. These questions do not seem to be matters of concern to the Tzeltal, perhaps in part because the origin and destiny of the *ch'ulel* are completely irrelevant to the circumstances of one's personal life, and vice versa.

There is a vague notion that the *ch'ulel* comes from the last of the thirteen levels of the sky (*lajibal lam ch'ulchan*, but this is a commonplace expression that does not allow further clarification), descends to earth, and introduces itself into the fetus during the early months of pregnancy. Its presence is felt once the child begins to move about in the womb. This is a key moment because from then on, there is the ever-present risk that the soul will part company with the fetus.

In the days or months before the body dies, that is, during the body's agony, the *ch'ulel* leaves it for the last time and spends a number of days (twenty, forty) wandering about what was its home. During this period, the *ch'ulel* poses some danger, because since it is always emotive, it may try to induce other *ch'ulel* it is fond of to join it. A prayer may be said that gently but firmly persuades the deceased's *ch'ulel* to take leave of this world once and for all. This will come about when it passes through the wooden cross with the stone base in the church atrium in Cancuc (in other versions, the *ch'ulel* slips behind the church's main altar), through which the *ch'ulel* of the dead (*ch'ulelal*) cross over to the otherworld. This place is called *k'atinbak* (literally "bone burned to ashes") and is to be found deep in the heart of the earth. As sunlight never reaches that spot, it is cold there, and the *ch'ulel* warm themselves around fires made from bones—which are their firewood—they have extracted little by little from beneath the graves to serve as their kindling. The *ch'ulel* return to the surface of the earth just for a day, on the first day of the month of *pom* (in 1990, this was October 26), to visit the *ch'ulel* of the living and to collect food from them. They can see each other, but they cannot speak. It was explained to me that no harm can come from the dead, and that offerings are given "out of affection" to thank the fathers and grandfathers who ceded the land. It also gives the members of a *jun kuil mamil* an opportunity to meet and decide which plots of land are going to be farmed by each domestic group during the coming season.

However, the *ch'ulel* can expect a fate rather different from those who go to *k'atinbak*, depending on the circumstances of death. Lorenzo Lot once heard his mother say that the *ch'ulel* of those who were murdered or drowned (*mililetik*) find their way into the ground at the precise spot where they met their death, ending up as peons in the service of the Mountain Lord. According to Rominko Extul and others, the *ch'ulel* of murder victims, suicides, and those who have died in either of the two wars that can be remembered go up to the sky, where they walk side by side with the sun and the *ch'ulel* of the saints from churches that were burned to the ground by Mexican troops during the "second war" (the Mexican Revolution). They may be the stars. It is said their bodies are not given the customary burial that others receive, but are arbitrarily thrown into any deepish hollow (*suklej*) in the limestone rock of the landscape (and in fact, half-buried human bones can be seen scattered in some of these areas—a disturbing sight for the Tzeltal). Despite the different resting places, the final destiny of the *ch'ulel* is regarded as a matter of little importance. Nevertheless, given that this kind of death is always premature, it is a death that the Tzeltal would prefer not to meet.

Floating invisibly somewhere halfway between the sky and the earth is a destination for the soul that is sometimes identified as *rapicha* ("sugar mill," *trapiche* in Spanish), and other times referred to as *chu'te'* (literally "wooden breast/nipple"). In actual fact, it is a sugar mill composed of several wooden rollers with teeth (these teeth are called *chu'*, "nipple" in Tzeltal), like those used in Cancuc to manufacture cooked sugar, although from the way it is constructed, it bears more resemblance to a replica of the sugar mills from the old sugar plantations (the owners of which will be discussed later), because it has more and bigger teeth. This "suckling" contraption is the destination of the *ch'ulel* of small children who die without having spoken their first words, that is to say, who have not committed any wrongdoing (*mul*). "Wrongdoing" in this case is not understood as "sin" in a Christian sense of the word, but as a debt of reciprocity, of verbal exchange, contracted on speaking for the first time. There they spend an indeterminate time suckling and crying, and in one version, in the guise of (or inside?) black flies (*us*). They wait for some woman to become available into whose womb they enter, ejected from the mill's rollers. Nevertheless, they will still have to be born, die, feed at the sugar mill, and return there four times; not until they return for a fifth time will they have the chance to grow normally.

The *lab*

The third type of soul residing in the heart is known as *lab*. It also leads a dual existence akin to the *ch'ulel*. On the one hand, it may be a "real" creature (an animal, for example) that lives in the outer world. On the other hand, it also has a double inside the human heart of an individual, whose profile is identical to the creature living outside of it, except that it adopts the form of vapor with a shape.[9] The *lab* is a very mixed bag, and it does not conform to any rigorous system of classification of its types. However, from descriptions of it, certain tacit criteria of order, based on Tzeltal common sense, may be recognized and are described below.

Lab That Are Animals

Virtually any animal (*chanbalametik*) can be the *lab* of a person. These include insects, birds, mammals, and even animals as hard to find in Chiapas as whales and tigers.[10] However, in practice, there are certain limitations in the designations. Given that knowledge about the *lab* is basically casuistic, the kinds of animals that are *lab* are reduced to those that intervene in some kind of incident affecting people, be it in a state of wakefulness or in a dream.

Therefore, the *lab* animals that intervene tend to belong to a variety of categories. Most cases are dominated by the feline family, including the domestic cat (*mis*), the ocelot (*tsajal choj*), the puma (*choj*), and the jaguar (*balam*). Other sorts of *lab* animals belong to diverse groups: birds of carrion; the pigeon (*palóma-mut*), which even if its body may be chopped to bits, it does not die because the pieces put themselves back together again; the hawk (*likawal*), who possesses amazing powers of vision; the larger eagle (*kok mut*), capable of stealing the silver coins that are kept in San Juan's coffer—otherwise known as *me'tak'in* (mother-money), perhaps because it appears as the national emblem on Mexican coins; the hummingbird (*kaxlan ts'unun*); the opossum (*uch'*), a highly intelligent animal, which perhaps explains why two months in the Tzeltal calendar bear its name ("little opossum" and "big opossum"), and one that is also able to breathe through its anus; ants of the *baj te'* class, which are the army ant; the fox (*tsajal wax*); and the coati (*cojtom*). Less often one hears of the woodpecker (*ti'*), the coyote (*ok'il*), the agouti (*jalaw*), the odd species of spider, the squirrel, the weasel (*saben*), certain caterpillars (*chup* and *bulub sit*, the latter capable of sipping milk from women's breasts), and butterflies.

There are numerous examples of happenings, even recent ones, in which the death or injury of an animal is related to or implicated in the injury or death of a human being. For example, a person may be discovered to have a wound at the exact moment when, somewhere else, another person may have struck some vermin with a machete for wrecking his cornfield; and the wound is located exactly on the same part of the body as the animal's.

But there are times when these incidents are much more elaborate and interesting. Antonio Lamux heard from his former wife's brother, who lived in another village, that his wife was a puma. The husband discovered it one day when he was walking back along the path from the town of Chenalhó. He bumped into some friends of his, and they began to drink liquor by the side of the path, where they ended up completely drunk. Meanwhile, his wife was waiting for him at home, but he didn't turn up. So she waited and waited, but still he didn't show up. Finally, when he arrived the next morning, his wife was so angry that she refused to prepare him food. The man became angry as well, took his axe, and went off into the forest near Keremtón Mountain to cut some wood. There he was, when all of a sudden he saw it, the puma, on top of a rock, and he stared at it as it moved its tail. The man thought to himself, "It's enormous! Its tail is longer than my arm!" Then he yelled obscenities at the puma, "*Pinche vieja! Vete cabrón!*" (Damned hag! Get the hell out of here!), in Spanish. He added, "I've got my axe with me!" Nothing happened to him; his wife only wanted to scare him. When he returned home with the wood, he said to his wife, "You were just trying to scare me!" Some months later, he was on the way to Yochib (the site of a weekly market where liquor is sold and consumed), when he passed by the mouth of a cave. The puma was there again, its eyes shining brightly. He threw a stick at it, but it didn't even flinch, so he had to run for his life. It was then that he let Antonio Lamux in on the secret that his wife was a puma, and that he was unable to do anything to risk angering her because each time he did, he came across "her power" in his path (especially when he was drunk, that is). The next year, Antonio saw this man again. By this time, his wife had died, and the widower told his version of the event. At a certain spot in Pantelhó (a neighboring village where there are cattle ranches owned by Spanish-speaking people), a cowhand discovered a pair of pumas, one male and one female. He went to his ranch to get a rifle and two big dogs, and then he went after them. The male managed to escape, but the female fled to a treetop, where the cowhand shot her in the back and killed her. His wife died, too, her parents saying that it was from losing too much blood because of her period. . . . But no! The hole in her back made by the Mauser bullet was plain for all to see.

Of course, not all pumas, hawks, opossums, and other animals are *lab*; only some are truly *sénte* (from the Spanish word *gente*, which means "people"). However, there is nothing distinctive about *lab* that identifies them as such at first glance. Their nature is not essentially any different from other members of their species. Their appearance is the same, as is their habitat, while their habits are, if not identical, very similar.

Most of the time, just as the Tzeltal rarely manage to find out what and who their *lab* are, so the animals are unaware that they are the *lab* of a "Christian" (*kirsáno*). But mishaps suffered by man or beast in the form of injuries, sickness, or death affect their counterpart immediately; the pain one experiences is felt instantly by the other, and in an analogous part of the body. In fact, what facilitates this connection between man and animal is that the names given to the parts of the animal's body, even those to all appearances as different as insects, have an equivalence in the parts of the human body. According to Lamux, that explains why both of them, man and *lab*, find themselves sharing a *pajal* relationship, a relationship "on the same horizontal plane." In the *kuxlejal* prayers, which are prayers of protection offered by the head of a household two or three times a year, there are entreaties not only for the crops and the health of the various members of the domestic group and their *ch'ulel* but also for the *lab* (whether animal or of another sort) they might happen to have, "because they may fight, fall, get hurt," thus causing suffering to the body in Cancuc.

There are some people who manage to identify not only the species of their *lab* animal but even the specific animal that is their *lab*, going so far as to build up a friendship with it. Exactly how this occurs is not entirely clear. In fact, cases of it happening are extremely few and far between, both because they are extraordinary events and by virtue of the fact that they are hardly spoken of at all. The person and his/her *lab* animal are then to be found at night in desolate spots at crosses that mark a spring, a cave entrance, or a simple crossroads. People take advantage of the opportunity to give the animals advice: not to go wrong, not to eat Christians (if the animal is carnivorous, of course), not to fight with other animals, or not to let themselves be seen. If it is a butterfly, for example, the person might tell it not to go too close to the flame of torches, because it may burn itself, "because if you do, you (we) aren't going to live long."

Some years ago, Lorenzo Lot spoke to an old man who used to communicate with his *lab*. The man lived alone, with no family, in an isolated house on the riverbank, not far from where Lorenzo grows chili. His *lab*, an animal in which he took fierce pride, was, as he explained to Lorenzo, a jaguar. It lived in the jungle, but every year it came to pay him a visit. To get to Cancuc it traversed underground passageways until it surfaced, always at night, at a cross near his house. On its arrival, the old man would give it something to eat (raw turkey), he would stroke it, and they would play for a while ("as if it were a dog"). Then the old man would give it the odd bit of advice, the most important being not to go anywhere near humans, because jaguar pelts are highly valued and they might kill him for it. Finally, they would bid each other farewell until the next year.

Water *lab*

The *lab* of the realm of water (*slab chanul ja'*) are mostly freshwater snakes, only remarkable in that they have a metal tool instead of a head; the handle is the body of the snake. These water *lab* include the following in Tzeltal: *machite chan* (*machete* serpent), *acha chan* (axe serpent, Sp. *hacha*), *pala chan* (shovel serpent, Sp. *pala*), *piko chan* (pickaxe serpent, Sp. *pico*), *chixnabal chan* (sewing-needle serpent), *maro chan* (hammer serpent, Sp. *marro*), *tijera chan* (scissors serpent, Sp. *tijera*), *pokol chan* (metal-grill serpent), *bareta chan* (bricklayer's-hammer serpent, Sp. *barreta*).[11] In fact, any metal instrument that may be used in Cancuc will find itself swelling the ranks of this kind of *lab*. Someone even mentioned *xarten tak'in*, "metal skillet" (Sp. *sartén*) as a *lab*, but it is not certain that it is a river creature: It is a *lab* said to be of the utmost use when defending yourself from gunfire. These creatures are *at'eletik*, "laborers," because incessantly but almost imperceptibly they toil away at eroding the banks of streams and rivers until they end up pulling down trees and causing cave-ins and landslides. Nevertheless, apparently their activity is regarded as beneficial, since it helps the drainage of water through the valleys and prevents flooding. Apart from that, they are retiring creatures that hardly bother humans; further, on account of their prudence, they do not endanger the well-being of the persons whose *lab* they are. They live in four deep pools, *k'ib'al lukum* (pool of snakes), one for each

Cancuc lineage (*chejeb, ijk'a, chijk',* and *boj*), "because those who are not relatives cannot live together." One of these pools is a lake located on Cancuc land where strong eddies are formed, making swimming unadvisable; the others are in rivers in unknown parts of the world. On the eve of the rainy season, a great fiesta is held at each pool to celebrate the imminent rise in the river level.

The *tsuluchan*, whose head is like a goat's but with only one horn that grows at its forehead, is also a water *lab*. Its body has never been seen, for it lives in the water and only its head emerges from the surface from time to time. Not long ago, someone saw how one such creature saved one of the hanging bridges that was threatened by the river's rising swell by lifting it up with its horn.

Meteor *lab*

The third distinct group of *lab* souls are forms that reside in "the upper space," *kajal*, in the "atmosphere," higher than any bird can fly, but never so high as to touch the sky. This group encompasses the bolt of lightning (*tzantzabal*); the *xojob*, a light beam that is kindled from above and which, when it settles over a house, is a sign that someone is about to die there; the rainbow (*sejkubal ja'al*), one of the ends of which blocks the mouths of caves to stop more clouds from emerging; the *k'anchixalton*, "stretched-out yellow stone," which are shooting stars.

Winds (*ik'etik*) are *lab* of a most violent disposition. They come from the east; blow for short, intense periods of gusts and squalls (they are storm winds); and are not to be confused with the west winds, which are softer and more consistent, as well as not being "people," but only air in motion. The *lab* winds are divided into four lineages, Cancuc's lineages, although they apparently all live in the same place, in the cave of a mountain (*luch'ub*) on land belonging to the Tzeltal town of Tenango, less than a day's walk east of Cancuc. Cheerful after having a big fiesta, the winds emerge from there in small groups from April onward, crossing the valley from east to west until they reach Tenejapa, where they veer away to the south, toward Teopisca, Amatenango del Valle, and Comitán, where they come to a virtual standstill, before returning unseen to their mountain. They are *lab* only for the people of Cancuc; other villages may well have *lab* winds, but if so, they live in other mountains.

Lightning is divided into two classes: red (*tsajal chauk*), which are *lab*, and green (*yaxal chauk*), which belong to the Mountain Lords. Along with the green bolts of lightning, the Mountain Lords also send up through the mouths of caves the low clouds that pour forth the most rain. In this guise, the Mountain Lords are known as *ánjel*. Curiously, it is not the color but rather the effect of the flashes that distinguishes between the two classes of lightning. Red lightning is considered much more powerful, and the time that elapses between the flash itself and the clap of thunder is shorter. From roughly August to March, they remain inactive because they are barred from living in caves (presumably because the green lightning bolts, with which they are quite incompatible, reside there); so they remain asleep inside plants (orchids or moss, the latter called "orchid of Castile") that grow on the big trees in the tropical lowlands.

During the rainy season, winds and lightning fight against each other. The former, in cahoots with the green lightning bolts and the storm clouds, try to wreck cultivated fields by knocking down the stalks of corn; meanwhile, the latter defend the annual harvest by attacking the aggressors with shots from their muskets. Yet the sequence of the battle seems highly ceremonial. Shortly before the rains begin, around March, all the red lightning bolts assemble (they are also divided into lineages) at a fiesta with gunpowder rockets, liquor, dancing, and music, at the end of which each one receives from the "mother of lightning bolts" (*sme' chauk*)—considered the highest authority among lightning bolts and herself some woman's *lab*—a red uniform and a musket (*mécha* or *chajan*). They are also given the season's orders regarding shifts and the locations where they are to lie in ambush for the winds.

Those Cancuqueros who suspect that they themselves may be meteors recite standard songs with the specific objective of convincing their *lab* not to expose themselves to any unnecessary danger. If the *lab* is a wind, for example, it is reminded not to enter empty tree trunks, as they are easy targets for lightning; and not to seek shelter in rounded stones, but rather in sharp-edged ones that will disperse the shots. An appeal is also made for the lightning bolts to stay asleep in their orchids, to forget the date of the annual call to their general meeting, not to check the date of it in their books, even for the ink in which it is written to be erased, and so on. This concern is more than justified, as a wind hit by a flash of lightning will almost certainly die. The same will happen to the person in Cancuc, or at least part of his body will show signs of burning. The chances of it happening are not as remote as one might imagine. The year 1990 was, according to the Tzeltal, not especially remarkable for the amount of red lightning, but at least five people died from this cause. Accidents such as someone drunk falling into the hearth in his home and ending up badly burned are not uncommon.

Death from or signs of burns is a frequent symptom of being a wind. Particularly well remembered is an event that occurred one June in which three or four men were busying themselves with the first weeding of the cornfield, when suddenly a violent storm broke out, forcing them to seek shelter beneath a tree. At length, one of them decided not to wait for the storm to subside and instead set off for home. Later, when the others returned along the path, they found him dead, burned to a cinder. They carried him home, and he was buried the next morning. But when they had finished filling in the grave, a myriad of lightning bolts began to strike the site, bolts flashing in the sky and then striking, flashing and striking. It was believed that the lightning bolts were showing their joy at having put a wind to death. If there are no winds, the red lightning bolts do not appear, although in 1990, winds flattened the cornfields while red lightning did nothing to prevent it. A *principal* dreamed that the mother of lightning had died that season without having designated any successor, which is why the flashes of lightning were wandering around disconcerted; there was also talk of some old woman who had recently died, but no conclusive explanation was ever reached.

The "Illness-Giver" *lab*

The fourth and last kind of *lab* souls are a mixed bag of beings, different only in appearance, since they all share the condition of being *ak' chamel*, "illness-giver." If the *lab* we have mentioned thus far are capable under certain circumstances of harming humans of flesh and blood, most of the time the risk they imply is passive, that is, someone grows ill because one of his *lab* has died or has suffered in some way. By contrast, these kinds of *lab* are different from the rest in that they actively seek to cause illness; they are homicidal *lab*, even if their motives cannot always be understood.

The most outstanding of these characters goes by the name of *pále*, from the Spanish *padre cura*, "father," also referred to in chant couplets as *kelérico*, "clergyman" (Spanish *clérigo*). They are about one meter tall, chubby, bald, with ankle-length vestments and shoes. There is no doubt that they are Catholic priests, with whom they are explicitly compared. A man explained to me how he had once passed by the village church of the town of Oxchuc where he caught sight of a *pále*. It was not, in fact, a *lab* at all, but a real Christian, praying in the atrium, although he really did look like a *pále*—fat and bald, with multicolored clothes.

Actually there are several kinds of *pále*. The most common are the "black fathers" (*ijk'al pále;* also known as *tsots' pále*, "father-bat"). Their clothing is black, and according to some, they are only active at night. On the other hand, the "daytime father" (*k'aalel pále*) is clothed in a white habit and is completely bald except for a thick band above his ears. Sometimes he wears a hood that conceals his head and face. To help me get a good picture of his appearance, Lamux gave me as an example the statue of a daytime *pále* in the city of San Cristóbal—a bust sculpted in commemoration of Fray Bartolomé de Las Casas, bishop of Chiapas and "Defender of the Indians"—where he is shown complete with tonsure. The leaders of the *pále* are the *wispa*, "bishops" (Spanish *obispos*), plumper in appearance, probably because they wear several garments, one on top of another, each item of a different color; they also wear very shiny black shoes. Much rarer is a fourth type of priest: the *jesúta*, that is to say, "Jesuit" (Spanish *jesuíta*); according to Xun P'in, he is a more solitary being. He is also different in appearance. No one knows what he wants, but he is taller and extraordinarily thin, with sunken eyes and a fine long nose.[12]

In all their versions, the *pále* are slaves to an indomitable desire to eat meat. They have a weakness for fowl, especially for the Bird of the Heart, in other words, the soul of each Indian. This makes them truly terrifying beings. It may be said that whereas felines invariably give rise to fascination, and meteors are spoken of with an ambiguous reverence, when it comes to *pále*, it is not unusual for the characteristic self-restraint in the conversation to be replaced by an excited, jumpy tone, not unlike someone describing the species of animal to which he feels the strongest aversion. The *pále* are the only beings capable of extracting the Bird of the Heart, by means of strange songs and whistles. They do not whistle like Indians, with a simple shrill note, but rather they compose a melody that the bird cannot resist. Earlier we saw how the Bird of the Heart is extracted from the body, converted into a larger size, and cooked with hot water, a procedure in which a simulacrum of the process of baptism can perhaps be recognized. Moreover, the *pále* inhabit the woods and the caves of the cold land; watchful and slippery customers, they prefer not to be seen (although, along with the other *lab*, they frequently appear in dreams, where they travel by mule, cart, or motor car). Nonetheless, there are a few tell-tale signs that give away their proximity: an acrid smell of burnt tobacco, for example, because they smoke a lot. But they have actually been seen a few times. An elderly woman told me how, one night when she could not sleep, she had gone out to the patio of her house and there she came across a fat bishop sitting on one of her stools, peacefully smoking an enormous cigar. That is why leaving stools out overnight, or even neglecting to lean them up against a wall inside the house, is considered an invitation for this kind of being to visit.

The *pále* are often accompanied by a "Castilian dog" (*kaxlan tsi'*), which is a *lab*, too. They are tiny dogs, plump and furry, usually white, although occasionally black, that feed off the bones of the Bird of the Heart tossed to them by the *pále*. It seems to me that they closely resemble the dogs that are bred as pets in the city of San Cristóbal. What is certain is that they are different from Indian dogs, which are taller and scruffier and are never, understandably, given a bone to gnaw, just a corn tortilla every now and then.

The *eskiribano* ("scribe," Sp. *escribano*) type of *lab* is in many ways similar to the *pále*. It includes the *nompere*, from the Spanish *nombre*, "name" (almost certainly the same character as the one referred to in the prayers as *rei*, "king"). It is also a dwarf, dressed in black breeches and shirt and flat hat called *birete*, "biretta." In one of his hands he holds a feather, in the other a logbook (*jun*: "book," "logbook," "writing paper,' or "paper with writing on it"). As the term indicates, a "name" gives illness by writing down the names of its victims. He says, "Well, let's see, who am I going to give an illness to today?" before sitting down and carefully writing the name, the Tzeltal name, on a list; this action alone is enough to cause illness in the person named. However, in this case, the very body of the person falls victim directly, not his or her soul entities. It is more difficult to obtain a description of a second kind of scribe, the "professor" (*provisor* or *pofisol*, Sp. *profesor*).[13] Looking like a schoolteacher, to whom he is compared, he is said to spread illness by reading aloud from a book, apparently without having preselected his victim.

Priests and scribes do not get along; when, by chance, they do meet, they are capable of killing each other, obviously resulting in some Tzeltal falling ill or even dying. Both are alike in not having a body: beneath their clothing, there is nothing except handwritten or printed paper, rolled up in such a way as to permit them to stand upright. Lorenzo Lot compares them with the *xutax* (Judas) doll that is hung from a rope around the cross in the church's atrium every Easter Week. Its body is made of dried and pressed banana leaves, which are clothed with a hat, shirt, jacket, pants, and shoes; at the end of the week, it is burned. But in the case of the *lab*, it is paper with writing on it. K'aal relates the following incident that took place in another village and involved some acquaintances of his. The sun still had not set completely and the family was in the kitchen of their hut when they saw something approaching the house. What could it be? The thing was dancing and singing next to the wall, so the owner of the house took a bit of burning wood from the fire and hurled it with such force that it hit the thing right in the throat. The thing collapsed; it was a *pále*. So they set fire to it, and were able to see that it was paper. As it burned, they say, it gave off a foul-smelling white smoke.

The "Castilian" (*kaxlan*), another kind of *lab*, bears an unmistakable resemblance to a Mexican rancher, even though the details of his clothing vary from one description to another. He almost always wears a hat, leather pants, a shirt, and sometimes shining metal spurs and sunglasses. When seen in dreams, he often rides a horse.

Sheep (*tumin chij*, literally "cotton deer") and goats (*tentzun*) also belong to this group. Not all of these animals are *lab*; they are mostly ordinary animals, although after careful scrutiny, one may catch a fleeting glimpse of some sheep that seem to have a human expression.

Owls (*xoch'*, *totoi*, *k'ajk'al wax*) occupy a special place among the "illness-givers." Just like the *pále*, they are interested in eating the Bird of the Heart, but they are unable to extract it by themselves. They must position themselves on a branch and wait for the priests (the *pále*) to get hold of one and toss it up into the air to make it grow bigger. The owls then can grab it and fly away with it. But the owls also send illness to the bodies, so that the Bird of the Heart is released from the dying person. The owls do this by "speaking," that is, by repeating *kuts' kuts' kuts'*, an onomatopoeic word that recalls the first babbling words of a baby.

In fact, this is the feature common to the whole group of *lab* that are "illness-givers," whether human or animal in form: the faculty of language. The other *lab* may have at their disposal their own "languages" to communicate among themselves, or, at best, they may have a passive "understanding" of human language, without being able to articulate it. Words are, as shall be seen later, the principal vehicle of illness.

Finally, new forms of *lab* have come along to swell the ranks of the illness-givers. One such *lab* is music and songs similar to those performed by evangelical groups in their chapels and the songs currently making the rounds on cassette tapes played especially at night: the music of the guitar, bass guitar, and accordion, with a *norteño* (a popular type of music from northern Mexico) rhythm, which in actual fact are evangelical songs. At the end of the dry season, which in 1990 lasted longer than normal, it was necessary to wait until late at night to fill the pitchers at one of the very few springs that had not dried up ("even the men had to fill pitchers"). One could hear the *lab* musicians singing and playing their instruments as they came down from Chixtetik, where there is a Presbyterian church, to the lower limits of the inhabited zone, where another of their churches was located. In earlier years, these musical interludes coincided with a plethora of gastrointestinal complaints that were further complicated by a measles epidemic, killing several small children.

Earlier still, twenty or thirty years ago, another kind of *lab*, the *me'tiktatik* (mothers-fathers) appeared, which, with the passage of time, has become terribly morbid. They seem to take the shape of old men and women with gray hair and beards, but they are invisible. They usually sit on small chairs around a table in the middle of roads to eat and drink chicken, soup, liquor, and coffee. Any passerby runs the risk of inadvertently knocking over their food, which is invisible as well. In retaliation, the *me'tiktatik* remove the miscreant's *ch'ulel*, in order to obtain from the healing ceremonies food that is at least as good. Rominko Extul, for example, had one of these mishaps not long ago. He was returning home one night, very drunk. No sooner had he crossed the stream beside the small coffee warehouse than he noticed that something made him stumble and fall down. It was a bunch of *me'tiktatik*, annoyed because he had knocked over their food. He realized that they were holding him back by the ankle, so he spent the whole night there on the bank of the stream, amid the puddles. As he slept, he "saw" that they were demanding two liters of liquor from him; at sunrise, once he had managed to make it home, he offered up the liquor at his household altar. These *lab me'tiktatik* are *lum*, "earth," but they have nothing to do with the Mountain Lords. In a way, they are manifestations of the earth in human form.

The *lab* as Personal Power

Up to now, we have looked at the different possible kinds of *lab*. Let us now turn to how the Tzeltal use these *lab* in matters of personal power. Everyone has at least one *lab*, although most people possess more than one. One *lab* per person is considered a minimum, while the maximum number is thirteen, but people usually have "several," that is to say "two or three." It seems that any combination of *lab* types is possible within an individual, for example, a puma, a butterfly, wind, a schoolteacher, an owl, and a "mother-father." Even mutually incompatible *lab*, such as lightning bolts and winds, or priests and scribes, may occur together within the same individual. This notion led me to ask one day about the possibility of one person's conflictive *lab* types killing each other, but my query was met with bewilderment.

The numerical classifier used for *lab* is *kun*.[14] Such counters refer to a grammatical particle in Tzeltal that describes the shape or some other quality of the thing that is being counted. *Kun* is generally employed to count separate things that exist on the same horizontal plane and that possess some adjoining point of communication, like the rooms of a house, should it have more than one, connected through an opening, whether a doorway or another aperture. For example, if you say in Tzeltal that someone has three *lab*, you would say *ay oxkun slab te tul winik*, a rough translation of which would be: "He is/has (*ay*) three (*ox*) things joined horizontally (*kun*) that are his *lab* (*slab*), that being with a human form (*tul*) that is a human being (*winik*)." Nevertheless, I must admit the expression is a little forced, formulated as a response to the demands of my questions.

Broadly speaking, the term *lab* designates something hidden, veiled, as in the expression *slab k'op*, "language with obscure meaning." However, when referring to the soul entity, the word *lab* sounds too "strong" to use in conversation, and nowadays a common recourse is to employ other terms that are half synonyms, half euphemisms. For instance, the word *pukuj* (creator of illness or the very substance of the disease) is used if the *lab* is a threat; the word *ánjel* ("angel," which in fact designates any soul component) refers to one's own *lab* that are protective and benign; sometimes in songs, the semantic parallel to *lab* is *way*, the root of "sleep/dream." Nonetheless, the word employed most often is undoubtedly *yuel*, equivalent to someone's "power," "faculty," his or her capacity to affect others or to be affected.

In part, the *lab* are "power," due to the fact that some of their most characteristic faculties (depending on their kind) make their presence known in the body or, more accurately, in the person as a whole. Individuals whose *lab* are jaguars or pumas tend to be corpulent and strong; people with a hawk *lab* may have extraordinary eyesight; those who are water *lab* have no fear of swimming in rivers; those with wind *lab* are stormy by nature; Indians with "mother-father" *lab* are said to have above-average wisdom because "they can see what happens beneath the earth's surface." Additionally, some *lab* are accorded strengths that would never be imagined, judging from their outward appearance. For example, despite its delicate appearance, the hummingbird is considered to be a powerful *lab*, perhaps on account of its ability to penetrate diverse realms—mainly the earth's interior and the sky—realms barred to other beings.

However, as we have seen, having one or more *lab* constitutes a risk for the person's body. "They say that if more than half a man's *lab* die, the man dies, too; if not, he will live, and can go on living because he still has others left." It is not easy to decide whether it is preferable to have many or few *lab*. In principle, having many seems safer, but the chances of them being harmed and falling ill are also higher. And the picture is even more complicated than that, for what is at stake here is not only the number of *lab*, but also fundamentally their quality. The greater the *lab*'s strength, the greater the possibility that it will intervene in circumstances harming the person (and vice versa); but greater, too, is the risk of death if the *lab* are killed. What is certain is that these issues are no more than a schematic sampling of the intricate, almost arithmetical, calculations the Tzeltal are capable of making when weighing the pros and cons of having these soul beings. In other words, *lab* are power, and as such, what is being judged is the double-edged convenience of having power.

It is commonly believed that those who excel socially—whether because of their initiative, their de facto power, or because they hold office—have a high number of *lab*, including some strong beings. That idea explains both their capacity to act and their strength of character, as well as the high frequency with which they die prematurely (probably true statistically, given the endemic factionalism and the penchant for achieving a position of privilege by physically eliminating one's political opponents). Powerful individuals or figures of authority tend to be connected with certain *lab*. One of the shamans' many *lab* is a feline, almost always a jaguar. Elderly *principales* almost certainly have meteor *lab*; the fact that meteor *lab* are divided into winds (aggressors) and lightning bolts (defenders) throws into relief the deep ambivalence with which members of this group go about their business. What is at stake in their battles is no less than the corn harvest, the fundamental means of the community's survival. They (*lab* of *principales*) generally do not allow any young men to cease in their obeisance to them, and they are even suspected of attempting to annihilate the *lab* of newborn babies (especially those with thirteen of them) so that they die and thus do not pose any threat to their power when they grow up. It should be clarified that those who hold positions of authority do not benefit from their *lab* as "representatives" as such, but rather are driven by a power struggle in the realm of souls, a sort of soul despotism.[15]

Nevertheless, the inverse is also true. People who are vulnerable in society—elderly people living alone; young wives, particularly in the period between leaving their parents' home and having male sons of a certain age; widows or estranged women who do not wish to remarry—actively cultivate the belief that they possess powerful *lab*. As a matter of fact, people who are apparently weak are prominently featured in many of the events one hears, accounts that almost certainly were introduced or put into circulation by these same individuals. The fact that there is no sure way to identify personal *lab*, together with the power that their own position on the fringes of society gives them, makes it easier for them to wield this counterbalance of power to its limits.

Complete Human Beings

Men and women possessing thirteen *lab* are said to be "complete human beings" (*ts'akal winik*). Another formulation of the same idea says the group of their soul entities is a finished product (*ts'akal sch'ulel*). Only a select number of Cancuqueros have thirteen *lab*, "otherwise there would be many problems (*sk'oplalil*)." Once dead, these "finished" human beings await a different fate from the others. They go to dwell inside the earth, where they are spirited away not only as *ch'ulel*, but with their body as well, which does not decompose in the grave. Instead, they rise up, pay a farewell visit to their house, pick up their small gourd of ground tobacco with lime (if the family has forgotten to deposit it in the grave), and then enter the earth by way of a bottomless abyss, the entrance to which is not far from the center of Cancuc. If you stare down toward the bottom of the chasm at midday, you are supposed to be able to see little points of light that are the stars on the other side of the world, where at that moment it is midnight. The "complete humans" then arrive at the base of one of the four pillars holding up the earth's surface, where they join forces with the column. The pillars prevent the sea surrounding the land from overrunning it; and they are assisted in this enterprise by the sun that "burns" the water at dawn and at dusk, causing it to evaporate and thus preventing the level from rising.

Top shamans have thirteen *lab*, as well as *anejme'jtatik* (our mother-father angels), those slightly enigmatic folk entrusted with transferring the *ch'ulel* back to the patient's body once it has been liberated by the shaman's prayers. It should be noted that it is not these individuals' *lab* that do this work, but rather their *ch'ulel*. In lay circles, it is frequently thought that it is the very shaman's *ch'ulel* that makes the trip, thus discharging the ransom; but this is categorically denied by Xun P'in. The role of the *anejme'jtatik* is similar to that of the guardian angel in the Catholic tradition, but it is an angel linked to a kinship group, not an individual angel. Furthermore, there is one man and one woman for each lineage, making a total of eight. By night their *ch'ulel* make a round of the houses, one by one, to make sure that all is well, and if anyone feels threatened by night falling, he or she may pray for their protection. They are authentic Cancuqueros, but their identity is unknown. There is some speculation that the current female "angel" of the Chejeb lineage is a certain young woman, very beautiful and demure, who lives in a small village. As for the men, it is said with admiration that they dislike living with women, and if they do, they do not have offspring. Very rarely, and just for a few instants, the *anejme'jtatik* show themselves along the paths looking like a "Castilian," beggarly in appearance, shoeless, with clean but ragged clothing.

The Internal *lab*

Lab are scattered all over the face of the earth (*spamal lum*). Yet, as we may recall, they are at the same time doubled in an individual's heart and can, under certain circumstances, leave the body. This entails a whole new set of problems. In theory, any kind of *lab* may emerge, although from the examples given, it is clear that the Tzeltal have in mind strong *lab*, and most often illness-givers. Anyone will tell you that other kinds of *lab* have no reason to leave the heart, even more so if they are weak, because then they would be running an inordinate risk.

Let's look at an example of someone's *lab* that is a *pále*. In its "external" form, this being lives in the forests and may approach human settlements to give illness, but that same person also has a *pále* in the heart, the exact double of the other one. While the body sleeps (for the *lab* almost always steal away while the body is sleeping), the "internal" *lab* may leave from the individual's mouth, stroll among the houses, perpetrate his wicked deeds in the same way as the "external" *lab*, before returning at last to the heart. It may well be that the person's body has turned facedown during the *lab*'s absence, thus hampering its reentry through the mouth. Logically speaking, any mishap this second type of *lab* suffers has an equal impact on the body. It's not that the body's will plays any part in the misdeed—in fact, it does not have even the slightest inkling of what is going on—rather it is the *pále*'s own decision to leave. This point is crucial: there is absolutely no physical transformation involved in the process. The fact is that the *lab* is part of the *talel* of the person involved. The root of the word is *tal*, "to come," and when

applied to a person, means "what comes to him as given," "his character," "his way of being."

One gets the impression that activity on the part of the internal *lab*
is much less frequent than that of its external counterpart. For some
reason, they do not find it easy to emerge from the heart. However, the
chance that it may happen is terrifying, given that they do not come
out from inhabited places, but rather from "within." In such cases, the
ordinary precautions are useless, because the *lab* are already inside the
house. Obviously, domestic relations, and especially conjugal ones, are
placed in a difficult position, for there is no guarantee that a jaguar or
a Jesuit will not spring from the husband or wife sleeping peacefully by
one's side at night.

This overall picture is again complicated by some exceptions. Under
certain circumstances, the body's will is able to make direct use of the
faculties of its own internal *lab*. One man, for instance, explained to me
that his father was *xojob*, that is to say, a "beam of light," and that he
used him to light his way at night; the light poured from his mouth and
armpits. The contrary is also possible: the *lab* themselves make use of
the *ch'ulel*'s body and perhaps even its emotions, in other words, the rest
of the person. If anyone is offended by another flesh-and-blood person,
his *lab* might conceivably try to benefit from the occasion by giving the
offender an illness during the night. It is in this sense that the *lab* is regarded as someone's "power."

By way of examples, I present two accounts illustrating two possibilities. (It seems to me that both are more distant in time than is usual for
lab-related incidents.) The first was told to Xun P'in by his uncle, who
had witnessed the event, which must have taken place more than forty
years ago. It happened that there were some men who gave light with
the aid of "their power." They had been working on the fincas of the
Pacific coast as paid laborers and were returning to their communities.
Most were from the Indian town of Oxchuc, but there were a few Cancuqueros, too. The journey was a long one, and they had to walk day and
night. At sundown, complete darkness fell upon them, and they had no
pine-resin torches. They stumbled upon a deep, wide river and were unable to find where the path continued on the other side. A man jumped
in to find out and drowned; another jumped in, with the same result.
The group then sat down to decide what to do. They carried a little
liquor with them, so they mixed it with tobacco and began to drink,
whereupon one said, "We must pick the strongest (*tulan winik*), but who

would they be?" Another said, "I only have a little power, I'm *pále*," to which the rest responded, "Ah, but they can't help us." "I'm an owl," said another, but that was no good either. So they selected the four who were "beam of light"—that *lab* can illuminate like a flashlight and is also very strong. They stopped drinking and said, "Let's go," and then Xun P'in explained to me, it came out of the mouth, it came out like a gunpowder rocket, straight up, and, he said, the path was lit up as if there were a full moon. They waded across the river and continued walking, all the while accompanied by the beam of light. That is how it happened; they chose four men and saw how their power came out of them, out of their mouths. Xun P'in added that it's true that the *pále* give only illness, lacking any kind of benefit; but the beams of light, the lightning bolts, they certainly do have real power.

The second incident involves an unidentified man who fancied a certain woman. The woman was a relative of his, in the broad sense of belonging to his exogamic group. Once, the man trailed her to a secluded spot, where she stopped to wash clothes in the stream. Then, in broad daylight, a jaguar leaped from his mouth and grabbed hold of the woman. "Leave me alone," she said. "I'm not going to leave you alone. I like you a lot, I really love you," said the jaguar. "All right, then," said the woman, for she wanted to save her life. Once the woman relented, they say, the jaguar was a jaguar no more, and only a man. And it is true that jaguars have a voracious sexual appetite, as well as incestuous tendencies.[16]

The Transference of *lab*

Opinions on the fate of the *lab* once the body dies are quite unanimous: they are passed on by the person who is at death's door to some child that is still inside its mother's womb. This transference can only occur in the event that donor and recipient are members of the same lineage. The *lab* leaves the body through the individual's mouth as if it were "smoke" or "steam" or a bright sparkle of light, taking the shape that corresponds to it. That is to say, it can be the somewhat blurred outline of an animal, wind, a bolt of lightning, and so on. The last gasp of life confirms the *lab* has been expelled.[17]

The operation by which one person's *lab* is transferred to another person is *nochtayel*, an expression that, as far as I know, is only used in this context, where its meaning appears to be "take the place of someone" or "supplant him." It tends to happen between alternate generations of lineal relatives, grandparents-grandchildren (that address themselves reciprocally as *mam*), regardless of the sex of the donor or recipient. On the other hand, the word *elol* means "replacement," and as applied to people, the *elol* is somebody with whom one coincides both in proper name and clan patronymic designation (which is not an unusual occurrence, bearing in mind the limited range of proper names available). In other words, here it essentially means "homonym." But in a much more precise and connotative way, someone's true *elol* is that person to whom the *lab* are passed on, in the strict sense, his "replacement" on earth. In actual fact, parents are in the habit of giving their children the proper name of someone in the generation of the grandparents on the father's side who had passed away while the infant was being carried in its mother's womb, clearly believing that the infant will receive the ancestor's *lab*.

However, this operation functions only as a conjecture. There is no way of checking which little boy or girl receives a recently deceased's *lab*, because, among other reasons, the will of the donor holds some sway in the fate of the *lab*. According to some accounts, in a final flash of lucidity, the donor infallibly identifies—he "sees"—his own *lab*. For better or for worse, the *lab* are a sort of legacy with which people may play tricks on their heirs. It is, for example, possible that in the haste of death throes, the *lab* may be transferred to the womb of the first available woman. Or, knowing himself to be the possessor of some *lab* types with a tendency to put the body in danger, the donor may, in a final act of vengeance, transfer them to the son of a personal enemy, so that the child runs the risk of dying prematurely.

Another very different option is that of obtaining *lab* by buying them. They are bought from someone who wants to rid himself of them in exchange for money or corn; but this is definitely an exceptional situation, because the transference, which requires complex ceremonies that few know how to perform, endangers both the donor's and, above all, the recipient's lives. The reason for this is simple: the *lab* is not his *talel*, he was not born with it; his body is not adapted to the *lab*.

In this regard, while several men were conversing, someone from another hamlet recounted in passing something that had recently happened in his land. A woman (her name and her husband's, and a few other details, were supplied so that she might be identified) was spread out on her fiber mat, at death's door. Next to her were her husband, her children, and other relatives. But the woman did not die, she just would not die, and suddenly, her youngest child, still a baby, began to tremble, moan, writhe, and roll about on the floor, shouting very loudly as if he were in great pain. This went on for a few seconds until all of a sudden, silence fell. Shortly afterward the mother died. The tale stopped there. There was a pause, and then the conversation took another turn. I never discussed this account with anyone, but it is, I think, easy to interpret: the mother attempted to cede her *lab* to her son, but his body did all it could to reject it, as the *lab* was not innate. What, perhaps, the episode leaves hanging in the air (very characteristically, it should be said) is whether the transference was finally successful or not.

In any case, the incident speaks eloquently of the concern regarding the possibility of mothers trying to pass on their own *lab* to their sons or daughters, grandsons or granddaughters. It is believed women would be "usurping" (*nochtayel*) the transmission of *lab* on the father's side, when they should in fact restrict their role in making the continuation of the father's line possible. It is taken for granted that an equal number and kind of *lab* is maintained among the lineages, but not among the clans composing each. On the other hand, some clans tend to specialize in particular types of *lab*. For example, a clan in which many members inhabit the valley slopes facing the town of Cancuc is said to possess *lab* of the "water beings" group. Indeed, some of them are specialists in swimming goods and people across the river. On the other hand, since the quota of *lab* per lineage is limited, its unstable distribution is subject to an underground struggle to reduce other clans' *lab* for the benefit of one's own clan's *lab*. This is done through the straightforward process of killing each other.

This is the only plane, the parallel world of the *lab*, on which one can note the influence of interclan politics. Apart from the odd, isolated episode, it all seems a bit distant when viewed from the perspective of ordinary life in Cancuc.[18]

Further Interpretations

So far we have seen all the aspects that exist in the general awareness of the people, which are widely known, even though they are not exactly publicly acknowledged. However, private conversations revealed that there were those who had worked out other relationships in much greater depth, though they were unable to refer to concrete "events" to back them up. These relationships, when heard independently, reveal some points of convergence. Two of these coincidences are especially revealing.

First of all, the true *ch'ulel* that dwells in the *ch'iibal* mountains also possesses *lab*. This means the *lab* that are to be found duplicated inside a human body are also to be found in his *ch'ulel* in *ch'iibal*. Secondly, the "external" *lab* have within them a reflection of the silhouette of the flesh-and-blood Tzeltal whose destiny they share ("silhouette," here, for what someone called *ch'ulel*—a very imprecise term in any case—and someone else called *noketal*, that is, a "person's shadow"). A new possibility may be inferred from these two explanations: an immediate relationship exists between the *ch'ulel* of the *ch'iibal* and the *lab*. If this is so, the relationships between the soul components may be imagined as forming a triangle, each corner of which—Cancuc, the *ch'iibal* mountain, the *lab*—is duplicated in the other two. Most Tzeltal only show some interest in two sides of the relationship, that is, between Cancuc and the *ch'iibal* on the one hand, and between Cancuc and the *lab* on the other. The third side, joining the *ch'iibal* and the *lab*, is not worked out so well; but the odd clue to its intervention in everyday life may yet be discerned. One possibility, for instance, one that not all Tzeltal are ready to entertain, is that the *ch'ulel* give their consent to some *lab* to harm the human body or make use of them to mete out punishment. Another possibility, one with even fewer supporters, is that the *lab* themselves are sanctioned on the part of the *ch'iibal*.[19]

CHAPTER 3

Souls and Signs

Behind the public face, other identities are always concealed, other beings that are in some cases, as we have seen, intrinsically hostile. But at the same time, the precise identity of those others lodged in the heart ("souls") is unknown to everyone else, as well as to oneself. Apart from a very few persons, usually elderly ones, who get as far as discovering the species of being that inhabits their interior, most of one's life is spent without getting to know one's own inner beings (that is, without knowing oneself), let alone those of other people. It would then seem to be inevitable that any relationship between Tzeltal individuals is fraught with wariness produced by that initial ignorance. What is certain is that it would be difficult to overestimate its importance, because many human relationships, if not the preservation of life itself, depend on recognizing the hidden identities of neighbors, relatives, members of domestic groups, and spouses.

Signs in Gestures

In all cases, just because the identity of the souls is anonymous at the outset and resists discovery, it is by no means a completely impenetrable realm. To understand how this works, a person's different identities would have to be imagined as arranged in layers, stratified. The topmost layer corresponds to the body. Beneath the body, the *ch'ulel* is found, and deeper still, the *lab*. (As for the Bird of the Heart, it is of no interest in this regard, as the matter at hand is what distinguishes one person from another, and the Bird of the Heart is replicated identically in every person.) In principle, only a person's top layer is known, but at some specific moments, or in specific ways, partial exposure of these other layers occurs that bespeak the other identities: traces, bits of properties characteristic of the souls that manifest themselves in the person's appearance. How can they be recognized?

To assess the degree to which these possible partial glimpses may be seen, it is first and foremost necessary to take note of the stylization and the strict control of personal expression cultivated by the Tzeltal, as is characteristic of many other Amerindian cultures. This effort leaves its mark on three areas of the person that are subject to meticulous public scrutiny. First of all, attention to bodily movements and the economy of gestures is extraordinary (particularly if the ethnographer comes from a Mediterranean background). The way of sitting, leaning, standing; hand movements; facial expressions—everything should transmit the impression of serenity and self-control. There is a constant concern with maintaining a vertical position and corporeal symmetry. Walking is typically a regular, graceful, solemn gait. Few things are more ridiculous than tripping or falling in public. From an early age, girls and boys are taught to tread gently, without disturbing the earth. There is no place for brusque or excessive gestures either, as they are strongly viewed as improper, actually immoral.

Secondly, strict control is expressed in the fervor shown in matters of personal neatness and clothing. Clothes are, aside from the difference between men and women, virtually a uniform in which very few variations are allowed. Special care is taken to avoid any kind of stain: earth, ash, mud, or anything else. It is amazing to behold how the Tzeltal manage to almost never splash their white tunics, however muddy the paths may be. In the same way, the fording of a stream is taken as a good opportunity to rinse one's feet. This zeal for personal tidiness is perhaps all the more remarkable for its contrast with household interiors: dark for lack of openings, blackened by soot from the fire, permanently damp; household utensils and a host of other objects of all kinds mixed up carelessly together, making it impossible at a first glance to see a clear distribution of space.

Finally, self-control must be shown when speaking. Certainly this means saying the right thing at the right time but also controlling the physical qualities of language: the timbre of the voice, tone, cadence, and so on. If a list were to be made of rebukes and derogatory nicknames used in Cancuc, those that are inspired by improper speech would assuredly figure among the most numerous.

The way to pose for photographs is a good example of what is considered an appropriate posture for the body. The portrait will preferably be full-length, with no limbs cut off by the frame. The subject would be dressed in traditional Indian clothes, clean and new, if possible, together with some accessories—a red cotton band knotted around the waist, a string bag slung from the shoulder to hip—regarded as part of the daily uniform. The body would be upright, with weight distributed evenly on both legs, in other words, with the body symmetrically positioned. The shoulders would slope forward a little, the arms glued to the body, thus preventing any chance gesticulation. Something might be held in the hands, usually something to do with social position, not personal whim. For instance, a grandfather might hold his little granddaughter, an *alcalde* his staff of office, and so forth. Of course, their mien is always unflinching.

With this ideal uniform and immaculate body as the stage, the task of recognizing the nature of each individual's *ch'ulel* entails some difficulty. As we have seen, the emotions are to be found stored away in the *ch'ulel*. In fact, in the Tzeltal language, emotions and feelings are defined as states of the "heart" (*o'tan*): *mel yo'tan*, "sad"; *lek y'otan*, "kindly"; *chopol yo'tan*, "wicked"; *bik'tal yo'tan*, "jealous"; *slab yo'tan*, "hidden, cloudy"; *k'uxul yo'tan*, "affectionate"; *p'ij yo'tan*, "intelligent"; *k'ixin yo'tan*, "violent"; and so the list goes on. Here, "heart" is synonymous with *ch'ulel*, its emotional characteristics defining both the *ch'ulel*'s transitory moods and its unvarying temperament, given to it before birth. This "character" in turn reveals itself piecemeal in idiosyncratic traits that distinguish one person from another: gestures, details of clothing or the manner in which it is worn, preferences of taste, and so forth. But of all of them, there can be no doubt that the most significant are those related to the individual's linguistic habits. Tzeltal concern for metalinguistics has possibly to do with the fact that it is through language that one inevitably discovers in front of others the character of one's own *ch'ulel*.[1]

If this happens in the privacy of one's own home, it is to a certain extent (but only to a certain extent) acceptable. However, allowing facial expression, for example, to reflect the emotions of the heart in public, thus attracting attention, perhaps in the center of town or in the marketplace, is a much more serious matter. In extreme cases, it may lead to *k'exlal*, a condition that is hard to define: something like a feeling of ridicule, embarrassment, but one that also engenders a homonymous illness (with the most heterogeneous symptoms). Although such a case only rarely brings about death, it leaves the shamefaced person—usually a woman—prostrate for weeks or months at a time. An intense case of *k'exlal* may actually go on indefinitely.

Discovering the precise identity of each person's *lab* requires an altogether more complex process, consisting of spotting possible similarities between the details peculiar to an individual—details that are usually, though not exclusively, physical—and those of a particular kind of *lab*. To put it schematically: physical defects are to the *lab* what idiosyncratic traits are to the *ch'ulel*. As if to compensate for a surprisingly superficial knowledge of the internal organs, the Tzeltal language possesses an elaborate vocabulary of physiognomy. Nevertheless, anatomical peculiarities are just as exposed to examination in public and merciless ridicule in private as idiosyncratic gestures.

Thus, one is perfectly entitled to suspect that the *lab* of a big animal, a puma or a jaguar, may correspond to someone who is heavily built; an intense, staring expression is also a mark of being feline. There could be something reminiscent of a goat in the hair on a man's chin, and hairy cheeks may have the look of a *lab* ocelot about them. Fearless swimmers of the river may be a metal tool (a water *lab*), and exhibiting an uncommon fondness for meat could display the *pále* within. Baldness or a potbelly, rare among Indians, could also be clues to a *pále lab*. All of these are examples pointed out to me in Cancuc to help me see the kind of partial exposure produced in people's appearance. It is largely a matter of reasonable guesswork, not ready formulas.

Out of the whole constellation of unique features that may be discerned in an individual, only some, perhaps only one, is a *sign*, something that indirectly evokes the relationship between the person's skindeep appearance and the deeper nature of the *lab* in his heart. The relationship presents itself in a *kuyuyil* way, in other words, by showing only one aspect of the group it belongs to, thus in a misleading way. The Tzeltal vocabulary compiled by Fray Domingo de Ara (1986) in the sixteenth century translates *cuy* (*kuy*) as "to feign to be something other than what one is. To compare." Later we shall return to this last word in greater detail.

For now, how can a mere individual detail be distinguished from a genuine sign, a signal of the presence of the *lab?* It seems to me that this cannot be established in advance, that there are no simple rules. For example, nicknames (*yixta biil*, "joke name," or also, and more suggestively, *nop biil*, "name learned or discovered after an investigation"), which are frequently used to identify individuals, may generally be traced back to physical traits. But by themselves, they do not have value as signs of *lab*. Just because someone is nicknamed *mamal t'ul*, "Mr. Rabbit," on account of his big teeth, does not mean his *lab* is—or is not—a rabbit. Whatever the suspected thing may be, it is nothing that can be spotted once and for all; it is not a sudden on-the-target vision by means of which we see, say, an owl in someone's face. In fact, personal interest and perspicacity are required if guesses are to be taken at all seriously and if one guess is to be effectively backed up by another, and vice versa—with time, there are gains both in consistency and direction. On the contrary, the suspicion does not go beyond a very vague level.[2]

Furthermore, this interest in ferreting around in the identities of other people's hearts—their *ch'ulel* and, above all, their *lab*—seems born of a need to defend oneself from, or to forestall, any act of aggression. Nevertheless, making inquiries into the half-concealed identities of others, as well as resisting or yielding in the discovery of one's own, implies a kind of game, an intellectual workout much to the liking of the Tzeltal. There is a children's game in which one of the participants hides some small object that the rest have to find using verbal or other clues, given by the person who has hidden it. Some clues are true, but others are deliberately false, and the game's difficulty and its fun reside in the untangling of the true ones from the others. In an analogous fashion, between adults this same manipulation of partial concealment and revelation plays a part in what one makes others believe about oneself with regard to one's own identity. Perhaps the sign that is made known is so obvious and conventional that it seems to be begging to be ruled out for that very reason. Similarly and inversely, precautions taken to guarantee one's self-control may seem so excessive that they are asking to be called a conscious bluff.

The opposite case, an open declaration regarding the identity of one's own heart, seems much rarer. That is why the following testimony given by the only person whom I heard identify his own *lab* spontaneously and without being drunk is exceptional. A man of advanced age, who lived a bit far away, was telling me of some events remote in time that he had witnessed—fights between factions in an attempt to seize control in Cancuc around 1920—when, for no apparent reason, he introduced into his account an autobiographical aside. He had belonged to one of those factions when it was ambushed by members of the rival gang. At sunset, as he was going to cross the stream, they rushed out from behind the vegetation, and he saw how one of his assailants' machetes was aimed at his head. He made an enormous leap that took him across the water. It was a leap that surprised him, and thanks to which the machete only wounded him in the arm. He quickly scurried away through the undergrowth in the forest. By nightfall, he was lost and losing blood. An ocelot appeared in front of him; it was not clearly visible, but its eyes, which were shining brightly in the darkness, highlighted the silhouette of its round ears. Instead of running away, the feline took up a position in front of the man and began to lead him along narrow paths. The whole night, he dragged himself after the animal, keeping a short distance behind him, until at the first light of dawn, they reached a village where some relatives took him in. When he looked around behind him, the animal had already gone back into the forest. That was how he knew his "angel" was an ocelot; they are very nimble and see perfectly in darkness. Thus, even in this extreme case of someone claiming to know his own *lab*, the recognition is not produced in any positive way, but just the opposite, in the form of a well-founded suspicion.

Signs in Dreams

Recalling and interpreting dreams is a valuable exercise in inspection among the Tzeltal, as among other Indian groups in the region.[3] That may partly be explained by the fact that dreams represent one of the routes that may give access to the ontological status of the souls. Oneiric activity, as will be recalled, originates in the *ch'ulel*, and probably in the experiences of the *lab*, too, though to a lesser degree. However, dreams also offer difficulties in decipherment.

In appearance, dreams possess a meaning known beforehand, and the application of a previously worked-out scheme is enough to understand what they say. Faced with my requests for examples, certain people had no choice but to hazard some sort of correlation between common dreams and their meaning. Most have to do with the harvest, future illnesses, or the death of some relative or the person himself. For example, the appearance in dreams of old buried coins means a good corn harvest. People from Oxchuc (a neighboring Indian municipality) or women with white skin mean a bad harvest (because they are in fact animals, rodents, birds, or squirrels that damage the cornfields). Someone entering by the door of one's house portends the illness of a member of one's family. The theft of a machete presages the death of a son; if a pitcher or some backstrap loom tool is stolen, a daughter. If one is very drunk in a dream, barely able to stand, it is a sign of a serious illness. Horses, mules, cattle, or sheep signal the coming of death itself. The steam bath (a small, low rectangular building next to the house, half dug out of the earth) foretells the burial of some member of the family. If a "Castilian" hands over to the dreamer a parcel or a book, then they are going to have many hens or a good coffee crop, or perhaps he is going to occupy some religious post or become a shaman.

In practice, however, a dream's meaning is not so easily revealed. A specific, but not completely exceptional, case will serve to illustrate this point. In Xun P'in's house, where I had spent the night, the women got up before dawn, as usual, and made their way to the kitchen—an area sheltered by some beams covered with a flat thatched roof, with walls of banana leaves and plastic sheeting—to stoke the embers of the fire, start making the corn dough, and warm up the coffee. We men joined them later and huddled around the fire to take the edge off the cold. Apart from Xun P'in and his wife, their four sons lived in the house, two of them with their wives and children. One of these wives, a very young woman, had a dream that night and told it to her mother-in-law, who in turn told it to Xun, amid comments of another sort, when he came into the kitchen. The second version of the dream's contents was roughly that she "had been speaking" with a "Castilian" (*kaxlan*), which could be understood either as meaning that she did indeed speak with him, or that she had sexual intercourse with him. In fact, the two meanings are not so very different in Cancuc, where a young woman is not allowed to converse with a male who does not belong to her own clan. As I later found out, this is a dream that recurs quite often among women, sometimes being interpreted as foretelling a miscarriage. Nor was it, I gathered, the first time that this woman had had such a dream.

Without attaching too much importance to the dream, Xun P'in still wanted to know more details. He asked the young girl to her face to describe the Castilian's appearance. Had she seen him before? No. What were his clothes like? She didn't remember very well, but he was wearing a shirt. An old shirt? Quite old, but it looked clean. Was he carrying a book or anything else? No. Where did the encounter take place? She didn't know. Near the stream? No, it seemed to be on a path. A big path or a little one? She thought it was a wide path. Was there a cross? She didn't recall seeing one. But was it somewhere in Cancuc? She didn't think so, she didn't recognize the place, but it was an open area. Did she have the dream early or late in the night? Shortly before waking up.

The young girl was giving brief answers in an appropriately garbled fashion. Then Xun's wife asked her something that I could not completely understand; it had to do with whether she had spoken with her mother about her current home. All this went on at length, interwoven with conversations about what everyone was going to do that day. The husband made fun of his wife's dream, and everyone laughed. A few minutes later, Xun recommenced asking questions, this time about what she had done in the last few days. Had something strange happened at the spring or the market? What did she eat at the market the Sunday before? Once breakfast was over, everyone went his or her separate way without hazarding an explanation for the dream.

Later on, intrigued by the whole incident, I asked Xun P'in to tell me what the dream meant. He was quite clearly the right person, not only because he was the "master of the house," but also because, as a shaman, his authority as a dream interpreter was well attested. Nevertheless, his answer was that it was difficult to know, that "dreams are hard to understand, strange." If the young woman continued to have similar dreams, perhaps they could know a bit more, but he would need more details of the dream and her conscious life.

In other words, to evoke the meaning of a dream is a matter of placing it in a wider context, in a way that permits the recognition of some of the rather scant details as significant (insofar as they show some kinship linking them to others). In that case, the question would be which details are significant, and then what are they signs of; or is it simply one of so many dreams with no purpose at all? Thus, strictly speaking, the future does not appear in dreams, for dreams are not predictions. Rather, dreams are of interest due to their capacity to partially uncover overlaps in the relationships between people—*ch'ulel* interacting with other *ch'ulel* or with *lab*, or, less clearly, *lab* interacting with *ch'ulel* or other *lab*. In a waking state, these interactions pass by unnoticed, masked by an appropriate attitude or an impassive face. Therefore, however much their interpretations are oriented toward the future, the Tzeltal are content to scan for signals that reveal what is in the offing for a person, in much the same way as atmospheric changes foretell storms.

As we can see, the discovery of the person's identity, as manifested on the stage of physical appearance or the meaning of dreams, is pervaded with the same interpretative attitude. We may proceed a little further in this direction.

"Comparing, Harmonizing like Voices"

The Tzeltal verb *nop* may be translated as "to learn," "to understand," but its semantic range is in fact much wider. The vocabulary of the Tzeltal language compiled in the sixteenth century by the Spanish Dominican friar Domingo de Ara—possibly around 1560 in the Tzeltal-speaking village of Copanaguastla, where Ara was, with a few interruptions, parish priest for almost twenty-seven years (Ruz 1986)—simultaneously broadens and focuses the meaning of the word *nop*. The following are some of the entries for this word (Ara 1986, 348–349):[4]

nopoghon   to approach, to draw near to

nopol   close. *Napal nochol*, something close like a relative

nop   to appreciate by showing appreciation. *Qnopztoghol*

nop   to compare, to harmonize like voices

nopob cop   comparison

nopol   neighboring

nop   to make up. *Qnoptalay*, like nicknames

nop   to insert one thing into another. *Znopzba*

nopil, nopol   inserted. *Znopbenal*, insertion

nop   to judge what one is ignorant of, *quo animo fit*

noptocabi   to think what is to happen

nop   to think or to seem

nopbiluc   little by little

nop   to suspect

nopcopnax   suspicion that I have

nopel tamulauegh   suspicious of whom one suspects

nop   to plan in understanding

nopben   thus planned

The subtlety with which Ara translates into Spanish the constituent parts of what learning and understanding is in Tzeltal is remarkable. Apart from his extraordinary mastery of the language, this may be due to a certain affinity between his informants and himself in the way of conceiving meaning. In other words, both he and they start off by comparing. In addition, they both use a process by means of which discrete features of the thing compared come to harmonize one with another, paralleling what happens with words. Certainly, the comparison process mirrors how words are imagined to have behaved in the sixteenth century: by "morphology," similarity of forms. Michel Foucault (1984, 43), on sixteenth-century understanding of language, states:

Language forms part of the mighty process of distribution of similarities and signatures. As a consequence, it too must be studied as something natural. Like animals, plants or the stars, its elements have their own laws of affinity and suitability, their own inevitable analogies. . . . Language isn't language because it has meaning; its representational context plays no role here. . . . Words group together syllables, and syllables letters, because the very qualities that distance them or bring them nearer are deposited in them, just as in the external world brand names oppose or attract each other.

I think that Domingo de Ara was right. In Tzeltal, understanding is not so much a matter of accepting conventional links and relations that have been established beforehand, as it is conjecturing a "meaning" or, in Spanish, a *sentido*. "*Sentido*" is used in three ways: first, the capacity to express something; second, to judge and appreciate; and third, direction, course—planning ahead in understanding. That is why Ara's image of "insertion" is so attractive, as it evokes the idea of a puzzle whose pieces (in this case, virtually infinite in number, mobile, and endlessly substitutable) have to be inserted one by one, *quo animo fit*, so that a pattern emerges. What is interesting here is the capacity to associate, to insert each piece into what comes before and after. Expressed in terms of figures of speech, things link themselves together by relationships of "analogy," where "in some aspect or part one thing is equal with respect to another" (Moliner 1975).[5] It is therefore not a metaphorical relationship, nor exactly a metonym.[6]

The standard used in a public ceremony—the snippet of a tale, the attributes of a *lab*, the accidents of a dream, the features of a Mountain Lord—does not represent, does not symbolize; nor is it a metaphor. On the other hand, if one discerns partial details in them that lead to similarly fragmentary details of other things, chains or networks of associations may then be set up that locate them in a wider context and give them a meaning (and it is precisely "analogy" that was once used as the grammatical term for what is now known as "morphology"). To resort to a conventional example, it is possible to set up an analogy between a house and the earth's surface, which is done in several prayers for household protection. Both are similar in having four corners, each the site of a pillar, and just as the pillars of the world are its "guardians," the posts of the house are conceived of in a ritual context (although it would be preferable to say "used," because their value is instrumental) as protectors. However, that does not transform the house into a small-scale representation of the world, a kind of "microcosm." Such a transformation would be nonsense, as was brought to my attention when I suggested the possibility. It merely smoothes the ground for a provisional concordance with a given purpose. In the same way, other separate features of the house (the door, the three hearthstones, and so on) serve to trace associations in other directions.

As in the case of the preceding example, some associations seem relatively simple, almost verging on a certain redundancy, perhaps the result of the polysemous nature of the Tzeltal language. At other times, the link is less evident and requires a much longer process of inquiry during which there is a progressive accumulation and insertion of "concordances" until intermediate transitions become possible. In any case, it is hard for the process to undergo serious contradictions, given that the associations are provisional and may be abandoned in favor of others if they do not yield any results. As shall be seen later, the diagnosis of illness provides one of the most eloquent examples of this attitude.[7]

The Person

Closely following the ethnography of Esther Hermitte (1970) on the Tzeltal people of Pinola, Julian Pitt-Rivers explains the beliefs about souls among the Indians of Chiapas, asserting that a man and his animal are the same person, that the man is the animal (1970, 201). However, it should be understood that the animal, or any other type of soul, is only one *part* of the person. We have to make an effort to cast off the European notion that a person constitutes an individual, that it is a physically and psychically integrated whole. Instead, we should come to terms with the indigenous image of a person composed of heterogeneous fragments, a heteroclite conjunction of beings, places, and times. Speaking of a person's moral nature as a general condition is, for instance, wide of the mark. Someone is not easily scared because he has a *lab* animal from a species known for cowardice; only a *part* of him is a coward, while other fragments of his being (other *lab*, his *ch'ulel*, his body) will have other qualities, perhaps including bravery. Moreover, the truth is that not even those pieces may be considered each as a unity in itself, because they are themselves fragmented into others, which are fragmented even more. Hence it is not easy to generalize about the moral characteristics of an animal either. If, from a European viewpoint, a lion may be said to symbolize "noble strength," a Tzeltal jaguar has an altogether more intricate nature.

The emphasis placed on the *function* of a person—the idea that instead of being conceptualized in essential terms, personhood is located in a set of concrete circumstances with respect to other persons, in relational and situational terms—may explain the importance attached to personal details, as if they were attributes intended to make the role of the person easier in a given context. Such a notion may best be seen in the case of supernatural figures or the main characters of a tale. It may be said that the complete image of their persona remains in shadow, while the description only spotlights one aspect at a time: a part of the body, a detail of clothing, a character trait. About one Mountain Lord, for example, you may hear in a description of him that his hair and beard are gray. About another, one hears that he wears a cowboy hat, and about still a third, that he addresses human beings with the words (in Spanish), "Hey, give me a cigarette!" But that is all we know about each of them. From a European perspective, there is always a maddening lack of details and certainly no form of general characterization. Clearly, it is all a matter of setting up a correspondence between this particular attribute and other similar ones in other beings. Everything else is beside the point. Even when descriptions do refer to more than one aspect, it is frequently the case that these aspects are drawn from apparently disparate beings: someone with an apparently human body has a big cat's claw in place of a foot.

Often these fragmentary details, rather than being categorically stated, are for the most part only insinuated. One story, for instance, refers to its main character at one point with the words, "he is like a little boy," without further clarification. This apparently superfluous feature actually encapsulates a detail that is decisive for an understanding of the character's strange nature, and one that must be easy for any Tzeltal trained in this sort of observation to pick up on: in this case, that the man is very small, a dwarf. Seemingly trivial details attract attention to themselves by running countercurrently (as, when writing, one sometimes employs parentheses to add emphasis, while at the same time feigning a desire to lessen it).

Words

The behavior of language is another version of this same argument. In the first place, words are not essentially different from anything else; although they are invisible, they possess sensible—and one might even be tempted to say sensual—qualities. Naturally, they can be heard, but words can also have animating properties: shape, temperature, sensitivity, motor function, and voice. Thus, words speak for themselves and consequently have an intentionality that is independent of the person who has uttered them, for all of their inability to shake off their first impression.

To make themselves heard, most words enter via the ear, but not all of them; under certain conditions, some produce illnesses. Actually, most if not all of these kinds of words are uttered by the *ak'chamel* category of *lab*. Those bodily complaints that are strictly physical and not the result of some disturbance of the soul components—aches and pains, rheumatism, difficulties when giving birth, infected wounds, and so on—are always the result of words uttered by someone with the specific purpose of causing harm. Once the words have been shaped on the lips, or sung in the voice of a priest, or written by a scribe's pen, they operate with a certain amount of autonomy. Following Paul Ricoeur's (1979) definition of the text, it can be said that these words function as a text because they have been detached from their author and develop consequences of their own.

In cases such as these, words have two ways of getting about. If the illness-giver's aim is to harm one person in particular—and the Tzeltal name of the addressee is added to the words—the "text" is carried inside small animals (*chanetik*) with the shapes of frogs, toads, various kinds of worms, snakes, donkeys, or horses, which work as emissaries (*pixan sk'opetik*, "word wrapping"). When the words have no named addressee, they are uttered without wrapping and wander freely through space at the mercy of the winds. They usually linger at crossroads or steal inside drops of water to then drip indiscriminately down from a tree's wind-ruffled leaves onto a hapless victim until, by some chance encounter, they enter someone's body through their joints (the most exposed parts of the body), usually at the crook of their elbows or knees, to end up lodged in the bloodstream.

However, words also work their effect without entering the body. It is commonly supposed, for example, that the reason why someone is injured with a machete, apart from that person being tired or simply careless, is that words have crossed the tool's trajectory. To exemplify the materiality of words, Lorenzo Lot assured me that if a *lab* owl is killed (or indeed, any *lab* of the illness-giving variety) and its corpse opened, a swarm of tiny beings would fly out of its interior, like black insects, which are nothing more than words.

When a shaman, in his role as diagnostician (*pik'abal*, from *pik' k'ab*, "touch the arm/hand"), takes a pulse by placing his fingertips on the wrists and ankles of the patient, he is actually engaged in the task of finding those words whose voice gives their origin away. However, the words show themselves in a *kuyuyil* fashion, only permitting a partial view of themselves. This is also the case with external signs of the *lab* on the body or the meaningful signals of a dream. That is why the curers press both left and right wrists and ankles, and sometimes the temples or neck; their purpose is to gauge, to the extent possible, through a meticulous comparison of the different pulses, the degree of pretense in the symptoms. Xun P'in can feel the words. Sometimes, he says, he only notices the shape of the animal bearer, but occasionally he can feel the outline of the word itself. Some are shaped like multipointed stars, others are stretched out in a zigzag, while some, similarly elongated, are gently curving, and others are shaped like a volute. Incidentally, these shapes remind one irresistibly of the speech scrolls painted in sixteenth-century Nahua codices to represent the act of speaking.

We may read that "the blood speaks" with regard to the shaman's pulse-taking in several ethnographies of the area (see Vogt 1969; Tedlock 1982). The expression, however, should not be interpreted as a metaphor, but taken literally. In the European tradition, it is common to consider the text after the model of the body. Our texts have headings, index, footnotes, preface: a well-articulated group of texts constitutes a "corpus." The "corporealization" sometimes is not only physical but also psychological. Letters, it is said, have characters. In Tzeltal healing logic, however, the inverse seems to occur. If Europeans "corporealize" the text (Mason 1990, 129), the Tzeltal "textualize" the body. It is as if, from an Indian perspective, words, particularly Castilian texts, cannot be "read" until they are inscribed in the body. The diagnostician's task of deciphering is probably comparable to a "reading," just as the reading of old pre-Hispanic books for divination can be compared to a diagnosis. In all strictness, they form part of the same hermeneutic matrix involving the activity of *nop*.[8]

Fostering Knowledge

The knowledge about souls is nurtured in the innermost, informal core of extended families or domestic groups. It should be recalled that the distance separating the home from the public domain is enormous, both physically and conceptually, and the latter's extension is extremely limited. Its location par excellence is the marketplace, but it also refers to the area of the plaza where the church, town hall, and other administrative buildings are to be found. To a certain degree, paths are also considered public places, and for women, the springs and banks of rivers where they collect water and do laundry. In sharp contrast, each domestic compound is a world of its own. For the most part, each domestic unit is composed of several buildings—a main room and a kitchen, and sometimes a building for each married son—and a fair amount of surrounding land. Preferably, each unit will be located a good distance away from the next, the farther the better. In the event that there is no enclosing wall or fence, everything is arranged—trees, plants, winding paths—in such a way that strangers will be unable to catch even the slightest hint of what is said or done within. Domestic protection ceremonies—generally conducted twice a year, but also when there is some sense of foreboding or someone has been having recurring nightmares—offer a good synthesis of this feeling of being cloistered.

The following are some extracts taken from a *muk'ul kuxlejal*–type prayer, by means of which the domestic space is "closed" (*ch'ul mak'te, ch'ul xoral:* "the sacred enclosure," "the sacred pen"):

> I put myself within an enclosure
> I put myself within a pen
> a big pen, now
> thirteen pens, now
> a pen of stakes
> a pen of wire
> where I am humbly
> where I live humbly
> sacred lord angel [of the lineage]
> sacred lady angel
> sacred lord
> sacred father
> I come with my humble word
> I come with my humble heart
> beneath your feet
> beneath your shoes
> I ask for my health
> I ask for my life
> my people
> my wife
> my children
> my women [his sons' wives]

my grandchildren
let them not come
let them not come near
the sacred enemies
the sacred gossipers
the sacred priest
the sacred king
the sacred bishop
the sacred goat
with the sacred dog of Castile
with the sacred hummingbird of Castile
four lineages, sacred mother
four phratries, sacred father
four sacred guardians
four sacred *mayordomos* [angels of the lineage and/or the house posts]
I give you your "alms"
I give you your words
visit me
help me
in a corner of my house
in a corner of my pen
my sacred enclosure
for life
for health

Nevertheless, within this hermetic space, individual privacy is virtually nonexistent. The sensation of the absence of privacy stems from the fact that ten or fifteen people sleep together in the same place, exacerbated at night by crying children, barking dogs, undercover conversations, restless sleep, sorties to urinate, and so forth. The steambath, in fact, is the only place that affords any privacy within the domestic compound, so it is often a place for amorous trysts. It should be recalled that domestic groups are not the continuation of lineages or clans on a smaller scale. In fact, in many respects, they are in open opposition to them. Nor can they properly be said to be units of production, although they can possess some sort of specialization. In reality, it would be better to describe them as gossip units.[9]

Exposing oneself to the gaze of others, consequently making visible traces of what is concealed in the heart, is to become the object of gossip, and in turn, gossip is primarily, if not solely, practiced within the home.

A young man repeated to me the two pieces of advice his father had given him as rules of life, that is, "to be able to continue living." First, never let other people find out what goes on in your own home; second (the logical counterpoint to the first, but much harder to follow in practice), never pry into or, above all, show any interest in public in what goes on in other houses. This attitude accounts for the ever-present dread in families that affinal relatives—nearly always daughters-in-law—may divulge the private goings-on of their home in the house of their parents, either when paying them a visit (something unadvisable) or when they bump into their mother or sisters in some public place, especially on the Day of the Dead. For largely the same reason, newlywed wives represent a fundamental source of intersecting domestic information, as if they fertilized those spaces that are otherwise almost impregnable.

So it is in this introverted, domestic context that the Tzeltal concept of personhood is in its element and flourishes. It is nurtured by means of an extensive but irregular range of daily habits, such as the interpretation of dreams, attention to personal appearance or lack of it, diagnosis of illness, healing rituals, word games, happenings, and so on.

Outside this environment, references to soul principles are even more uncommon. They usually only come up when someone is drunk, which is tantamount to saying, as a sequence of tacitly agreed assumptions, that they are unspoken but understood nonetheless, in a game that everyone takes part in and which is excused by inebriation. This is a fragment of a conversation:

> *First person:* It looks like they're saying someone has turned up with a burned leg.
> *Second person:* Haven't they said that he turned up with his leg burned?
> *Third person:* That's right . . .
> *Fourth person:* Who knows for sure whether he turned up with his leg burned?

And so forth. Everyone knows that the others are thinking the same thing: they all know that burns are a fairly reliable sign of having a wind *lab*, but no one makes the connection explicit. Any conversation, especially if liquor is involved, is permeated with these sorts of double entendres, which often serve to evade or at times produce partial misunderstandings. In fact, drinking is almost always a requirement for such conversations, because without drink, the dialogue would never get beyond a simple exchange of commonplaces and courtesies.

Through interviews, it becomes clear that, especially in matters of souls, the Tzeltal do not always share the same assumptions, and it is even possible for the same event described in the same way to give rise to completely diverging interpretations. However, it is certain that this inconsistency not only does not hinder communication but actually facilitates it. At one and the same time, and without having to say very much, it makes room for complicity and the use of intelligence in the interpretation of one particular episode or another. Prayers may well constitute the most systematic aspect of knowledge about souls (although, a very limited systematization when compared to, for example, a written text that progresses linearly and cumulatively), but gossip, for all its shortcomings in systematization, gains its communicability and texture precisely in its ambiguity and incongruent nature. Its details permit the tracing of a meaning.

CHAPTER 4

The European Within

An inventory of Tzeltal souls reveals a very extensive and detailed exotic geography, a discontinuous map of places that are alien to the everyday life of an Indian peasant from the Chiapas highlands region. Souls belong to the underworld, the atmosphere, the rainforest, the mountaintops, Mexican cities. . . . The species of animals of which souls form a part are usually found in the hot lowlands, considered by the highland Indians to be insalubrious and unsuited to civilized life. But this assorted gallery of strange beings is also present in the human heart. The heart, considered to be the innermost organ at the core of the body, has folded this exotic geography in such a way that what lies deep inside oneself forms an internal landscape that captures and replicates the outside world. Heart and world are superimposed, each mutually affecting the other. Between them there is a topological relationship through which personal destiny is linked to outside events; what happens to the jaguar in the jungle will affect the human body in the village.

Nevertheless, souls do not represent the facet of these beings that we would call ordinary or natural—animals, meteors, humans—but their other side, their reverse, sacred *ch'ul* condition. What is folded into the human heart is, so to speak, the interior of all these beings, the "other" of the ordinary world. As a consequence, their behavior, their habits, and their abilities differ in essence from the natural species that inhabit the heavy, opaque state of *jamalal*, the solar world. Evidence for this difference between the two sides of the being—the ordinary and the sacred state—is found in many aspects. However, this chapter is devoted to showing what is probably the common denominator of souls: their "Castilian" character and their association with the European or Mexican modern world.

The Magic Mountain

Indian descriptions of the lives of *ch'ulel* souls inside the mountain swing between two extremes. At one extreme, the society of souls lives in a perfectly ordered world—a space that is harsh, categorical, authoritarian—where there is differentiation between age groups and the sexes, but at the same time they are united by a common structure, the very edifice that gives them shelter.[1] This point of view conjures up in the imagination a closed-in, contained space with an architecture that cuts into it vertically, rather like a microtome that leaves the interior architecture of the mountain—levels, compartments, alveoli—on view. From the perspective of the other extreme, however, souls inhabit an open, unstable geography, as we are about to see, and have an abundance of industrial goods with which they live a life of extravagance and wastefulness: a nonplace where social code and bodily etiquette are systematically subverted and where the logic of kinship ultimately disappears. Each of these descriptions of the two forms of life lived by the souls pushes to the limit what the life of the Tzeltal in the ordinary world maintains in an intermediate state. The *ch'iibal* mountain is simultaneously normality and excess, containment and incontinence.

But in both cases, this other life of the souls is characterized by the adoption of a European or Mexican culture. The political organization of the authorities and the repertoire of signs proclaiming their legitimacy are associated with the Castilian world. One example is the chairs and benches on which they sit. The significance of these can only be understood when contrasted with those used in the Indians' ordinary life, where seats are rough stools hewn from hollowed-out tree trunks, or else tiny chairs. Inside the mountain, these have all been transformed into large benches or heavy high-backed chairs with armrests, in other words, into the furniture of the colonial Castilian councils.

In their dealings with the mountain, the shamans often identify themselves as European lawyers. They are not so much the defense attorneys present in a trial as they are the "lawyers" (*licenciados*) who are able to cope with the intricate labyrinth of Hispanic legal bureaucracy and obtain a prisoner's freedom, something historically closer to the Indian experience. There are some shamans for whom "defense" is no more than a healing ceremony before the altar in the house. Still others assert that their very soul visits the mountain to deal directly with the authorities. At times, it is the authorities of the mountain themselves who summon the shaman's presence through dreams.

In this case, the *ch'iibal* mountain is usually represented as a modern Mexican courthouse building. One shaman described the *ch'iibal* as being like a modern thirteen-story glass-and-concrete block with the lineage flag flying from a pole on one of its balconies. The soul of the shaman—the version found in the heart—enters through a revolving door; a receptionist hands him a ticket with the number of his turn, and he goes to sit in the waiting room where a great many shamans are waiting. When he is called, he takes the elevator. The lower levels are occupied by storerooms, archives, garages for cars and small airplanes. On arrival at a certain floor, he meets a secretary sitting behind a table who consults the case file. If the offense committed by the soul is too serious to be resolved, then the shaman soul must return to where he came from; in this case, the most likely outcome is that the patient will die. But if the way is cleared for him to proceed, the shaman will go to the three uppermost levels: the "big-small" level, the middle-aged souls' level, and finally the "mothers-fathers'" level. He will then go to the offices of the Great Mother, the president, and the trustees, and finally to the councilors' room. In each of these sections he will ask for a pardon and will offer liquor, flowers, and sometimes the soul of a chicken, substances offered up on the domestic altar that he has brought with him personally. He will make sure everyone gets a share. The idea that everyone receives something, regardless of their position or post, is fundamental, because if any vestige of antipathy or resentment remains, it will be easy for the illness to strike again. The shaman-lawyer can then argue that the accuser was only moved to act as he did because he held a grudge and that what he said about the soul of the patient is not completely true. However, the shaman's visit is not so much a repeat trial as a payment of a *ch'abajel* or "fine." This is to satisfy the authorities in a friendly manner in order to maintain calm and harmony, the ultimate objective being the granting of the soul's freedom.

What sort of justice is this? There is no doubt that the descriptions bear a resemblance to public trials held by *cabildos* or councils made up of the principal village elders and public officials. Nevertheless, there are some significant differences. In the first place, the most common cases of contention in the ordinary world involve marital conflicts and disputes over land inheritance and rights to resources such as water. But it is clear that in the mountain there are no married couples and there is no domestic ownership of resources, since there are no families as such. Instead, trials almost always involve personal aggression, usually consisting of disrespectful behavior, generally in the form of verbal offenses. Although such incidents also occur in the world of flesh and blood, it is evident that the souls of the mountain revolve almost entirely around codes of social conduct and personal etiquette. Secondly, it is a very harsh place as far as the meting out of justice is concerned. Unlike the village council, which is always prepared to accept compensation, however serious the offense, the Indians insist that the mountain court often refuses to accept offerings at the altar, and in such cases, little can be done for the sick patient. The intention of an Indian court, as Jane Collier (1973) points out, is to seek conciliatory solutions. In contrast, the court of the souls revolves around the idea of transcendent justice (although, as we have seen, inflexibility is not absolute), in other words, a European idea of justice that leans more toward punishment than settlement.

Descriptions of the *ch'iibal* mountain often portray it as a city, especially when it is the result of a dream. It is a modern Mexican city, complete with a proper street system, traffic lights, sidewalks, one-family houses with yards (rather odd in a place where there are no families), high buildings, shops, bars, gas stations, and banks. It is said that when one dreams of Mexico City or any other large city—something that seems to happen with frequency—the dream is not really about the cities themselves but about the experiences of the soul inside the mountain. It is the life of the soul: moving around by car, taking children to the adventure playground, visiting the zoo . . .

But the city can also be a universe in itself, with towns, villages, rivers, mountains, jungles, and oceans, although it all exists in unstable coordinates of space and time. The absence of the sun (there is only electric light) generates a heterogeneous and qualitative geography, a multidimensional space—like in dreams—as immense as it is diminutive, and the souls move around it freely, able to travel great distances in an instant. Instead of the homogeneous and progressive time of the ordinary world, we have a time that is discontinuous and flexible. Thus, in the mountain, the present coexists with extensions of the past and advances of the future; aspects of the ancient past live side by side with ultramodern features, forming a kind of collage of times and styles.

It seems this world is fundamentally perceived as co-extending to the ordinary world, as if it were the obverse of existence, a parallel but immaterial world. According to the reflections of a Tzeltal friend, this world is among us—we are among ourselves—but we do not realize this. During the night, however, when there is a blurring of the thin line of shadow that separates the two states, interferences (*kaxumtayel*, "crosses") sometimes occur between the two perspectives. The same friend saw at nightfall, when he was awake, a small plane-soul piloted by *ch'iibal* souls. He perceived it as a "good shadow" that flew in silence, lit by a huge light. Some of his neighbors also saw it as it landed in a nearby pasture, but, of course, when they went to look at it at daybreak, it was no longer there, nor were there any marks in the grass.

If there is anything that characterizes the cities from an Indian point of view, it is the abundance of commodities. Descriptions of the inside of the mountain emphasize the presence of a multitude of industrial goods. Certain descriptions confine themselves to the mention of simple everyday objects like thread, worsted yarn, combs, soap, bands to tie the hair back—items of personal grooming that are bought in shops in the mountain. But, more often, the Tzeltal take pleasure in enumerating the different types of commodities their souls enjoy—that they enjoy as souls: telephones and cell phones, cassette recorders, television sets, cameras, typewriters, computers, refrigerators, washing machines, ceiling fans, and air conditioning. There is also a good supply of cars and light aircraft in red, yellow, or green. Groups of souls will climb into a car simply for the pleasure of going for a ride, although sometimes they are drunk and have accidents. There is also money, in the form of banknotes, that some say is used to buy all these commodities, and which is kept in a bank.

While it is true that some of these objects, like thread, combs, and soap, have become mundane items in the ordinary world, others are very scarce. Even with the arrival of electricity, few homes have television, and only a handful of small shops have refrigerators for cold drinks. Other goods, like washing machines and fans, simply cannot be found and have only been seen on trips to the city or in photographs. "Now, in the *ch'iibal* there is everything. They have everything, everything those in the city have, everything the Castilians have; it's all there. They now know how to work these machines; they're ready to use them. They're images they have, things they imagine. They want everything. They buy it. It's like a city."

From the moment an artifact is manufactured in the faraway industrial world to the moment its existence is echoed inside the mountain, a certain time elapses. The word that expresses this duplication is *slok'omba:* "what comes out of oneself."[2] This is the word applied to the material figure of the saints in the church and any drawing, illustration, or photograph. They are "images," and the word could perhaps also be translated as "copy" or "reproduction." In principle, reproducing or copying these souls does not entail any difficulty for the *ch'ulel* souls; these are images, just like they are, images extracted from themselves.

Like the European original from which it is partially copied, the *ch'iibal* undergoes continuous transformation and modernization.[3] In the eyes of the Indian, the very faculty of copying, of using technical means to reproduce images of objects and living beings, constitutes an important quality of the European world.[4] The *ch'ulel* are understood to have means of reproduction at their disposal, such as books, typewriters, cameras, and cassette recorders, because in the mountain they imitate not only the Europeans but also their means of imitation. Indeed, much of the universe of souls could be described in photographic language, like the play of light and shade, reflection, refraction, emulsion, capture, exposure, developing, and so on.

A Perpetual Fiesta

For the Tzeltal, the one European feature of the mountain that stands out above all the rest is that it is a place for fun activities. Fiestas with dancing and music take place all the time, but these are not ordinary Indian festivities or ceremonies, generally dedicated to a saint or to specific political or social activities; the sole purpose of such entertainment is to ensure everyone has a good time and is "happy," one of the qualities most closely associated with "Castilianness."

As happens with the types of goods, the fiestas in some dreams are rather tempered events. The musicians drink liquor as they play the guitar, the harp, or the violin, and as they softly sing a tune, they display emotion—not unlike what happens in the ordinary world, except for the frequency. Nevertheless, it is much more common in these cases for the imagination to be given free rein, and the fiestas then take on the character of urban Mexico. Nowadays in the *ch'iibal*, common sugarcane liquor is no longer drunk; it has been replaced by beer; *comiteco*, a mixture of agave sap and sugarcane liquor that landowners in the region used to drink; and particularly tequila, brandy, and vodka.[5] The music is mariachi, *norteña*, or "tropical." Drunken male and female souls dance together noisily, touching and embracing each other like in a dance hall. Indeed, the mountain often appears in dreams as a huge saloon or an elegant bar or discotheque. There is always a bar where liquor is served and marijuana is sometimes smoked, a dance floor, and on the far side a jukebox into which the clients put coins to select music, which is invariably Mexican folk music or mariachi. At other times, the place simply converts into a brothel with a number of rooms where souls can have sexual relations. It goes without saying that the Indians of the region have nothing like this, at least for the time being.

One friend dreamed the following: A big fiesta was being celebrated in the mountain to which no less than three musical groups had been invited. The first group played *norteña*, the polka-type music from the north of Mexico and the southern United States that has become popular everywhere. The second was a "tropical" band, with guitars, electric keyboard, and a chorus of "dancers" clad only in T-shirts and shorts who moved their hips to the sound of the music, and the third group played a kind of rock'n'roll. All the souls were dancing frenziedly. Whenever one of the groups stopped playing, another would start up so the fiesta never ended.

There is no doubt that this type of dream takes its inspiration from the popular fiestas of the Spanish-speaking villages of Chiapas, especially those of the hot country. It is true that some Indian villages have begun to adopt these musical events as part of the festivities celebrating their patron saint's day, but the difference is that in Indian villages, when dancing forms part of the celebration, no one dances. The Indian public remain motionless for hours, either seated or standing, men, women, and children deeply absorbed in this live spectacle from the other world. The mothers take tortillas and tamales out of their bags to eat in the meantime. Only at the end of the evening may the younger men be sufficiently drunk to do a grotesque imitation of the dancers' movements or to try and jump up onto the stage. In the *ch'iibal* mountain, on the other hand, the souls do dance and, to judge from descriptions, they let themselves go even more than in Mexican villages. Another Indian dreamed that in the mountain they celebrate something similar to what is known in Mexico as the *quinceañera* that takes place when young girls reach the age of fifteen and enter into circulation as marriageable young women. Each girl wears a flounced dress and dances a waltz partnered by a *chambelán*, or escort, as if she were at a Viennese state ball.

Nevertheless, from the point of view of the ordinary world, all this merrymaking has a harmful effect, as it leads to numerous illnesses that affect carnal bodies. The reason for this is not quite clear, although I feel that here we come up against that old Mesoamerican equation consisting of fiesta, sacrifice, and death. In an immediate sense, it seems likely that the souls increase the number of punishments in order to obtain the liquor that is exchanged at shamanic ceremonies—souls always have a chronic deficit of liquor, despite the abundance of commodities. This way, they are able to continue their revelry, as if alcohol had a similar function to blood. Also, at *ch'iibal* fiestas, as at any party that ends in drunkenness, there may be fights and assaults; souls may get hurt, and this has repercussions on the ordinary world. But there appears to be a more general reason, although it is difficult to specify exactly what it is. In Indian terms, there is a very close association between fiestas, music, shouting, and noise in general on the one hand, and illness on the other. In the Tzeltal language, shamanic songs dealing with healing or prevention are called *ch'ab*, meaning "agreement," "concord," or "calm" between the different parties, though the literal meaning is "silence." The song cures illnesses by silencing the source of the noise. As in many other Amerindian languages, the term *k'op* means "word," "language," and "dialogue" as well as "conflict," "dispute." and "war." Health is silence, which is harmony, or the opposite of conflict, which is noise, the incessant noise of the *ch'iibal*. As the Tzeltal like to point out, shamanic songs are aimed at "switching off," as much as is possible, the fiesta inside the mountain.

We have discussed dancing, embracing, and even sexual relations between souls. It is evident that from the point of view of ordinary morals, *ch'iibal* customs are quite scandalous. Touching and kissing each other in public, dancing, singing, sitting at bars—all this implies breaking with the imperative of corporal continence. But what makes them particularly immoral, and therefore deserving of being dreamed, is their Mexican or European style. Their libertine character resides precisely in their association with the "other." And if homosexual relations are not mentioned in the *ch'iibal*, it is perhaps because in themselves they are far less conspicuous and more conventional than an erotic, European type of bodily attitude.

At the heart of all this scandalous merrymaking lies a more delicate problem. Souls that embrace call each other "sister" or "brother" among themselves. Even if coitus does not actually take place, the very acts of touching or talking together are considered to be overtly sexual. Kissing on the lips like the Europeans implies an exchange of saliva. As in many cultures, talking together is synonymous with having sexual relations (though in the case of the Tzeltal, perhaps not metaphorically). In other words, are we looking at incestuous relationships? It was quite telling that my question was not only uncomfortable for the Tzeltal but also rather disconcerting, maybe in part because perhaps it was the first time they were required to think about this in such an explicit way. But the difficulty also resides in having to decide. It is evident that relatives are involved who call each other *bank'il* and *wix*, "big brother" or "big sister," who, with respect to ordinary human beings, would therefore be transgressing an absolute prohibition. This is precisely the issue: they are not beings with bodies of flesh and blood. And since they do not have a carnal body, sexual intercourse cannot, strictly speaking, be considered incestuous. In this regard, the Tzeltal appear to subscribe to the definition of incest by Francois Héritier (1994) as "the coming into contact of identical humors." Insofar as a trafficking of bodily fluids—semen, saliva, blood—does not exist, it is inappropriate to talk in terms of forbidden exchanges. Souls cannot have "carnal knowledge," since such fluids are absent in them.

Even so, the unease faced by my informants when talking about this issue implies that the problem cannot simply be ignored. A certain "incestuous sentiment" lies latent in the idea of a closed world populated exclusively by consanguineous kin—dominated by the desire to be "among themselves," according to the well-known expression by Lévi-Strauss (1969).

Castilian Features in the *lab*

This class of soul is exotic to ordinary Indian life in a purely "natural" sense. But a second layer of estrangement within the group of *lab* has to do with the relationship—by resemblance or contagion—between them and the Castilian world. In some cases, like those of priests or scribes, goats or metal instruments, this is a self-evident dimension; but as a matter of fact, European features may be found in any *lab*.[6]

This can be seen in the specific choice of many *lab* animals. To take a few examples: not every species of the hummingbird genus (*ts'unun*) is actually *lab*; on the contrary, quite precise mention is made of the *kaxlan ts'unun* (*Chlorostilbon canivetii*; Hunn 1977, 165), a small hummingbird also known as the Fork-tailed Emerald, typical of the lowlands and rarely seen in Cancuc, whose local name, "hummingbird of Castile," gives it a clear ethnic concordance. Again, the *lab* species of vulture is the *k'ajk'al jos* (*Coragyps atratus*; Hunn 1977, 141), also known as the Black Vulture, a bird of prey that seldom shows itself in the valley of Cancuc but that abounds on cattle ranches, as well as on roadsides and at the trash dumps of the Chiapas lowlands.

One may further see it in their conduct, especially those that are among the "sociable" *lab* species (meteors, metal river tools, priests, scribes, and company), who have at their disposal books and notebooks to write in, chairs and rectangular tables to sit at. They are also often conceived of as holding fiestas. Even "happiness" and "sadness," like every emotion, are passed through a Castilian filter. In this regard, it may be worthwhile to reproduce a fragment of a shamanic chant where some *bajte'* ants, "happy" to have kidnapped a *ch'ulel*, throw a party. Characteristically, the text does not furnish a complete description of the scene, but that makes its fragments more meaningful. In a certain underground place:

> in the cold of their tables, now
> in the cold of their flat tables
> in a hollow mountain
> where they bound its [the *ch'ulel*'s] hands
> where they bound its feet
> how many evildoers there are
> how many there are wicked in heart
> how many there are lined up around the table
> how many there are sitting at the table
> now, they are dancing
> they are dancing and clapping
> to the sound of nine pieces of music
> the sound of nine dance entries
> with the noise of Castilian music
> with the noise of Castilian guitar
> the table is now set
> the chair is now set
> with fifty-five dishes
> fifty-five dishes piled high
> with chocolate
> with beer
> with tequila from Castile
> with liquor from Castile . . .

These *lab* ants are apparently involved in representing the scene of a European banquet or, more exactly, given that the table is laden with cups of chocolate, a Creole banquet in New Spain. Whichever way it is looked at (particularly from the perspective of dancing), to an Indian's eyes, the scene is outlandish and, to a considerable extent, grotesque. It is probably also over the top; and this lack of restraint is a characteristic shared by the *ch'iibal* and the *lab* alike. There must be some connection between the abundance of food and gestures, on the one hand, and the abundance of noises and words, on the other; and it would come as no surprise if the *lab* made speeches while seated at the table. Undeniably, the whole scene points up a sharp contrast with day-to-day custom, where eating is an activity that is not just private but almost intimate. Within each domestic group, each couple, together with their youngest children, eats separately, while single adults also eat apart. People eat at low, round, three-legged tables (*mats'malte*), with fingers for utensils and tortillas for plates, preferably in silence or, at most, exchanging a few short phrases.

In Cancuc, collective meals are highly unusual. It is a practice that is almost entirely reserved for holders of politico-religious office and is accordingly markedly ritualistic. Moreover, it displays many affinities with Castilian banquets, and by extension, with those held in the *ch'iibal* and by the *lab*. Meals are at a rectangular table with long benches (in some ceremonies, in the town square itself with the big table and chairs on loan from the town hall building). Food is served in small, industrial ceremonial aluminum or enamel bowls; even the food has some "Castilian" ingredients.[7] Here, too, the fact that the diners may serve themselves several helpings and even keep the food they are given to take home with them is in rude violation of the norms of dietary frugality and verbal restraint. Like the public fiestas they form part of, these kinds of meals are essentially an imitation of what is European; but, again, like any fiesta, it never goes beyond a poor imitation, far from the sumptuous feasts that are held in gatherings of the *lab* souls.

Castilianizing nuances can even be identified in the smallest of details, one of which will serve as an example. We know that during their annual period of inactivity, *lab* lightning bolts reside in plants called *kaxlan ech'*, "orchids of Castile." I am not certain of their identification; it could be moss or perhaps mistletoe. If it were the latter, it would be no more and no less than the "golden bough," that branch of Virgil's that spurred Frazer on his worldwide investigation of magic and souls. Frazer himself (1980, 786–796) furnishes us with many examples of places in the world where these plants are associated with fire, Europe among them, and where mistletoe, which grows on oak and ilex, is commonly given the name "lightning broom." But in Cancuc, thanks to its contradictory nature of being a plant that grows outside the ground, its popular name of "orchid of Castile" has prevailed. This designation is possibly due to the fact that Spanish speakers of the region use the plant either to decorate the Christmas crèche (moss) or to decorate their house fronts during the Christmas season (mistletoe).

The Ethnic Contrast between Heart and Head

This clashing gallery of other beings is also to be found within the body. Evidently, the variety is a crucial aspect of the concept. The upshot of these replications is that the person is a bundle of different beings and wills: the *lab*, the *ch'ulel*, and the Bird of the Heart (which is not given too much importance, but whose madcap character puts itself and its host body at risk). These three intentionalities are not to be confused with the consciousness of the head; and this is a contrast that merits further attention.

Taken as a whole, the inside of someone's heart is, as we have seen, his *talel*, "that which comes as given," in other words, the character bestowed upon him before birth and therefore formed a priori. On the other hand, reasoning and discernment are a function of the head. But the head is not formed at the moment of birth, and children learn slowly because their brains (*chinam*) are still tender. Only with time, by means of learning and experience, is the brain gradually toughened up, filled out, and given shape, a process that is enabled by the working of the senses—sight, hearing, smell, and taste—that also answer to the head. It is no coincidence that when the head is spoken of as one of the centers of consciousness, the word *sitkelawtik*, which literally means "my eyes-face" (that is, the part of the anatomy that includes the face and the neck), is used more often than *jol*, "head." I take this to be a way of emphasizing the head's role as the center for sensory perception, a perception in which sight is of paramount importance.

Lorenzo Lot distinguishes between the activities of the heart and the head (what each one "does") by explaining that the first is *bi ya jk'antik*, "what I want, desire," while the second is *jnopibal, ay bi ya jnoptik:* "my understanding," "what I apprehend, understand." The head knowledge is designated with the verb *nop*, "to understand," "to learn," but with the host of nuances we saw in the previous chapter. Heart knowledge, however, is normally, but not exclusively, expressed with the verb *na'*, which implies a type of knowledge that either exists beforehand or is acquired independently of sensory experience; in effect, *na'* has a retrospective character, as if something that had been learned beforehand is brought to memory at a given moment. In Tzeltal, "oblivion" is *ch'ay ta o'tan*, "to fall from the heart."

In a strict sense, it is a type of primitive knowledge related to the emotions and inclinations that has to be concealed through the will of the head. This is perhaps seen most clearly in the field of language. Words well up from the inside of the heart, where they exist as mere raw materials; when speaking, the words must pass through the head to be formed in the mouth, being modulated basically on the lips, which give them their appropriate (Tzeltal) form. That is why the presumably more educated language of adults should not betray any hint of emotion or be accompanied by gesticulations, whereas young people still resort to *ixta k'op*, "informal speech" or "jest", although they are better speakers than children. Apparently there is no widespread opinion on whether undifferentiated words exist in the heart or whether they pertain to a specific language. In this regard, we could mention an interesting detail: It sometimes happens that children utter words in Spanish, odd words, often insults, that they strongly accentuate on the first syllables; without doubt, they have heard their parents using them and repeat them because, as their parents find it very funny, they are quick to discover it is a sure way of getting their attention. On the other hand, Sebastian K'aal cites this as evidence of the very poor self-control of children, that is, the still relative dominance of the heart over the head.[8]

Thus, what lies behind the contrast that distinguishes the heart from the head is an ethnic counterpointing: the heart is Castilian, while the head, together with the body, is Indian. Having said this, let me hasten to clarify a point. Clearly, it would be absurd to pretend that the souls of the Tzeltal (and therefore their hearts) *are* Castilian, or even that they are like Castilians. Their "Castilian" character should be understood in a purely analogous sense; in other words, in line with the thesis underpinning the whole of this study, the heart shares some attributes, partial ones, with Castilians, sometimes many. In short, no one in Cancuc is born Indian; the acquisition of a cultural identity runs parallel to the acquisition of a body and a social identity, and is a long, continuous, and arduous process of differentiating oneself from the previous identities that one is born with.

It is by no means easy to determine the type of relationship this ensemble of heterogeneous wills maintains with one another, inside the space of the body itself. They do not seem to be in opposition to each other by definition—at least not in the Cartesian dualist manner of a body/soul or matter/spirit dichotomy—nor do they seem to complement each other in any meaningful way. Rather, each goes about its business quite independently of the others, except in certain circumstances or cases when they coincide or actually diverge. The following expression can often be heard in Tzeltal: *ya sk'an te ko'tan pero max xu kuun,* "my heart desires it, but I can't (mustn't)." I have heard it, for instance, on those rare occasions when someone turns down a drink of liquor; logically, it is the *ch'ulel* that desires the liquor, and the head that refuses it. This is a case of divergence; but in other circumstances, the different wills may coincide. Convergence is perhaps the explanation for the extraordinary event we came across in Chapter 2, where a man with a jaguar *lab* raped a woman. But which part of the person is really responsible for such a misdeed? In principle, it is the animal; but for such an act to have taken place while the person was wide awake and to have been accompanied by sweet talk (*mero ya jmulat:* "I really like you"), the wills of three beings, three intentionalities, three interests, must have come into conjunction: the jaguar's lust, the *ch'ulel*'s romantic emotion, and the head's tacit acceptance (if not, as seems much likelier, its active involvement for some motive that escapes us).

What seems certain is that the inside of the heart is a legacy that cannot be escaped, and it is neither lost nor affected in its essence by the passage of time or by maturation. The *ch'ulel* provides biographical events in the shape of a memory, but this does not affect the nature it started out with (sad, happy, generous, vengeful, etc.); it is highly unlikely that its emotional character will be transformed in the course of a life. The *lab* are even less likely to change. Occasionally, people warn the external version of their *lab* not to reveal themselves without good reason; but it would be naïve to assume that a jaguar would do what it was told; jaguars pay little attention to reason. To sum up, the body neither represses nor stifles the others within its heart, contenting itself—with a greater or lesser degree of success, depending on its age and level of Indian education—with keeping them invisible. And the head's ascendancy only has to slip a little for the inside of the heart to show itself at once.

Loss of the Senses and Exposing the Heart

The loss of body consciousness may occur spontaneously when asleep or after imbibing alcohol. Chicha, based on fermented corn, or, more usually, aguardiente, liquor made from sugarcane, is consumed. The effect of either is obviously not to stimulate sensory perception; instead, they bring about partial drowsiness. In fact, drunkenness, which is well established among the Indians and can go on for several days, at times reaching extremely high degrees of intoxication, gives rise to a radically different mode of behavior, worthy of further examination.

In a state of inebriation, there is a constant alternating between emotional extremes, such as laughter and disconsolate tears. The individual yells; sits down with his legs crossed; and even enters the doors of houses without announcing himself from the mandatory distance, banging on the door with his fist; and the like. Drunkenness leads one to lose a sense of proper modesty. Romantic love is spoken of, or amorous disappointments, even though Tzeltal lacks precise vocabulary to express these feelings. What may happen, as I myself have seen on occasion, is that men may suddenly become affectionate, trying to touch, hug, and even kiss their wives in public, just like Castilians (who, in this respect at least, resemble nothing more than dogs sniffing each other). Clothing, generally impeccable white tunics, is dirtied to unheard-of extremes due to frequent falls. It is not unusual for a man to pass out right in the middle of a path—not on the side, but quite specifically spread-eagled across it.[9] Sometimes hours go by until he is able once more to stand and continue wandering—erratic movement seems to be an outstanding feature—around the paths that lead from one house to another. It is also easy to lose items of clothing during the binge and not to remember where they were left afterward.[10]

Perhaps to be expected, the ethnic identification of the *ch'ulel* may perhaps best be seen in the speech of drunks. The higher the alcohol content in the body, the more control the lips lose of speech, which begins to be sprinkled with words in Spanish.[11] For example, a group of three men (one over forty, designated "First person" below, and two young men) who are, as far as I know, completely monolingual (in Tzeltal) when sober, are now in an advanced stage of drunkenness and are chatting loudly in my house:

First person: . . . *ja jich*, the disicrimination of the sociality . . . eternal, *ma xu kuun, ma xu* . . . is checked. . . . Attention! Left right left right left right . . . because water is coming down . . .

Second person: 's difficult, that's how it is . . . national commission . . . son of bitch.

First person: . . . more eternal disicrination, more natural disincrination . . . this country, this world is already dying, eighty, sixty, *kaxlanetik* . . . already sixty percent, eighty percent water level . . .

Third person: Great, great! A municipality now . . . Indian people's history rights . . . Mexico . . . practices and customs . . . it's, then . . .

First person: . . . more natural . . . political water . . . Cancuc history . . . world-level history, republic level . . . it came right out that foreign debt, no, no, I ask. . . . Does the soul exist? . . . *ma xa jnoptik* [we haven't found out] . . .

There can be no doubt that the Tzeltal understand more Spanish words when they are sober than they are prepared to admit. As a matter of fact, they are exposed to Spanish in several ways. Young children hear it at school, where instruction is bilingual (in fact, the "left right . . ." could be connected with school discipline); adults hear it in political meetings of the powers that be, who are usually bilingual, where there is an abundant use of Spanish expressions, although they don't seem to have much to do with anything. It is also heard on the radios, which, in the houses that actually have one, are frequently left on all day—out of a kind of sonic *horror vacui*—and spew out words in Spanish and *ranchera* or *norteña* music. At the time of the conversation reproduced above, the only two radio stations that could be picked up in the valley had been broadcasting exclusively and uninterruptedly for days on end the speech given by the governor of the state of Chiapas on the accomplishments of the first year of his term of office. For weeks in Cancuc, that speech kept cropping up time and again, parts of it frayed and woven together with other source material, in a host of alcohol-inspired monologues.

Drunkenness allows for a partial exhibition of one's freedom from cultural restrictions. But it is plain to see that there is more to it than that. In many respects, cultural convention does not evaporate, but rather subverts itself from within, so that any gesture, attitude, or action seems to want to be taken for Castilian or, to be more precise, to want to concord with the traits that constitute the Castilian stereotype. Nevertheless, there is no element of mockery in the "imitation"; a drunk's behavior may sometimes verge on the pathetic, but it is never comic; and generally speaking, amazing consideration and patience is extended to the inebriated. In a way, the reason is quite simple: one's self is not responsible for one's alienated self.[12]

Closely related to the loss of senses (sleep or drunkenness) is the loss of bodily uprightness, a factor distinctive enough to merit consideration as the second axis around which the exposure of the content of the heart occurs. The loss of verticality may be total, as when lying down on one's back, which is when the *ch'ulel* or the *lab* gain complete autonomy from the body and are able to separate themselves from it. But this independence may also only be partial; this is a more interesting possibility, because like drunkenness, it shows how the heart acts on the body.

Stumbling, falling over, limping, hobbling, or walking in a zigzag are all signs of internal alteration. In some cases, the imbalance is spontaneous, but it may also be induced. The Indian dance may be an illustration of this second possibility. It is almost always performed by women (although it is not forbidden to men), always by the wives of religious office holders as part of public ceremonies. It takes place inside the church or else at night inside the head *mayordomo*'s house, which is lit only by the glow of the hearth. The least that could be said of its movements is that they are strange. They consist of repeatedly letting the weight of the body fall onto one foot, while raising the heel of the other a little and tilting the head, first to one side of the body, and then to the other— all of this without moving from the spot and to the accompaniment of background harp, violin, and guitar music, although music is not essential. In other words, it is a kind of "limping dance." This rhythmic movement can go on for very long periods, each dancer in a world of her own, and if she is sufficiently inebriated, humming under her breath a piece of music that usually has only two or three words—for example, *kampana nichim*, "flower bell"—that are repeated over and over.[13] Indeed, there is an inverse relationship between the verticality of the body and the horizontality of the soul. While one is on one's feet, in the daylight hours, one's own shadow, projected by the *ch'ulel*, keeps itself horizontal, clinging to the ground, but when the body is horizontal, the *ch'ulel* raises itself up.

In fact, as Indians continually point out, one of the most unmistakable characteristics of the European is his clumsy, rolling, unbalanced gait. My nickname in Tzeltal, Petul Ach'al (Peter Mud), refers directly to the fact that my boots and trouser bottoms were always muddy, implying that I did not know how to walk carefully enough to avoid getting dirty. Whenever I appeared in public, everyone was waiting for me to stumble or slip in the mud (which can be as slippery as walking on ice, something I can vouch for), so when it did happen, nobody missed the opportunity to whoop and guffaw. On a hypothetical list, there is a good chance that nicknames and epithets referring to ambulatory difficulties would come second only to those having to do with anomalies of speech.

In more general terms, there are certain activities that require one "to reveal oneself," that call for one to cast off the culturally decorous attitude and "show the heart." Occasionally, the only objective is a more intense social relationship, such as a more interesting, less inhibited conversation, for which drunkenness is necessary. In other cases, inebriation is called for by particular tasks, like the shamanic healing ceremonies or the rituals of politico-religious office holders. As a matter of fact, rituals demand vast quantities of alcohol, ground tobacco (which is chewed or lodged next to the gums, which produces numbing of the tongue, lips, and part of the face), going without sleep, fasting, cold nocturnal baths, and sexual privation (except in the case of homosexual relations, which are acceptable in periods of intense and prolonged ritual activity, because unlike relations with women, they are not strength-sapping, but they are considered a sign of immaturity). The aim of these substances and actions is to place the person who consumes or performs them in a state analogous to those "other" beings with whom he must talk, negotiate, or cajole—in a word, with whom he must act as mediator.

Shamans and office holders also cultivate a mild "Castilianism," which they flaunt every so often in their day-to-day lives. But it is the caciques (the word commonly used in Tzeltal) for whom "Castilianism" remains a perpetual mark of their identity. Their "charisma," their ability to sidestep cultural conventions, hinges especially on their capacity to be "Castilian." And it is this transgression that sets them apart as "others." One of the most noteworthy cases in recent times is that of Miguel Ordóñez, whose political biography has been charted by Henning Siverts (1965). He was the de facto and uninterrupted wielder of power in Cancuc from the early forties to the end of the sixties, when he died a natural death (a rare occurrence), leaving no male offspring. He held various political and religious posts, but his real power had two bases: his band of armed followers (independent of kinship bonds), which he used to defend himself from his enemies, and more importantly, the fact that he was considered by the authorities of the state of Chiapas and the Department of Indian Affairs as the perfect interlocutor in any matter relating to Cancuc. The fear and fascination he exercised is still palpable today among Cancuc's adults. He was the only Indian who celebrated his birthday.

By the time of Calixta Guiteras's stay in Cancuc in 1945, Ordóñez had already turned himself into the town's strongman. Guiteras has left us a magnificent portrait of him, which cannot be improved upon as an illustration of corporeal Castilianization, in this case, in the service of a strategy of political control and fear:

> Miguel Ordóñez, member of the Chic clan, is a man of between forty
> and forty-five. He is the feared cacique of Cancuc. He goes about armed
> with an old Smith & Wesson revolver and prefers American bullets to

those of his own country. Always clean, almost always drunk, he serves at the bidding of the "boss" [Chiapas Delegate for Indian Affairs]. . . . He attended school for some months, learning rudimentary reading and writing, which made him a scribe, "servant of his town," and attorney for his people and his own interests before the Ladino authorities in Tuxtla and San Cristóbal, where, in addition to Ocosingo, in recent times, he has been afraid to visit because of the multiple charges of armed rebellion and murder brought against him. Violent by nature, he shouts, gesticulates, and insults those who do not carry out his orders or do not answer him with due speed. He is as fearful of night and "ghosts" as of his political enemies. He is intelligent and discharges carefully and painstakingly his duties as deputy agent, a post he has been given so that he may be kept, as far as possible, under the watchful eye of, and on good terms with, Ladino authority, for he is indispensable as a collaborator and dangerous as an enemy. In order to conduct the village census in the short time I had available, I had to give him a huge bottle of swill (twenty liters of cane liquor), and, bottle in hand, he tagged along with the president and other Indian officials, making a house-to-house tour, toasting the men, cracking jokes, forcing the others to ask the questions, and translating the answers for me. (Guiteras 1992, 41)

Those positions in society that involve a high degree of "Castilianness" are, at least fleetingly, necessary to maintain lines of communication with the outside world, but they are not models for conduct; or if they are, only by default. The very fact that they persist in the collective memory (as is the case of Ordóñez and other caciques) is proof of their anomalous quality. A proper Indian, that is, someone who has managed to become a good Indian, is soon forgotten, once dead, and it should not be any other way.

Summing up, the self is composed of various intentionalities that cannot be reduced to one or another, although they may be bound up one with the other. If their varying degrees of visibility are anything to go by, they occupy distinct planes: one public and completely exposed that corresponds to the domain of the head (body); another intermediate one, which is the *ch'ulel;* and a third, much more hidden plane, which is that of the *lab.* However, their distribution is not equitable; some people possess up to thirteen *lab,* others only one; in some cases they are "strong" *lab,* in other cases, "weak" ones (to play host to a mouse can never be the same as hosting a bishop). Therefore, some people are more affected by alterity than others, or are affected by it differently from others. This state of invisibility or clandestinity offers a perpetual challenge to be discovered, which in turn compels one to explore the field of oneself/one's "other."

The "other" is the ethnic "other," the European; or, to be more precise, Europeanness impregnates all that is "other." We have seen the extraordinary receptivity that the Tzeltal have developed in relation to specific aspects, practices, or objects of European culture, and how they are emulated by the *ch'ulel* and the *lab*. We can see this ethnic difference in the *ch'iibal* mountain, a place located beyond everything on account of its categorical excess. We can also see it in the universe of the *lab*: in this case, a negative "beyond," a sort of bestiary whose only common denominator is its Castilianness.

But the fact that the "other" is also inside the body means that the self/"other" contrast is not external to the person. That the person is imagined to be composed of several beings is a key feature, for, in contrast to the modern European concept according to which anyone at any given moment can possess only one identity (unless he is mad or ill), in the Tzeltal scheme of things we have been examining, a person, by definition, simultaneously has different identities—he *is* different beings. The "other" is already present within the self.

CHAPTER 5

Animism as History

It is not difficult to recognize the relationship between certain Tzeltal souls—in their conduct, their attributes, and their very titles—and the Indian historical past. Characters in this repertory of souls include livestock from the Old World, tools known to be from Europe because they are manufactured of metal, Catholic priests, royal officials, Mexican cattle ranchers, schoolteachers, and evangelical musicians, among others. In other words, there are perceptible concordances that transform the interior of the heart not only into a discontinuous repetition of exterior geography, but also into a mirror, so to speak, of the past, a kind of historical memory.

We should recall that virtually all these "historical souls" are *lab* from the "illness-giver" group (*ak'chamel*), a category that is unique because its common denominator is not ecology, as in the case of other sorts of *lab* (animals, meteors, river creatures), but rather the faculty of language, through which they inflict illness. This type of being, with its intrinsically wicked character, seems to have a long history. For example, in the Nahua tradition prior to the Spanish Conquest, the horned owl was a creature especially feared by humans, for it was a *nahualli* into which some individuals transformed themselves to inflict illness upon others (López Austin 1980, 87). There were also sorcerers who magically devoured the *teyolia*, which were soul entities that resided in the heart and were transformed into a bird at the individual's death (1980, 256); this ancient soul entity displays features suggesting a distant forebear of today's *pále*. In the case of the Tzeltal, however, the category of illness-givers seems to have evolved to inordinate lengths. Availing themselves of human language, or one sufficiently analogous to give illness, the *lab* of this group add a considerable extra burden of suffering to the range of "natural" ailments that may afflict the Indians. In fact, the words that penetrate the human body to produce illness are precisely the words that come from or are related to the world perceived of as European.

Thus, there is a link between illnesses and a propensity for historical time. In the following, I shall make this connection clear by examining the relationship that possibly ties these souls to the historical circumstances from which they were born. I will also shed light on some of the possible reasons why these souls have ended up assuming such a high, palpable profile in Tzeltal experience. I do so by tracing the thread of possible affinities based on conjectures and retrospective probing, rather than by adhering to a strictly linear, chronological scheme. I will deal with different categories of historical significance in an effort to make connections with this peculiar assortment of illness-giving *lab*.

Birds of the Heart, Livestock, Metal Tools

The first group is composed of illness-giving *lab* that are all clearly associated with European commodities that were brought to the New World to serve the Spaniards. In addition, each bears an inherently negative significance. The Bird of the Heart may be a hen or a rooster, a grackle, or a pigeon. In Tzeltal, the full name of "hen" is *kaxlan me' mut* (mother bird from Castile), while "rooster" is *kaxlan kelemut* (male bird from Castile).[1] Clearly these were animals of European origin introduced at a very early date into Indian communities. Furthermore, the "Castilian hens" play a prominent role in any list of contributions that the native population were obligated to give to their parish priest during the viceregal period, so it is not at all surprising that the Indians attribute a predilection for these birds to the *pále* (the priest *lab*). After examining how the *pále* are said to act, a guess might even be hazarded as to the Indian interpretation of the sacrament of baptism. They say that the Bird of the Heart is drawn out by the priest (in all probability, the song charming the Bird of the Heart out is a Catholic liturgical chant), magically enlarged, and finally cooked in boiling water, following a procedure that enables its literal embodiment in the form of the priest, as well as its posthumous incorporation into the society of the Church.

As for the pigeon, different types are recognized, all of which are given distinct names in Tzeltal. However, the Bird of the Heart is specifically called *palóma-mut* (*paloma* in Spanish), clearly referring to the domestic pigeon (*Columba livia*; Hunn 1977, 155).[2] Introduced from Europe, it was used as a messenger by Spaniards and it can be seen today in the public squares of any Mexican town. The Tzeltal regard it as a revolting animal; in the town of Tenejapa, an alternate name for this bird is *satanas*, also a loan word from Spanish: *satanás*, meaning "Satan." The grackle is a black bird (*Molothrus aenus*; Hunn 1977, 197), whose Tzeltal name is a loan word from the Spanish *zanate*; this derivation is indicated by the stress the Tzeltal place on the penultimate syllable, *sanáte*.

A brief note of clarification on language is in order at this point. Although the Tzeltal language has borrowed many words from Spanish, the number of loan words skyrockets when it comes to terms related to souls or all that is sacred (*ch'ul*) in general. What is significant is that in Tzeltal, all words are routinely accentuated on the last syllable. However, some loan words preserve their identity and thus may be recognized as such, thanks to the fact that they continue to be pronounced with the accent on other syllables, despite the difficulty this represents for the Tzeltal. For example, Tzeltal speakers immediately identify the word *pále* (from *padre*, "father" or "priest" in Spanish) as a Castilian loan word. In fact, we know that the word was being pronounced this way by the indigenous population in the Chiapas highlands since as early as the sixteenth century. Therefore, even vocabulary can be invoked in the service of the historical record.

Sheep and goats are also considered repugnant: malodorous, flea-infested, and naturally incompatible with cornfields. Surely they were introduced in small quantities in the Chiapas highlands during the sixteenth century by Spanish colonizers, and over time they were adopted by some indigenous groups (Perezgrovas 1991). Cancuqueros do not possess any of these animals, although they are familiar with them because women in some Tzotzil communities not very far away raise small flocks. The Tzotzil only use the wool from sheep, and, significantly, in Cancuc, wearing wool jackets is the exclusive prerogative of the *principales* and town hall authorities, who purchase them from the Tzotzil. On the other hand, the Tzotzil do not consume the meat, although there is a suspicion on the part of Cancuqueros that they do so secretly.

The Tzeltal principle underlying their refusal to eat these animals is quite simple: the human body literally incarnates what it ingests. Therefore, according to Lorenzo Lot, Indians are essentially composed of corn and beans, plus a pinch of chili to give color to the blood, and a little bit of fruit and greens from the forest. Lot described how in some chants, maize is referred to as *ch'ul chu', ch'ul bak'etal* ("sacred breast," "sacred meat"), and beans as *sch'alel yok sk'ab* ("corn's second arm"), regarded as its ornamentation, because of the way bean plants twine around the corn stalk and because of its flower. It is commonly supposed that if one fed on sheep continuously, one's body would become polluted by their European animal nature and transform into a European body itself.[3]

Nor should we overlook the contribution of the singular position these animals occupy in European culture in influencing Indian identification of birds and livestock as souls, whether through Christian narrative and iconography, or directly from Old World culture and folklore. Perhaps the representation of the Holy Spirit may be recognized in the pigeon; in viceregal religious art, the dove is a standard image for the Holy Spirit entering the bodies of the faithful. Moreover, it would not be out of place to recall the metaphor of the free reception of Grace and the gifts: "the love of God is poured out by the Holy Spirit in our hearts. . . ." Indeed, in the metaphorical language employed by the missionaries, Christian evangelists sought to pour their message into the hearts of Indians, as repeatedly reinforced in sermons and confessionals. The rooster occurs in a similar position as an element of the Passion, or the lamb as one of the main dishes of Easter supper. The goat might be compared with the Christian devil in his guise as a billy goat in more informal descriptions. In Tzeltal, the goat is called *tentzun*, probably a word of Nahuatl origin, but it may, to the Tzotzil or Tzeltal ear, overlap with the Spanish word *tentación*, or "temptation."[4]

Finally, turning to metal tools, it should be recalled that they are conceived of as the head of river snake *lab*. Today, machetes and axes in particular form part of everyday life and labor in Cancuc. However, during the sixteenth century, when metal tools replaced stone and wooden implements, they became a permanent source of dependence on the Castilians. This is due to the complete control exercised by Castilians over the manufacture of metal implements. After the indigenous uprising in 1712, for instance, the Spanish authorities impounded all the Cancuqueros' metal tools, perhaps in order to avoid a situation in which they could be used as weapons, or perhaps as a straightforward punishment, or both. Actually, it is interesting to note that during the rebellion, sticks, slings, and the odd stolen rifle were used, but not *machetes*. In any event, the lack of metal tools to work the fields exacerbated the cycle of famines and epidemics that followed in the wake of the rebellion (Viqueira 1997, 400). The role of indigenous access to these tools in their nominal acceptance of Christianity has yet to be fully investigated. However, it is known, for example, that during the seventeenth century, the Indians from the jungle, who were not subject to the Crown, and therefore not Christians, made long journeys in order to trade wild plants and animals for salt, silver coins, and agricultural metal tools with Christian Indians in Santa Eulalia, in the Cuchumatán mountains of Guatemala (Vos 1980, 132).

Priests

The distinction between the diurnal *pâle lab* dressed in white and the nocturnal ones who wear black may simply be the result of a tendency to discriminate between categories on the grounds of color differences. However, it is also possible that the distinction is related to the difference between the white vestments of the Dominicans and the black of the lay clergy. If this is the case, as I am inclined to think it is, then it is a good indication of the level of detail achieved in historical distinctions deposited in the heart.

Descriptions of the bishop *lab* highlight their ostentation, their multiple garments of different colors, and their shiny shoes. It is not difficult to imagine why. Not only could bishops be seen in Ciudad Real (San Cristóbal de Las Casas), the episcopal seat since the sixteenth century; they also made tours through villages (the *visitas*, or "inspections"), traveling on a litter or, in rugged mountainous regions such as those found in the Chiapas highlands, conveyed about in small *mecapal* chairs (a chair borne on the back of a porter, sustained by a tumpline), with the bishop and his entire retinue carried by Indians. In the early seventeenth century, English traveler Thomas Gage recounted the following:

> . . . Most of the bishop's income is in the form of large offerings received annually from the main Indian towns, where they go once a year to confirm and augment the bishop's income, for he will confirm no one who does not offer at least four *reales* together with a white candle with a bow. I have seen the wealthiest [Indians] offer [the bishop] a white candle of at least six pounds in weight and a bow two yards long and twelve pennies wide, surrounded from top to bottom with one-*real* coins. Even the poor Indians are proud to make this offering the chief masterpiece of their vanity. (Gage 1987, 260–261)

According to Xun P'in, the Jesuits are an entirely different case. However, it appears unlikely that the Cancuqueros had any prolonged contact with them at any time in their past. For part of the seventeenth and eighteenth centuries, there was a Jesuit school in Ciudad Real, where the children of Spaniards were taught moral theology and grammar, and since 1958, there has been a Jesuit mission in the Tzeltal village of Bachajón (Maurer 1983, 444) that has extended its activities to other Tzeltal villages in the lowlands, although they have never reached Cancuc, as far as I know. In any case, the school existed only a short time, and its relationship with the indigenous population must have been minimal. The mission is too recent to explain the precision with which the profile of the Jesuit *lab* is delineated. On the other hand, it is certainly possible that awareness of the not entirely good relationship between the Order of Preachers (Dominicans) and the Company of Jesus (Jesuits) led to the Dominican friars themselves delineating for the Indians such a precise portrait.

In general, judging by their preeminence in the heart of the Indians, the Catholic Church and its priests, of all the colonial institutions, have been the most powerful force that has affected Cancuc. Since the middle of the sixteenth century, when the Dominican friars established themselves in Cancuc, until the expulsion of the last priest at the end of the nineteenth century, the presence of the clergy has been one of the most palpable signs of indigenous subordination to colonial power: the alien in the very heart of the community. During the three centuries of subjugation to the Spanish Crown, priests were the only Spaniards who were legally permitted to reside in Indian villages. In fact, they actually took up residence in the social center of the community, in a room attached to the church building that is still today known as *komento*, from the Spanish word *convento*, referring to "convent" or "monastery." In the eyes of the Cancuqueros, this detail is particularly significant, because as we shall see later, the church—along with the other buildings around the plaza, including the town hall—is the unmistakable heart of the community and is simultaneously a place reproducing power that is alien to it.

The central region of Chiapas was finally conquered by the Spaniards in 1528 and from that moment, the indigenous population became tributaries of the Spanish Crown. As a result, indigenous society was gradually worn down by disease and the exaction of tribute, but it was not radically transformed (Wasserstrom 1983, 24), except perhaps by the swift weakening of the Indian nobility, once it was partly deprived of its former tribute (Remesal 1988, 1:243). In 1545, the first contingent of Dominican friars arrived in Chiapas, fresh from Castile, accompanying the first bishop of Chiapas, Fray Bartolomé de Las Casas. It was the friars, taking refuge in the well-known division between the "Republic of Spaniards" and the "Republic of Indians"—and bearing responsibility for this second "republic"—who took upon themselves the task of initiating sweeping changes in indigenous society and culture.

Fray Antonio de Remesal, the Dominican chronicler who wrote about Chiapas in the second decade of the seventeenth century, making free use of texts contemporaneous with the events, recorded the following description of the first steps taken and the initial intentions. Prior to the friars' arrival to the province,

> the Indians lived in their heathendom in different villages, with different names, different lords, different governments, different idols, and different languages, and all as different as one domain or kingdom from another; and because the villages are not arranged by streets and neighborhood, as in Europe, there was one house here, another one there, and yet another a distance away, with no pattern, and for this reason a place of five hundred or fewer inhabitants, which in those times was very few, occupied one league of land, and this is why they are not very sociable among themselves, and earlier they were continually involved in wars, factions, and disputes among themselves. (Remesal 1988, 2:243)

Then the chronicler describes how the first *reducciones* were undertaken:

> . . . The priests began to try to unite villages and arrange them in the manner of a sociable republic so that they would be more quickly assembled at mass and sermon[s], and all that was necessary for their government. For this purpose, first they made a plan, so that everything would be built the same. First they established the church, larger or smaller depending on the number of inhabitants. Next to it, they placed the priest's house, in front of the church a very large plaza, different from the cemetery, opposite the house of the *regimiento* or council, next to that the jail, and near that the inn or hostel, where visitors would find lodging. The rest of the village was divided by a rope, the streets straight and wide, [running] north to south, east, west, in a grid. Once this was done, the most important part remained, and this was making the Indians want to move in. (Remesal 1998, 2:243–244)

In Cancuc, they finally moved into the town, although I am unaware of the exact date. Today in the center of town, part of this original layout is still faithfully reproduced. There is a small plaza with the church and opposite it the town hall, with its jail. However, the missionaries left no mark beyond the confines of this rectangular space. Beyond it, there are no blocks nor streets, nor any semblance of a grid. The houses are as far apart from each other and positioned as randomly as in the old days of heathenism.

Remesal goes on to detail the attempts that were made to change habits, especially those related to the appearance of the body, in regard to which the fathers played the role of "mothers":

> ... Thus these priests, in order to lay hands on the Indians, who with difficulty, seeing them as from the Spanish nation, persuaded themselves to believe that what they were doing to them was for the love they had for them and for their own good, they acted as if they were their mothers. They combed and cut their hair, they clipped their nails, they washed their face and body, they dressed them in shirts, they put flared pantaloons or breeches on them, they fastened the clothes, they belted them, they taught them to tailor and sew; nor did they neglect to tell them how to discharge their bodily requirements decently, they built them houses, they drew plans for them, they got everything ready for them. (Remesal 1988, 1:484)

All the while, the missionaries did not overlook the reconstruction of the heart, for they were convinced that this was where the principal obstacle to true conversion could be found. So the fathers:

> ... entered as if into a thick woodland full of underbrush and brambles, to open a trail and path there, to remove the brush, plow it, cultivate it, and to make the land that was so rocky, dry, and barren, like the hearts of these miserable [creatures], become fertile with the preaching of the Gospels and bring forth a plentiful harvest of faith and good works that would bring them to everlasting life. They were like a few extremely perfect joiners who entered to destroy these hard and shapeless bits, to introduce into them the form of Christians and of courteous men and people living in republican harmony; and how well they have achieved this end, experience showed us many years ago. (Remesal 1988, 1:472)

Nevertheless, today Cancuqueros still prefer to wear their hair and nails long. Instead of trousers and shirts (except when worn for doing chores or as the garb worn by "captains" of festivals), they dress in tunics, and cotton clothing continues to be woven on the pre-Hispanic backstrap loom.[5] As for the heart and the success of its "fertilization," Remesal got ahead of himself, because even two and three centuries later, Cancuc parish priests continued lamenting again and again over the same problem: the hardness of the Indian's heart.

The gradual changes in the priests' attitude toward the Indians did not differ substantially from what occurred in other areas during the viceregal period, although the tempos are somewhat different. During the sixteenth century, the Indians were, in the eyes of the Dominicans—the majority of whom arrived from Spain and were strongly influenced by Las Casas—creatures without will, "meek sheep," the passive stage on which the new episode of the age-old struggle between God and the devil is played out. The triumphs of the friars' mission of evangelization were all God's doing: "This is the finger of God. This is His hand. This is His power, because it is impossible that this life be lived without His personal aid and this doctrine be imparted without His personal light," said an astonished inspector of the order repeatedly while on a tour of Chiapas to verify progress in evangelization (Remesal 1988, 1:212). In contrast, the devil lurked behind each of the friars' failures: "This was the devil, mortal enemy of the health of souls and much more so of those of those Indians, whom he had held in thrall for so many years, and appearing to them where they were to enter the Church to participate in God's most divine sacraments, it was that of baptism, he was so successful in defaming Him and in placing Him in such low repute in the eyes of the Indians that there was scarcely anyone who wished to receive Him, and they would sooner have their eyes struck out than give over one of their children to be baptized" (Remesal 1988, 1:488). The devil "grew so fond" of his little triumphs that he was inspired to develop new ruses. Among them is an attempt to discredit the friars by making "priests" appear at night, wandering between the Indians' houses, as the Indians themselves complained (Remesal 1988, 1:494)—an incident that could be early evidence of the activity of a *pále*.

After roughly 1600, the priests begin to concede greater initiative on the part of the Indians. Little by little, the province was dotted with the discovery of episodes of idolatry, mainly the cult devoted to "idols" hidden in caves or incidents of "nagualism." The fathers tended to interpret these occurrences not as the result of a continuity in native religious practices, but rather as regressive lapses, tinged with demonic relations to which the Indians inclined of their own volition. These practices, or perhaps simply the repression of them, increased in the second half of the seventeenth century (Wasserstrom 1983, 96–98; Aramoni 1992).

Perhaps in tune with the zeal of the Inquisition deployed years before by Bishops Bravo de la Serna and Núñez de la Vega, the first decade of the eighteenth century saw a new shift in Church-Indian relations in the highlands region. Miraculous apparitions of images of the Virgin or of Catholic saints began to crop up in some Indian villages, especially Tzotzil-speaking ones. As a result, cult associations, with varying degrees of formality, quickly sprang up around these visions. In most cases, the Indians tried to obtain ecclesiastical recognition for their new cult, which was denied to them, while parishes dismantled the sites of worship, usually located outside the center of the community (Ximénez 1931, 257–282). Finally, a new apparition of the Virgin in 1712 in the village of Cancuc itself, once again discredited by church officials, sparked a major Indian rebellion.

I will only provide a brief account of the events here, given that they have already received considerable attention in the historiography of Chiapas.[6] With Cancuc as its logistical and military center, the rebellion spread to thirty villages in the province of Chiapas, including Tzeltal-, Tzotzil-, and Chol-speaking communities, which managed to raise a sizable army, although a poorly armed one. During the opening weeks of the conflict, the rebels attacked villages and haciendas inhabited by some Spaniards and "castes" (a term referring to a wide variety of mestizo peoples), who were killed, while women were taken captive. In fact, they ended up taking almost complete control of the region. Ciudad Real, the provincial capital, where the Spaniards had dug themselves in, came under serious threat, until a partial defeat of the rebels at Huixtán briefly detained their assault on the city. At the same time, the Indians organized themselves politically. The leaders of the movement, most of whom had been Indians associated with the Church—sacristans, choir teachers, priests' stewards, and the like—some of whom could read and write, adopted a quasi-ecclesiastical pecking order, undoubtedly reflecting the Castilian scheme of political hierarchy they were most familiar with. They named themselves bishops, with vicars for each village, and performed the proper liturgical duties: masses, confessions, baptisms, marriages. The army, commanded by Indian captains, was also organized along the lines of the Spanish model. The whole movement was directed, from Cancuc, by a select group of people connected to the shrine of the Virgin that had appeared. Her messages were interpreted by the young woman who had first discovered her, who had taken to calling herself María de la Candelaria. However, the rebellion did not last long. Roughly four months after it started, Spanish troops from Guatemala (led in person by the president of the Audiencia, the Spanish council that oversaw the colonies at that time) and Tabasco managed to storm Cancuc, thus stamping out the movement. From then on, only a few isolated groups that had taken refuge in the mountains continued to put up any resistance (Ximénez 1931, 310–360; Viqueira 1997).[7]

What stands out in this account is that one of the first actions of the rebels was to attack the haciendas belonging to the Dominican friars, located in the fertile valley of Ocosingo. Each hacienda had its sugar mill, manned by an Indian work force. Significantly, not a single mill was left with its wooden presses intact, for they were all burned to the ground. Therefore, it does not seem far-fetched to assume that those very mills inspired the Tzeltal transfiguration of the mill in the ancient pre-Hispanic tree of breast into the limbo of children's souls. As for the parish priests in the region, they either fled under threat of death, were forced to continue administering the sacraments (also under threat of death), or were killed and flung into a deep fissure in the ground. Such drastic actions may have been triggered by a fear among the Indians that if the rebellion failed, the priests might become informants, given their knowledge of their languages and leaders. But, one might ask, why this particular end? To accompany the sun on its movement through the heavens? To lend support to one of the four pillars that hold up the surface of the earth, in the event of their having thirteen *lab?* The latter idea is not so far-fetched, as we shall see later.

It is not clear whether, in the aftermath of the 1712 rebellion, political and doctrinal control over Indian communities in the Chiapas highlands slackened or became tighter. In any case, one result of the secularizing spirit of the times was that other villages came to be administered by lay clergy (Wasserstrom 1983, 79). Cancuc, considered an unappetizing posting after the demographic and economic disaster following the Indian defeat, remained, if not a Dominican curacy, at least in the hands of friars of the order until the nineteenth century. For many years (even until today among the Ladino population), the Cancuqueros had to bear the burden of their bad reputation as instigators of the rebellion and therefore as "mutinous Indians."

The letters exchanged between the episcopal seat and the Cancuc curacy (preserved in the Archivo Histórico Diocesano of San Cristóbal de Las Casas, and the bulk of which date from the mid-eighteenth century to the end of the nineteenth) also reveal a change in the attitude of the priests of the period. Of course, the Indians were no longer viewed as easily malleable subjects, as they had been at the beginning of the evangelical mission. Nor were they regarded as hardened idolaters, as they had been in the seventeenth century. Instead, they became viewed as irrational rustics whose obstinacy aroused exasperated comments, a vision that makes perfect sense, given that this is, after all, the Age of Reason. According to one of Cancuc's parish priests at the end of the eighteenth century, the moral state of his parishioners "is as they have preserved it since time immemorial, for they do not advance from their rustic customs, because with respect to piety, they do not know it in re- ality, not for lack of warning . . . ; but because they are, on the one hand, steeped in the customs of their forebears, and the little or no discipline they have received from the different teachers these villages have had, has exerted sufficient influence for the purpose." Furthermore, if they do uphold a minimal degree of morality, it is due to the "constant zeal I show in their regard." Nevertheless, the Cancuqueros appear to have kept up a reasonable observance of the sacraments, and the priests leave no indication of having detected any overly non-Christian activity of any kind.

An apparently unremarkable incident recorded in parish correspon- dence with the episcopal seat in Ciudad Real illustrates the type of rela- tionship to which their priest had Indians subjected. I refer to the case "on the taking as confirmed the death of Nicolás Sánchez, husband of Rosa Vásquez, Indians of the village of Cancuc" in the 1809 files on Cancuc. At the beginning of May 1809, a man and a woman, one Rosa Vásquez, Indians who wished to be married, went to see the priest of Cancuc, Fray Feliciano García. The woman had been widowed a short time before. Her former husband had allegedly drowned in the river while attempting to cross it. He had been out with his brother-in-law, and although the level of the river was on the rise, he had stripped and dived in, whereupon, before his brother-in-law's eyes, he had been swept away by the current. After several days, the river returned to normal, so the whole family went downstream in search of the corpse. But they were unable to find it. A small detail aroused Fray Feliciano's suspicions that the deceased, Nicolás Sánchez, had not actually died at all. Some months before his alleged drowning, the priest had noticed that Nicolás had let his hair grow long ("in the manner of the Ladinos of Tabasco"). This, he feared, meant that the Indian had fled Cancuc and gone into hiding in Tabasco, where, thanks to his flowing locks, he would go un- noticed by the Spanish authorities.

The priest wrote to the bishop in Ciudad Real to ask for instruc- tions on how to proceed. The reply he received on July 8 told him he had to state in writing the names and surnames, marital status and age, rank and position of all the subjects who had anything at all to do with the case (there were fifteen of them). He was further instructed to take their statements (in writing) one by one, asking them for all the details surrounding the event, as well as the grounds they had for their declarations, and so on and so forth, taking special care that Rosa Vásquez should not come into contact with her suitor. Once this had been completed, he was to send the results of his inquiries to the bishop as soon as possible under seal.

Fray Feliciano did as instructed. He heard lengthy statements, which, once written down, he read back to the witnesses up to three times for them to ratify, although they did not sign them, as they did not know how to write. Although the testimonies revealed that the married couple detested each other and that the alleged deceased was a strong swimmer, that was all they revealed. No further light was shed on the matter. Fray Feliciano married the woman on July 21, "but always with the suspicion that the husband has taken flight." At the beginning of August, he received another missive from the bishop declaring the marriage unauthorized and telling him he had to continue with his investigations. Among other things, he was told he had to find out whether Rosa had made any "show of emotion, or of pain . . . whether she had complained to the justices, or to other Indians; or, on the contrary, had, to the admiration of her neighbors, remained quite unmoved by the whole incident; and if at the time of the event, she already had a relationship of friendship with the suitor. . . ." Rosa's statement was to be witnessed, and the other Indians had to make fresh statements. What is more, Rosa would have to "be held in a secure place, under strict supervision of the village justices, as is the custom in cases where there is similar risk of absconding. . . ." Fray Feliciano spent all of August taking down new statements, before sending his findings to Ciudad Real. In September, he received a new set of questions to put to the parties involved: establish the relationships of kinship and friendship that bound them all, and recognize any sentimental ties they might have. In the meantime, Rosa was to remain in the charge of some honest Indian woman, because until the whereabouts of her previous husband could be ascertained, a second wedding was out of the question. As for the suitor who had sprung up overnight, as it were, the bishop wrote that discretion was to be exercised in the search for a new woman for him; it could surely not be hard to find another one in the village.

So the hearings continued, even though it was becoming more and more difficult to extract any new information. Twice more, correspondence was exchanged with the bishop. Fray Feliciano García's final letter concluded with these words: ". . . and thus I beg that your piety and patience stoop to forgive whatever faults these findings may have, for I am of scant experience, and of none at all when it comes to paperwork, and I am of the opinion that a trial ad infinitum is much more likely than my ever succeeding in completely tidying up the investigations."

The phrase, ". . . cases where there is similar risk of absconding," is particularly revealing in this exchange. At that time, the relationship between priests and the Indians under their sway was no longer one of protection, if indeed it ever was. Far from being a region of refuge, given that haven was more easily found in the Spanish cities where one could pass unnoticed, Cancuc had become a place of confinement; Indians do not just leave Cancuc, they flee from it. The sour irony of the bishop or his secretary who assumed that Rosa's suitor would encounter no difficulty in finding other women to marry is certainly justified, given that women greatly outnumbered men, because men habitually disappeared to dodge tax charges, among other reasons.

In 1821, Chiapas won independence from the Spanish Crown, annexing itself shortly afterward to Mexico in 1824. These events do not seem to have substantially affected relations between Cancuc's priests and Indians, which remained unchanged until the consolidation of liberal power beginning in 1855 and the anticlerical measures that accompanied it (Benjamin 1990, 44). From that time forward, parish records reflect the rapid and progressive erosion of the priests' authority in Cancuc. In 1860, after learning from civil authorities that it was no longer obligatory, the Indians withheld from their priest any type of sustenance or alms. Shortly afterward, they were no longer taking him seriously, except when they could take advantage of him to oppose the district's liberal political authorities. By 1868, the *principales* did not even let the priest use the keys to the church, which led him to write to the bishop bemoaning the fact that no one kept up the observance of any sacrament and that "they drink and dance and light fires inside the church, and it fills me with dread, because I have been in some preposterous villages, but God forbid there be another like this! They do not believe in the holy sacrifice of the mass for all the fervor of their prayers in sound mind to some of the images, and no sooner does the celebrant of mass appear than they rush out as if chased away by someone, or they stay and show their back to the high altar." A few years later, a lay priest became the last priest in Cancuc, when he finally managed to leave once and for all, after several attempts and prolonged absences.

The practically enforced departure of the priests brought to a close a long parentheses that had been opened 325 years earlier, when the first Dominican missionaries had settled in the valley (inventing Cancuc as a settlement in the process). Despite the passing of time, that the Indians continually conceived of the priests as agents of an occupying force is a constant source of wonder. There is no doubt the priests were feared, but their sovereignty was never truly recognized. From that time, no priest has ever returned to Cancuc on a permanent basis; in fact, none would ever be permitted to do so. And then the Cancuqueros stopped observing all sacraments. Even kinship through godparents, considered an essential part of Mesoamerican Indian social life, is nonexistent in Cancuc; only the names of godmothers appear in the parish's eighteenth-century baptismal records. The only exception is the group of new Catholics who are paid an occasional visit by priests or catechists, who generally prefer to avoid the center of Cancuc, and go by the hamlets instead.

Scribes and Writing

The Tzeltal undoubtedly were familiar with writing as a skill. The remote cultural ancestors of the Maya Classic period were renowned for producing the most advanced writing system in pre-Columbian America. In fact, pre-Hispanic Tzeltal groups employed books that Ruz (1985, 232) suggests were used to make predictions about the destiny of each child at birth, perhaps in the same way that the *tonalamatl* (260-day ritual-divinatory calendar) was used by the Nahua. Even well into the colonial period, toward the end of the seventeenth century, Bishop Núñez de la Vega remarked (in a quotation that evokes the ethnography of the *lab* in Cancuc) that ". . . they do the same in compendiums and superstitious calendars, where according to their proper name, they have written down all the *naguales* of stars, elements, birds, fish, wild beasts, and different animals, with the useless observation of days and months to indicate to the children who will later be born which *naguales*, according to the calendar, correspond to the date of birth . . ." (Ruz 1985, 232). Moreover, during the colonial period, obviously, and down to the present, the Tzeltal engaged in European writing, some of them using it to learn to read and write Tzeltal.

In light of this evidence, it seems unquestionable that the written word must have been familiar territory to the Tzeltal. However, this is not the case in Cancuc. Among the Cancuqueros, writing is always considered an attribute of others. It is basically viewed as the property of the Castilians and inherently as the "other," and thus sacred in itself. Some quick observations may serve to illustrate how this is possible.

As is well known, some Indian villages in Chiapas have a collection of books, mostly colonial ordinances, although most Indians are unaware of their content, as they are usually not read by local inhabitants. Instead, they are stored in a coffer, as if precious relics, becoming the focus of ceremonial attention once a year when they are perfumed with incense and paid reverence with earnest phrases. Although no such thing has been preserved in Cancuc, each house has its assortment of old papers eaten away by damp and old illustrations ripped from books, kept in a small wooden box. From time to time, I was asked to read and translate them. They turned out to be licenses from the Instituto Nacional Indigenista, receipts from the municipal authorities of Ocosingo for a birth certificate or the like, and, the oldest of all, civil marriage certificates from one hundred years before. The value of these papers clearly resided not in their content, but in the fact that they were steeped in alterity.

A second case, extraordinary on multiple grounds, shows how writing is not only powerful as an object in itself, but also as a skill, because of its capacity to "reproduce." In one version, *pále*-type and scribe-type *lab* lack any form during their periods of inactivity; only their clothing exists, hidden away in some nook of the wood or a cranny in a cave. Once they decide to spring into action and give someone an illness, they write on some pieces of paper, out of which they go on to shape their own bodies. In other words, they invent themselves, by writing themselves. In a way, this is a logical extension of the mimetic abilities of sacred *ch'ul* beings.

One hears in a certain prayer:

> ... that's how it is, sacred lord
> that's how it is, sacred president
> white man, father
> white man, lord
> white Castilian, father
> white Castilian, lord
> he has a position in Mexico (City)
> may he grant
> my honest word
> my heart (my desire)

how many children you have!
secretaries
lawyers
deputies
sacred scribes, father
sacred scribes, lord
there, before the sacred president
in Mexico, beseech before his heart
in Mexico, beseech before his heart

he who expounds the word
he who expounds the speech
may his lips not take fright
may his heart not take fright

These are brief fragments from an extremely long chant of the *bik'tal ch'ab* ("shrink," "prostrate") category that Cancuc's *principales* have to perform, to the accompaniment of a lengthy and complex series of movements, before a delegation of them is sent to deal with Mexican political authorities. The explicit function of the words uttered is to break the will of the civil servants in the forthcoming talks. They demonstrate once more the intimate relationship imagined between the power of the state's civil servants and their ability to use writing.

It is in this highly charged field where power and writing are inextricably interwoven that *lab* scribes take on meaning. Both "name" and "professor" are designations for *lab* that are linked to the past and present procedures of European political dominion, thanks to their faculties of writing. The appearance of "name"—besides using a book and a quill, he wears black clothes and a biretta on his head—resembles that of a Crown functionary, and, as mentioned earlier, he often goes by the name of "king." He may well have been inspired by a judge or royal official. His manner of inflicting illness by writing down names in a register would appear to suit him. In fact, throughout the viceregal period, the economy of the Chiapas highlands was largely based on tribute, continuing as such until long after the royal institutions withdrew. Under this system, the Indians had to turn over food (corn, chili, beans, honey), make cotton mantles (the so-called labor draft, or *repartimiento*), and work periodically on haciendas and in sugar mills (generally owned by Dominicans). There were even periods when they were required to pay in coin, which left them no choice but to find jobs outside their communities in exchange for a wage at certain times of the year. The colonial tributary system required a census. Records of contributors (an exact record of the number of Indians, together with their classification according to age, sex, and civil status) were necessary for the region's economy during the viceregal period. To compile these records, certain Crown officials in charge of assessing and collecting taxes had to travel to Indian villages on periodic tours of inspection. This type of functionary might very well be the one that became fixed as the image of the "name" *lab*.

The concept of an individual "name" and writing it down has even deeper resonance among the Tzeltal. Until the last General Census of the nation in 1980, when the agents began to tour the houses, I was told fathers would hide their children, sometimes their wives, too, among the vegetation near the house, thus helping them escape being named and counted. In fact, widespread fear of having one's name written down still characterizes encounters between Indians and "Castilians," or any outsiders for that matter.

For their part, "professors" appear in Cancuc's history much later. Following royal decrees, the first schoolteacher was appointed in Cancuc in 1800 to "teach reading and writing, as well as give instruction in the Castilian language in order to perfectly achieve teaching and understanding of the Christian and Civil Doctrine among the people" (Archivo Histórico Diocesano, Cancuc VII). However, throughout the nineteenth century, the presence of elementary schoolteachers seems to have been intermittent. In any case, their work must have enjoyed only modest success, because nobody, with the exception of a select group of Indian "scribes," can even write their signature. While they were there, the teachers acted more as representatives of the liberal administration (from 1855 onward), and consequently as political adversaries to the priests. The documentary evidence makes plain that Cancuc's *principales* took advantage of this rivalry, taking the side of one party or the other, depending on the circumstances and the relative power of each. That historical dimension may explain why the *lab* scribes have been fixed deep in the memory of the Tzeltal as the bitterest foes of the *pále;* if they meet, they may even kill each other. Or perhaps the bad blood between them has more to do with the rivalry between the clergy and functionaries of the Crown over the extortion of Indian labor.

Around 1950, the figure of the schoolteacher underwent a drastic transformation. The Instituto Nacional Indigenista promoted a campaign to train Indians to be bilingual teachers. After a short period of instruction in special centers in San Cristóbal and elsewhere, they were returned to their communities of origin (Köhler 1975, 193–199). I had the opportunity to speak to one of the first two bilingual teachers to return to Cancuc. He explained to me how they had been openly entrusted with the mission of breaking the Indian cacique Miguel Ordóñez's hold on power (see Chapter 4 on Ordóñez) and how they had been fairly successful at it after several years of political tug-of-war. Other teachers followed them, maybe not all of them Cancuqueros, but always Tzeltal speakers, and now the bilingual teachers have come to monopolize the positions of political power in Cancuc.

Every morning, in the yards of every hamlet's little school (often an ordinary house of adobe and thatch), the children parade in military fashion and raise the Mexican flag. Incidentally, because of its rigidity in the use of joints and the fact that the children's movements are all synchronized, and thus too similar for comfort to the "dance entries" that we have already noted in the fiestas of some *lab*, military marching is a type of movement antithetical to the Indian aesthetic and ethic of decorous walking. That is why parents find themselves trapped in a difficult dilemma: either stop their children from attending school, which means missing the opportunity to learn the basics of reading and writing and the chance that offers for steering one's way through the Mexican world with some measure of confidence; or else force them to attend and be contaminated in the process with Castilian traits. A fairly common solution is to send only one child (almost always a boy) and withdraw the rest as soon as it is possible.

In her 1944 ethnographic report on Cancuc, Guiteras refers to the existence of a "*lab pofisol*" (professor) "who is also a wee fellow, dressed in black like the *pale* itself, or also all in white" (1992, 226). This early report suggests that its existence as a soul predates the arrival of bilingual teachers in the 1950s. On account of the appearance of its clothing, it apparently originated in the figure of non-Indian teachers, which was then fixed in the memory by that time. Nevertheless, by 1990, due to extant power hierarchies, discussing "professor" *lab* had become an extremely sensitive issue. In fact, I was never able to hear a detailed description of its appearance.

Cattle Ranchers

During the viceregal period, the majority of land belonging to the Indian peoples was legally protected as communal property. In the more open, milder valleys, there were haciendas for cattle raising and other activities, generally under the ownership of the religious orders that depended on the forced labor of Indians from the surrounding communities. However, from the eighteenth century and, above all, in the nineteenth, many lands that had formerly belonged to Indian villages or that the Indians had been cultivating without title became large estates or small family ranches, often cattle ranches, where the Indians would work as farmhands, on many occasions tied to the ranch by the bondage of debt (Wasserstrom 1983, 156–158; García de León 1985, 126–128). Although the Indians reproduced some of their own domestic culture on these estates and farms, they were also subjected to a different work regime and culture based on cattle, imported from the Old World. The *lab kaxlan* (Castilian), described as having the attributes of cowboys, is presumably related to this world.

However, the valley of Cancuc never fully became an out-and-out ranching zone, thanks, in part, to the tenacious resistance put up by the Indians to the loss of their lands. During the nineteenth century and early twentieth, the history of Cancuc is largely a series of legal battles over the ownership of land. My knowledge of this has been gleaned from a few documents kept in Cancuc's town hall: title deeds to common land, public land purchase certificates, district court rulings, appeals, and an official survey plan. They are stored in total disorder in small boxes, and it is not easy to obtain permission to gain access to them, because they are surrounded by a certain aura of power and risk (especially the plan). It is thought that if they were to be stolen or to disappear, the Cancuqueros would be in danger of losing their lands once more.

Taken as a whole, they span the period from 1848, when the title deed giving Cancuc's lands over to common ownership was issued together with the plan, to the 1930s, when the agrarian reform laws of the Mexican Revolution began to go into effect. The picture they paint is one of never-ending legal battles, starting more or less in 1860, coinciding with the liberal Reform Laws. On one side stood the Mexican ranch owners in the neighboring municipalities of Chenalhó and Pantelhó, who reported some plots of lands in Cancuc as being unworked and therefore susceptible to being adjudicated in their favor, and on the other, the *principales* of Cancuc, who maintained, through lawyers from San Cristóbal, that those lands belonged to them and had been used by them since time immemorial. The court cases ran on for decades, and once lost, it was usual for the land to be bought from its most recent owner. Nevertheless, some ranches were set up as *baldíos*, uncultivated common land, where Cancuqueros would work. So in effect, they were "uncultivated common-landers," that is, they would work their own land as best they could and work a few days of the month for the landowner. On one ranch, a chapel appeared where the ranch owner's wife had to be godmother to the children of several Indians (the baptismal records in the episcopal archive only record the godmother's name and the child's mother's name).

For some time now, the world of the rancher has not posed a threat to Indian life in Cancuc. In fact, ranching has been in rapid decline all over the Chiapas highlands. This probably helps explain why this type of *lab kaxlan* (Castilian) is barely a menace anymore. It has all but stopped causing illnesses.

Christian Music

Around 1944, in Oxchuc, a Tzeltal municipality near Cancuc, the Summer Institute of Linguistics began activities of evangelical proselytization. After a few years, and some initial setbacks, a Presbyterian church in embryo had been created in Oxchuc, which provided free medical assistance and formal training in some trades (Siverts 1969, 175–178). Just ten years later, around 1955, almost half the population of Oxchuc stated allegiance to the Presbyterian church (Harman 1974, 28), which began to spread rapidly through other Indian townships. Even so, its introduction to Cancuc was relatively late; it was perhaps not before the early 1960s that it finally managed to mold the first Presbyterian group out of several families who, due to their beliefs, had to endure violence and repression for some years at the hands of the town's traditional authorities.

For the other Indians, as for me, and maybe for the evangelical ones too, their most characteristic activity is the endless singing and music that can be heard every Sunday in the small chapels. That is how the *lab* evangelicals have been defined: as musicians who play string instruments and the accordion while they take nightly strolls. The style of the music, as I mentioned, is *norteño*, a lively northern type of Mexican dance music, but its words, didactic in intention, are texts with biblical allusions translated into some Indian language or other. One is forced to listen to taped recordings of the songs in any outdoor market in the region or on any bus journey; it is said to be *bien alegre*, "very enjoyable and lively."

These musicians are *lab* of recent appearance in Cancuc, and it is true that some of their customs are indeed new. But their history in the Chiapas highlands probably dates back much further. For instance, this event that occurred in the Tzotzil municipality of Chamula, as related by William Holland, is of interest:

> A Chamula also thought he had seen [the illness] some years before, when one night he went out with one of his friends to the fields to hunt foxes. While they were walking along the deserted paths, they suddenly saw a group of Chamula men and women who seemed to be very happy, as if they were on their way back from a fiesta. The men were playing guitars and the women followed behind carrying censers. When the Chamula and his friend passed by the group, one of them was struck and fell to the ground; the other hunter tried to lift his companion to his feet, but was unable to and went off for help. Returning after a little while with some other Indians, they found the man to be still alive and carried him back. They realized that the group of people had been *me'chamel* [mother-illness], as they always go around very happy and carrying lots of censers and guitars, as if they were going to a fiesta. (1978, 129)

This procession of musicians (and Holland does not specify whether his narrator considered them to be "souls" or some other kind of supernatural being) has all the appearances of the typical "company" of an Indian *cofradía* (a sodality) that moves in a procession with the image of a saint. In Cancuc, such processions are confined to the center of the village, but in other places like Chamula, the saint's retinue starts out from the surrounding areas and ends up in the main square, and in others, like San Andrés Larráinzar, the group also takes part in the ritual visits to saints of different townships (Ochiai 1985). Advancing in single file, the entourage usually includes the following components: someone (a young man or woman) carrying a burning censer, the man in charge of the fireworks, the musicians (violinists, harpists, guitarists) who go along playing nonstop, the image of the saint on a litter carried by the *mayordomos*, and bringing up the rear, more men to act as relief and the participants' wives with more censers.

There is every likelihood that today's evangelical *lab* musicians in Cancuc are a recent refinement of other retinues of *lab* musicians who must have made nocturnal visits, and that they in turn were inspired by the ritual corteges of flesh and blood that accompanied the saints in processions. Thus, this type of soul is more broadly connected to the system of Catholic *cofradías* that was introduced several centuries ago and that has come to be known in the ethnographic literature on Meso-america as the "fiestas system," which had the blessing of the Church and continues providing a livelihood for Spanish-speaking traders and artisans who are the only suppliers of the indispensable ritual objects for these activities.

The essential affinity that links the *lab* entourages to Christian ritual (in the two versions, Catholic or evangelical) is established through music. It should not be overlooked that all the instruments played come from the Old World, in just the same way that the music (which is what pleases the saints and is, for example, danced to by the women) is Castilian music of the seventeenth and eighteenth centuries, albeit considerably modified. Yet, there is another kind of music, Indian music, played on flute, drum, and, sometimes, turtle shell, that is completely different and is not performed to gladden the heart but to indicate certain of the ritual's movements and phases. However, unlike the former kind that pertains to the heart, this music does not inspire any emotions nor is it capable of causing any illness.

The *lab* "Mothers-Fathers" and Coffee Cultivation

The *lab me'tiktatik* (mothers-fathers) are invisible old folk who set up their little tables and chairs in the middle of pathways, so that when a passerby inadvertently knocks over the food and drink, they make off with his *ch'ulel*. Like the musicians, they are a recent phenomenon. They are clods of earth, in a way, personifications of the soil, and as such, perhaps they are not so new after all. If lately they have turned especially hostile to the Tzeltal, there are some reasons to suspect that this change in attitude is related to the beginning and rapid expansion of coffee cultivation.

In the first place, Cancuc shamans first identified them as a completely new and certainly very powerful illness some twenty or thirty years ago, immediately after the introduction of coffee growing in the valley, initially a slow and gradual process, undertaken with considerable reluctance. Today, perhaps more than half the families of Cancuc grow coffee, in large or small quantities, which, along with honey, is their sole source of cash. Disorders of the soul that are attributed to the *me'tiktatik* have undergone a corresponding increase. Secondly, as far as their form is concerned, the provenance of these *lab* coincides with the provenance of coffee, which started to be cultivated in the Tzeltal municipality of Tenejapa before Cancuc, but whose actual origin, it is believed, is the coffee plantations of the Pacific coast of Chiapas, also suspected to be the place of origin of the "mothers-fathers." Thirdly, encounters with these *lab* frequently, though not always, take place on paths or at crossroads near small coffee warehouses where the crops of different groups of hamlets are stored together until sold either to individual Ladino buyers or to Mexican government agencies.

Thus, the "mothers-fathers" are the demanding counterpart of what, in the shape of coffee, is taken out of the earth, at a high cost, incidentally, as only the seed or bean of the fruit is sold (extracted with depulping machines donated by a government agency), while the fleshy pulp goes to waste. As a matter of fact, coffee is today the only crop of any importance in Cancuc that is not pre-Columbian. What is more, not only are its growers made to depend on the market with its fluctuating prices, all too familiar to the Tzeltal, but its cultivation also reverses a relationship that had been established in the last century whereby the Indians left to join the payroll of the coffee plantations on the Pacific coast or in the lowlands farther north. This sudden turnabout in the relationship (the substitution of work in an alien land for the alienation of one's own land) could be the explanation of the unusual circumstance that the *me'tiktatik* appear to be the only *lab* that live in the very hamlets of Cancuc (coffee is often grown right beside houses), literally obstructing traffic on the paths joining households to each other.

Soul History and the Body

The link between these diverse "illness-giving" *lab* and Tzeltal history (at least since the European conquest) is plain to see. But what kind of past are we dealing with? What sort of chance events and states of being are "remembered" in this kind of internal playback? As I understand it, the *lab* embody certain strategies of power—institutional, political, cultural, technological—adopted by Europeans in their attempt to transform Indian life and subject it to the conditions of the new political order. It is a kind of memory that is apparently not so concerned with highlighting the overt, violent forms of domination as it is the less easily perceptible ones: reeducating the individual, remaking the conception of selfhood, altering the most immediate day-to-day environment from which he sustains himself.

On the one hand, the soul record possesses considerable temporal depth and a complex system of strata. It includes the old criteria the Spaniards put to use in the sixteenth century to distinguish a barbarian from someone who lived according to "Christian propriety." For example, these traits include skills and trades (based on the use of metal tools), Christian ceremonies, European music, urban planning, clothing, and so forth. But it also includes later criteria that are in a way proper to the modern nation-state, such as education and medicine. In this regard, there are indications that one of the next *lab* that could be formulated might be a doctor; he is described as a "Castilian" who carries a doctor's instrument bag. Although there has been a small Mexican Social Security clinic in the middle of Cancuc for some years, this doctor figure seems more inspired by private dentists, who travel to Indian hamlets, taking out molars or replacing teeth with pieces of gold-plated metal (a touch of vanity). They are sometimes referred to by the name of *unam*, almost certainly taken from the acronym of the largest university in the country, the Universidad Nacional Autónoma de México, from which some of them might have graduated.

On the other hand, the veritable repertoire of transformation skills called upon by the souls is as precise as it is subtle. It encompasses activities related to religious practice or bureaucratic institutions, as well as activities to which historians usually pay much less attention. In fact, this Indian soul history seems particularly concerned about the social implications of the choice of certain technologies. For example, there seems to be concern about the effects the use of certain tools, crops, or cattle might have on bodily movements, food, population density, or work; or else the crucial role of language (speeches, texts, sermons, loan words) in the implantation of these forces. Hence, perhaps we can understand the paramount importance of writing, by means of which those who wield it, the "Castilian" *lab*—priests, scribes, professors, and company—imprint on their language a much greater force, and therefore more illness.

At first glance, the internalization of this history may seem the result of a slow, accumulative process of "sedimentation" through time. However, this image is overly passive. It would be more accurate to interpret it as an active procedure of folding, whereby, as we saw before, the "other" is internalized and distinguished by a painstaking process of minute differentiation. Consequently, that Indian/Castilian contrast within each person, which initially appeared to be merely a cultural distinction, takes on a political connotation when considered from a historical perspective.

It is evident that Spanish hegemony over the Indians was (or should have been) based not only on practices of economic control and institutional dependence but, above all, on the Indians' acceptance of the values, conventions, classifications, interpretive categories—in short, of the culture (or a version of it)—of the Europeans. However, for domination to be complete and the exercise of power to be truly effective—as Comaroff and Comaroff (1991, 19–27), following Foucault and De Certeau, have pointed out—the symbols of that control must become to all intents and purposes invisible; they must permeate the daily routine and the conscience of the dominated so deeply that their eyes no longer "see" them or recognize them for what they are.

What frustrates the chances that this suppression might succeed among the Tzeltal is that the symbols of domination, rather than being resisted externally, are transferred to an internal plane. Locked up within each person's heart, where they are attributed the additional factor of intrigue (for their identity and number are a mystery; it is only known that they present a threat), those symbols are the object of scrupulous and sustained examination by everyone, and this forces them to remain permanently visible. They may be practiced (or perhaps one should say "imitated"), but precisely for that reason, they never become *habitus*; they can never be accepted as a group of habits of thought or normalized as ordinary, everyday procedures; they are always kept distinct, shown to be alien, made to speak and identify themselves as such.

In this regard, given music's avowed capacity for seduction, we may recall how the soul repertory devotes considerable energy to exposing Castilian string music or the religious songs of the evangelists as nothing more than strategies of co-optation. This is not to mention liturgical chants, which, for all their beauty, may result in the loss of the Bird of the Heart and the concomitant loss of life at the hands of a Christian priest. We might also recall at this point the "speech" of the drunk man that I transcribed in Chapter 4, the words of which are an imitation (albeit a watered-down one reduced to a few fleeting details) of Mexican political functionaries and especially speeches concerning the "Indian question." So long as they are copied in this fashion, it will never be possible to "confuse" that vocabulary and style; they will always be recognized not only as alien but also as a potential danger. And of course, it is edifying to discover that the official indigenist discourse (itself in a relationship of osmosis with academic discourse) loses any pretension to legitimacy and is radically incapacitated and exposed the moment it is copied (not even mocked, simply copied) in the words of those it is meant to be concerned about and protecting.

The main target of this generalized monitoring seems to be the body and, taking into account Tzeltal canons of beauty, elegance, and manners, everything that comes into contact with it. Any sign of Castilian contamination, however small it may be (showing an excessive desire to eat meat, walking carelessly, using Spanish words), immediately takes on a greater resonance. Just as the inside of the heart seems doomed to saturate itself in Castilian culture and history, the rest of the body must struggle to preserve itself undefiled by it. There can be no doubt that this is because that last state of being, a decolonized body, constitutes the principal means of defense against the procedures of political subjugation.

The case of the Tzeltal seems to stand in stark contrast to those of many other colonized peoples, who did not immediately yield when first subordinated politically or accept Christianity from the outset, but who later went on to be radically transformed on account of their relationship with the Europeans or else were wiped out entirely. The Tzeltal submitted to the Spanish Crown relatively quickly and at least nominally accepted Christianity and the policy of physical concentration, resettlement, and European administration that went along with it. But with the passing of centuries, they have preserved a day-to-day existence that is still essentially non-Hispanic. In such a situation—a simultaneous movement of integration and differentiation, of tacit compromise with the imposed order, but not with the logic that justifies it—the Tzeltal must have used first the colonial institutions and later the republican ones, right down to the present day, in an attempt to exploit them for their own benefit when defending themselves. For example, in Castilian courts, they were used to denounce the abuses of priests, obtain legal recognition of their ownership of land, or receive allowances from the Instituto Nacional Indigenista. To make all that possible, some Indians had to, and still have to, act as if they were Castilians: sacristans, interpreters, keepers of the peace, choirmasters, scribes, caciques, schoolteachers, Catholic catechizers, Presbyterian deacons, nurses, delegates from the government party, representatives of the official peasants' union, and so on. They form an impressive column of "insiders" to be reckoned with.

It is highly likely that the transcendence of the *lab* that we have been examining is not so much the reflection of a direct relationship with European social order as a procedure, so to speak, to confine in parentheses that "danger zone" that Indians, in their own opinion, occupy in their role as mediators. It must be a fear not so much of others, but of that part of others they may have within themselves. Thus, the assumption is that illnesses never come directly from Castilians, but more precisely, from Indians in their role of others, of Castilians.

CHAPTER 6

Narrative, Ritual, Silence

The Past in Narrative

In her ethnography of the Tzotzil people of San Pedro Chenalhó, Calixta Guiteras (1965, 251) wrote: "So much emphasis is placed on continuity and equality that it would seem that life in the village of San Pedro would have gone on forever, more or less undisturbed by events that, as far as is generally believed, form part of other creations or pertain to other people."

My own conversations in Cancuc left me with an impression very similar to the one recorded by Guiteras. Time past, whether recent or remote, is in moral terms essentially the same as the present. "Before," the Tzeltal lived neither better nor worse, neither longer nor shorter lives; there was neither less illness nor more rich people; nor, as strange as it may seem, were things any cheaper. As for the future that awaits everyone, there is no reason to suppose it is to be feared or preferred, because it will not be any different from the past and the present. For anyone versed in Spanish tradition, in which comparisons with the past are fertile ground for moral judgments, the idea that both time past and time to come appear to form part of one single and immense present continuum is always disconcerting. Nevertheless, just because a comparative examination of past and present does not provoke the formulation of value judgments, it need not prevent us from holding a general opinion about both concepts. On the contrary, for the Tzeltal, their history—their narrative history—is nothing more than a never-ending list of hardships.

Stories about past events are generally called *k'op yayej me'el mamaletik*, "word that exists from the elders." As the title suggests, narratives contained within this genre possess a separate existence, which is thought to be independent of the narrator. They differ from everyday conversation in that they are composed not so much of "spoken" words (words that are spoken back and forth and, therefore, immediately interchanged/exchanged), but of "given" ("donated") words, going only in one direction, which gives them an authoritative weight lacking in formal or informal conversation. Everyday conversation all too often loses its thread because of *chopol k'op* (gossip, mockery, criticism, verbal attacks); in other words, it is communication with a hidden agenda, which tries to elicit information and may be deceitful or deliberately false. In contrast, those stories included in *k'op yayej me'el mamaletik* are considered true, in the sense that the events to which they refer are deemed real. Were it otherwise, their existence would have no justification. It is useless to explain that a story may lay claim to existence even if it is a piece of fiction dealing with imaginary happenings. The events of the past are not remembered because they are true; they are true because they are remembered. That is why a story's narrator will usually conclude his account with the disclaimer that he has simply transmitted the words as he himself heard them, no more and no less, possibly excusing himself in the process for any omissions, as well as making it plain that any attempt to decipher the donated word would be superfluous. The narrator's role is limited, or should be, to updating the word so that the listener will, in turn, update it in the future. That may be why so much reliance is placed on a direct style of speech.

Unlike what happens in the prayer genre, which forms an admittedly interesting contrast, narrative lacks any consistent classification. Similarly, the stories themselves have no precise titles by which they may be identified. In any case, two types of narrative about the past may easily be distinguished by their form and the time they refer to.

In the first type, elderly people recount events that they have been able to see in their lifetime, or events that they have heard about from people close to their parents' generation or, more rarely, to their grandparents'. The defining feature is that what is told "has been seen": either the narrator has been an eyewitness of what is being told or he or she has heard it from a witness close to the speaker, who will often be named and paraphrased. It is an "open" story, following the format of a conversation in which the listeners participate, fill in gaps, give a different version. Often biographical details slip in, and the whole will last as long as the audience is interested. The subject matter is fairly broad, but there is a marked tendency to include the infighting and power struggles in Cancuc. The limit of memory at the time of my interviews was around the 1920s, the period of the revolutionary war in Chiapas. It is clearly a kind of movable frontier in time, the position of which depends, among other things, on the age of the narrator; the elderly push it further back in time, while younger people recount, most of all from a stylistic point of view, events of a few decades ago as if they pertained to an ancient era.

The second type of story takes us back to a time far beyond the recent, familiar past of lived experience to a succession of outstanding events stretching from the remotest past to the beginning of this century. The series of events are not invariable, because some Tzeltal barely mention some occurrences, while others may add more incidents to the list; nor is the order in which they appear immutable, as positions in the chronological sequence are sometimes changed, especially the order of those accounts of the earliest events. The following list comprises the stories, which is tantamount to saying the events, that, as far as I can tell, most adults would recognize:

—"When the burning happened" (*k'alal k'ax te k'ajk'el*). A rain of fire reduced the center of the earth's surface (the present site of Cancuc) to ashes, destroying those who lived there.

—"When the flood happened" (*k'alal k'ax te pulemal*). A continuous rain flooded the earth's surface, drowning its inhabitants. The few survivors turned into monkeys.

—"When the first war happened" (*k'alal k'ax te kerae*). The president of Guatemala attacked Cancuc in search of treasure, and the Cancuqueros defended themselves under the leadership of the hero Juan López. In the end, López was killed and the soldiers conquered the community; repression ensued, and the location of the church was changed to its present site. (This is the story of the Indian Rebellion of 1712.)

—"When the animals came" (*k'alal tal te chanbalametik*). Certain monstrous animals, who came out of the jungle in the tropical regions or so-called hot country (*yaxalum*) and who devoured "Christians," threatened to invade Cancuc, but ended up turning into stone. Some of their petrified forms and paw prints (apparently feline) stamped into the rock can be seen at a spot on Cancuc's valley floor.

—"When the great smallpox happened" (*k'alal k'ax te muk'ul chuel*). Many died; others became so weak that they could not tend their cornfields and starved to death; children died because their mothers were unable to suckle them. (This probably refers to the smallpox epidemic of 1860, which caused an enormous loss of life in Cancuc, according to documents in the Archivo Histórico Diocesano of San Cristóbal de Las Casas.)

—"When ash fell" (*k'alal yal tan*). Huge quantities of ash blocked out the sun; noon was as dark as midnight, and the whole earth was covered with a white blanket. (This is the eruption of the Santa María volcano, around 1903.)

—"When the hot cough happened" (*k'alal k'ax te k'ajk'al obal*). (This is probably the devastating influenza epidemic that spread through Mexico in 1918.)

—"When the war returned" (*k'alal k'ax te kéra yan wélta*). This was the war between Generals "Karansa" (Venustiano Carranza) and "Pinera" (Pineda), when they came face-to-face in Cancuc and its vicinity; the latter shot "four hundred" Cancuqueros beside the church. The war "calmed down" when Carranza's troops joined with women from the Tzeltal community of Altamirano, thus losing their strength. (This episode refers to clashes between the Mexican revolutionary government's army and soldiers of the region's landowning oligarchy between 1918 and 1920.)

—"Slavery" (*mosoil*, from the Spanish *mozo*, or "servant"). The "Castilians" forced the Cancuqueros to work for barely any pay; they were pressed into transporting packs or people along the pathways, the latter carried in chairs tied across the bearer's forehead and back. (This possibly refers to the period from 1923 to 1926. "In 1926 Cancuc's Indians complained that their municipal agent made them carry loads for less money than they had earned before 1910, that they were also forced into servitude for their debts, as well as the fact that the agent earned his money by selling then liquor. According to them, the Revolution's reforms had 'only served to make our situation worse'" [Chiapas Historical Archive 1926, XII, quoted in Benjamin 1990, 238].)

—"When the locust happened" (*k'alal k'ax te k'ulub*). A plague of locusts devastated Cancuc's crops, and for a year, hunger reigned; they had to eat the very locusts that destroyed their food supply. (Perhaps this refers to an event that occurred some time in the 1930s.)

Two features of this sequence deserve particular attention: the instigator or source of the event and the succinctness with which these momentous episodes are recounted. First of all, the obvious common denominator of all the stories is an intrusion from outside: plagues, war, hunger; forces of disorder and destruction, in the face of which the Tzeltal seem almost defenseless. The elderly *principales* can and must pray in the church during preordained periods, or when danger is imminent, but one cannot always be confident that the prayers will bear fruit and that danger will be detained or will pass. In any case, the impression it produces is one of an epidemic that arrives and moves on, or one that simply comes to an end; it dies out not because it meets with any resistance, but because it is extinguished by its own force. In fact, when these previous events are related, it is not unusual for the word *ch'ab* to be used to indicate that the misfortune is finally abated, be it hunger or servitude. The word *ch'ab* means something like "to stop something, diminish it in intensity, cool off," and it is normally heard when someone wants to say that an illness is subsiding. It also means "prayer," the kind uttered before a cross, and it crops up in the root of the word for "healing ceremony" (*ch'abaytayel*). Another one of its meanings, significantly, is "silence."

The past seen as a series of intrusions is probably a common denominator in the Mesoamerican historical imagination.[1] Nevertheless, I am struck by the acute disinterest shown in Cancuc for origins; everything seems to exist from the beginning, nothing ever seems to have been created, even less in a progressive manner.

The incidents presented in the list above could hardly be the result of some supposed initial act (akin to an origin myth, for example) that is earlier and more basic, because no such event is ever acknowledged. The incidents are interconnected by the reiteration of the intrusion scheme, not by possessing any temporal direction or sense of sequence of events. Disconnected, they take on the form of a discontinuous, random series of happenings, separated by intervals of time about which nothing is known; it is like an archipelago rising crystal clear out of a uniform ocean of absence. Its islets lack precise coordinates, for they cannot be located on a "map" of time; in other words, no chronological signifier exists on which they may be superimposed. Seen from this perspective, the burning of the earth by a rain of fire could have occurred eighty, eight hundred, or eight thousand years ago: it does not really matter. (It will be seen that I have yielded to the temptation to assign dates to some of the events, clearly in a concession to the practice of European historiography.)

Returning to the second feature of their narrative development, the least that could be said about these accounts is that they are frugal. They allude to an event, for instance the flooding of the earth and the disappearance of its inhabitants, without any further explanation. Why did it flood? Who (if anyone) decided it? Who were the "people" who inhabited the earth at that time? What were the flood's consequences? These questions are never raised by the tellers or the listeners. A typical account of "when the animals came," for example, would be as follows:

> Well, they say that long ago (*ta namey*) some animals came out of the jungle, they left from Yajalón. They were man-eating animals, they only ate human beings. Well, they first went to Chilón, and they began to eat up Christians, then they went to Sitalá and also ate up the Christians, then they arrived in Guaquitepéc and also ate up the Christians. Everywhere they went, they ate up Christians. Everyone had to flee their homes, they had to hide in caves. Well, then they headed to Cancuc. But it's said they never got this far. When they were in the vicinity of Tzajalchén they turned into stones, they say, they were petrified. That's what they say, nothing more, that's what they've told us, just that.

I made several attempts to find out the enigmatic reason for the petrification of these creatures, but on the rare occasions an answer was ventured, it was clearly ad hoc, an ill-fitting explanation that satisfied no one.

Characters are conspicuous for their absence in these accounts, and nothing of what happens appears to have any further consequences, or at least none that go beyond the simple observation that some happenings have left a mark on the landscape, no doubt lending them an added verisimilitude: the ruins of the old church, for example, the clay vessels containing human bones that are occasionally found at cave entrances, or buried grindstones. However, these vestiges will never be abundant in a place where objects of daily use and buildings are quick to decay because of the perishable materials of which they are made (wood, earth, vegetable fibers) and because of the damp. In fact, not only does human activity leave no trace, it is actually geared toward not leaving any at all. One only has to consider an Indian grave to become convinced of the desire not to leave the trace of any individual in the memory. A small bit of dug-up ground is sometimes, but not always, marked with a small, crude wooden cross that will end up rotting away; the conception is entirely different from the solid, elaborate stone tombs seen in Mexican cemeteries.

So there seems to be no interest in developing the events in themselves, for weaving a historical narrative; it is enough to note the incidents. How can this absence of narrative structure be accounted for? With respect to European historical discourse, Hayden White (1987) has remarked that behind the refusal to narrate events lies the lack of any need to dispute something. As there is no quarrel, there is no need to create an explicative framework, that is, to make the historical events "speak for themselves," to present them as if they could relate their own history. The Tzeltal narrative record of the past may thus be interpreted as a group of events that shun dispute. However, in this case, as I understand it, it is not due to the fact that "reality" is not considered problematic, but rather the contrary: "reality" is simply *too* difficult to confront.

In short, what the events cited earlier do *not* quarrel with are the Spanish and Christian versions, whether regional or universal, of historical events, and above all, the notion of history that those versions presuppose. In fact, if one takes another glance at the events on the list, it will be found that there is nothing that is strictly non-Christian, nothing that might contradict, so to speak, the version of a Dominican chronicler or, by virtue of the same of argument, a modern historian. Neither is there anything that would corroborate such a version. In this respect, the narratives are for the most part neutral, with only two exceptions that merit closer scrutiny.

Exceptions to Neutrality

There are two important exceptions to this generalized characterization. The first is the story of the Indian Rebellion of 1712 ("When the war happened"), which offers a partial contrast to the other events recorded. It is in harmony with the series insofar as it deals with a violent intrusion from outside Cancuc, but it differs in being a story that is complete in terms of narrative. Furthermore, the narration nicely fits Ximénez's chronicle of the rebellion (1931). The following is a synthesis of the story.

News comes to the president of Guatemala of hidden treasure in Cancuc, and he marches off with his soldiers to steal it. The Cancuqueros decide to thwart him and prepare to defend themselves. Their leader is Juan López, a man whose origins are unknown in most versions of the story, although one or two say he is the offspring of a chance encounter between a Tzeltal Indian from Bachajón and a "Virgin," or woman of European appearance with magical powers. (As is to be expected, Juan López is distinguished from the other Indians by certain signs that, instead of manifesting themselves openly, are insinuated in the course of the narrative: he is almost a dwarf, he gets caught up in incest, he has difficulties engendering a son, and on his head he wears a hat, which from some descriptions would appear to be a helmet that makes him invulnerable to bullets.) Then the Indians block the paths leading to the town with stone walls. The Guatemalan soldiers are prodigiously defeated by Juan López, who collects their bullets in his hat and throws them back at them, killing them. But after the battle, Juan's attitude begins to change; he no longer wants to continue working the land but demands more and more money, food, and wives. Cancuc's *principales*, fed up with the burden he is becoming, plot to kill him and throw him into a hole in the ground. Juan ends up inside the earth, where from that time on, he helps hold up one of the four pillars that support the earth's surface. In effect, Juan López is a "complete man" in possession of thirteen *lab*. Informed of his death, the president of Guatemala returns, and this time his army manages to breach Cancuc's defenses (the narration harps on the fact that the defeat was due to the Indians' lack of firearms and books) and enter the township, which is duly conquered. The invaders destroy the town center and force the Cancuqueros to move the site of the church to the valley floor, in tropical humid land. Then they depart, taking with them the treasure and a Virgin from the church. Years later, a delegation of *principales* from Cancuc make for Guatemala City and obtain permission from the president to move the township to its current site.

Thus, whereas the other events from the past may be summarized in a few words, with no defined beginning and especially no conclusion—they simply end—the account of the "first war" contains a finished story, which is therefore closed in narrative terms. It boasts a beginning, a development with plot, and a conclusion, resources that allow the marshaling of events as in a "tale." The fact that the account is also known as "the story of Juan López," after its main character, furnishes from the outset a clue as to its legendary nature. It looks as though so important a fact as the war of 1712 (about which the Tzeltal know there are both oral and written Spanish versions, and which the friars seized every opportunity to remind them of) was unwilling to be consigned to oblivion, or to survive in the Spanish version only.

The second exception, the story of how the sun appeared, or the story of Xut, is an account, save for some small variations, that is known (or fragments of which are known) throughout the whole Tzeltal area and, more generally, the Maya region of Chiapas and Guatemala. Although it is set in the distant past, it does not fit in the above-mentioned series (the Cancuqueros are unable to position it between any two of the events: it belongs on a completely different plane).[2] The bare bones of it are as follows:

A woman (*me' ixim*, "Mother Corn") was married to Beetle (in those days, Beetle was of course like a human being). Each leaf on every corn-stalk that grew in their field brought forth a cob. One day the woman went to the field to fetch some cobs, but when she returned, her husband said she had taken too many and he hit her until her nose began to bleed. She dabbed away the blood from her nose with one of the cobs, which is why there are corncobs with red bands. Then the woman left Beetle's house, leaving her two sons behind, too—one quite grown up and the other, Xut, the baby of the family, still very young—and went to live in the house of her brother Vulture. But before she left, she made a magic cooking pot of clay for her sons; when their father went to work in the mountain, the boys only had to touch the pot four times, and tortillas, beans, and all the food they could want would appear. As the days went by, the father couldn't understand why he was so hungry, while his sons seemed so well-fed. So he decided to spy on them, and he saw how they took food out of the pot. But the pot looked small to him, so he smashed it and decided to make a bigger one. He touched it four times, but the only thing that appeared was shit. This was his punishment. Then the boys decided to visit their mother. They asked her for more food, and she gave them half a corncob to plant, so that they would have to work. But on their way back, a crow appeared and stole it. They returned to their mother's house, but this time she only gave them a few kernels, wrapped up in her sash. When they arrived home, their father tried to steal the grains, and they had to run away. Then their uncle, Vulture, took them up on his wings, the big boy on one side, the little one on the other. That's why, from that time on, the vulture flies on the tilt. Then they went to live with their mother in a cottage and grew a new cornfield. But the elder brother mistreated the younger one. Once, while they were working, they saw a beehive in a tree. The elder brother climbed up and began to eat the honey; the younger brother asked for some from down below, but the elder only tossed him the wax he had chewed. That's why Xut became angry. Then he saw some little animals around him, gave them some stalks for teeth, and the animals, now rodents, began to gnaw away at the root of the tree. It toppled to the ground and the elder brother died. But his blood that had spilled over the ground turned into the weasel, the coati, birds . . . an infinity of animals. The little brother went home. When the elder brother didn't turn up, his mother began to cry disconsolately. Then the little boy told his mother to put some corn in front of the house so his brother would reappear. And in fact, all those animals appeared. They say that then Xut decided to go up to the sky and turned into the sun. From then on, there has been day and night. His mother went with him and became the moon. With her assistance, women count their months of pregnancy.

In this way the sun first made its appearance; and that is also the origin of the animals—or perhaps the *lab* animals.

Ritual

In common with the other Indian communities of the Chiapas highlands, Cancuc has elaborate and profuse public rituals. In the course of the year, in addition to the two weeks of Carnival (February), five major feast days are celebrated (Christmas, Easter, San Juan, San Lorenzo, and the Virgin Mary) that bring together Cancuqueros from the hamlets and the head town itself at a market more bustling than usual. The ceremony, in which only religious office holders and their wives (each saint's *mayordomo*, string musicians, flautists, and drummers, and so forth) participate, goes on for several days in the houses of the *mayordomos*, normally near the square, and inside the church. The culmination of each fiesta is at midday on the final day, when there is a spectacular procession of saints carried on litters through the square in a short circuit that is witnessed by some members of the public, most of whom will have come from the market, which is practically empty at that time.

Other, lesser ceremonies also take place, including the washing of the saints, the counting of coins in San Juan's necklace, and other subordinate festivals. Several other ceremonies are also held: the handing over of public offices, the main one around the end of December, beginning of January (coinciding with the European New Year); offerings to the Mountain Lords of Cancuc's main mountains (*mixa*, from Spanish *misa*, "mass"); and the beginning and end of the school year, both in the head town and in each of the hamlets.

It is immediately obvious that the festival cycle revolves around the Gregorian calendar. It is essentially a "Christian year," whose function resides in marking the main red-letter days when fiestas and other public events with historical ties to the European world are held. Until a few years ago, specialists in each of the public ceremonies (*slok'ijwenta*) found out the dates in the Christian calendar by consulting the Indians in the village of Tenejapa, where there was a permanent colony of Spanish-speaking Ladinos. Any other type of activity that calls for some differentiation of units of time is governed by the Mesoamerican calendar of eighteen twenty-day units, plus a unit of five days that brings the annual cycle to a close. This is the calendar (*bats'il ajta k'aal*, "the true day count") that provides a guide for the approximate calculation of the times when the different tasks in the field should be performed (there is no shortage of cases of farmers who applied the "Castilian day count" and ended up with a blighted corn crop), the month a child will be born, or the dates of the household protection ceremonies.[3]

The ethos that permeates public ceremonies is to a degree indigenous. However, in general, each ceremony's practices and rules are those proper to Christian liturgy: processions, days of abstinence, octaves, vespers, and so on, or else episodes taken from Christian festivals in their popular Mediterranean or New Spanish form. Moreover, it is highly likely that divergence from Catholic liturgical canons is considerably less in Cancuc than in Spanish-speaking parts of Chiapas. Undeniably, in Cancuc, some elements of the ceremonies "grate" with Hispanic ritual experience, and seen with modern European eyes, they have an exotic air, although perhaps they are no more exotic than a sixteenth-century Christian ceremony might look to us today. (It should be pointed out the celebration of Carnival appears completely odd if compared with European Carnivals.)[4] Nevertheless, generally speaking, the schematic expression of ritual movements and the objects used in public ceremonies in Cancuc are not substantially different from the fiestas conducted in other rural communities, Indian or not, in the rest of Mexico. In fact, the Cancuqueros consider their public ceremonies to be a local version of fiestas and rituals celebrated by other Indian or Ladino peoples, including the people of San Cristóbal de Las Casas, viewed as the "Castilian" town par excellence.

One characteristic shared by all these public ceremonies is more intriguing: they are bereft of any meaning. The Tzeltal, even the ritual specialists who keep careful watch to see that the ceremonies are faithfully reproduced, do not know why they are performed. Someone, without too much confidence in what he was saying, suggested they are held to celebrate the birthdays of the saints. Moreover, there is a widespread lack of understanding of what each particular action within the ritual signifies. Despite the defensive tone adopted when faced with my persistent questions in this respect, they usually do not even venture an interpretation. The degree of exegesis is nil.

The following episode, recorded during Christmas (*pásko*, Spanish *pascua*,), a term used to refer to church festivals commemorating Christmas, typifies this. On December 24, at night, the *mayordomos* put "something" together inside the church that consists of a low table in the middle of which they position three statues of saints; two of these are small, and are known as San Antonio (St. Anthony) and San Miguel (St. Michael), and the third is an anonymous oversized head, perhaps a fragment of a complete figure. Two big branches from a banana tree, from one of which a bunch of unripe bananas still clings, are arranged in the form of an arch over the table. That same day, the image of a small child is taken from the house of the first *mayordomo*—where it is kept for the rest of the year in a box—to the church, where it is placed next to the saints. There it will remain for a few hours until its eventual return to the *mayordomo*'s house on Christmas Day. The whole montage is dismantled on December 26.

Anyone brought up in the Catholic tradition would recognize this grouping, from the day, place, and arrangement, as an admittedly rather disfigured "nativity" scene. The nativity scene is open to a wide variety of interpretations, as are other episodes from the same ceremony. But what I find interesting is the absence of meaning for the Tzeltal. We may recall in this context Wittgenstein's remark that ritual and the ideas associated with it simply coexist: "Wherever that practice (the ritual) and those ideas (about the ritual) converge, the practice does not arise from the ideas; simply, both elements are there" (1985, 11). One may presume that since that time long ago when priests were denied the possibility of staying on in Cancuc, the *mayordomos* continued repeating their yearly building of the nativity as faithfully as they were able. But their execution of it, now as in the past, is so devoid of intention that they commit such feats of misrepresentation as the substitution of the Virgin Mary and Joseph with other images.[5] Why? "We don't know, it's the *kostúmbre* [custom]." What shines through this response is not perplexity, but rather an indifferent inhibition. It is not that they confer another meaning to a Christian ritual, as some theories of syncretism or cultural synthesis would have it; they confer no meaning to it at all.

Christian Rituals, Indian Simulation

In this light, the previous considerations may seem irrelevant. After all, a similar disinterest in exegesis could easily be explained as a consequence of a broader Tzeltal urge not to "rationalize" cultural practices.

There is nothing extraordinary in this attitude in itself: There is not always a need to translate the meaning of a cultural activity into another "language." Not even in the distant land where the ethnographer comes from are the ceremonies in which one takes part always or universally interpreted.

Nevertheless, what led me at an early stage to take this negative attitude seriously is its partiality. In other words, it is only adopted in relation to public ceremonies, not domestic, private rituals. Everyone is perfectly acquainted with the "meaning" of the latter: why and how they are performed. To put it another way, why an inauguration ceremony is conducted in a house, why a ceremony of offering is held to the *ch'ulel* of the dead, why a healing ritual is carried out, and so on, hold clear meanings. Perhaps most important of all, it is clearly understood why some movements and not others are executed, why these decisions are made, why those objects are used, why such and such words are spoken. In the practice of domestic and healing ceremonies, there is something difficult to define, but which is nonetheless evident—a kind of "spontaneity," a noticeable aplomb. There is, for instance, an ease and confidence with which objects and substances are replaced: Coca-Cola for sugarcane liquor, cigarettes for traditional tobacco, and so forth.

In this respect, the fundamental divergence from public ceremonies, the meticulousness of which leaves absolutely no room for any improvisation, could not be greater. Those in charge of public rituals exhibit a manic will to produce a copy of the ceremony of the previous year that is identical right down to its most trivial details. These ritual specialists are not given the title *slok'ijwenta* in vain; *wenta* means "respect for something," in this case for *lok'*, "going out," "replicating" (the same root we found in the term *slok'omba*, "image," "photograph"); the title may thus be translated as "he who guarantees repetition." What is most developed in public ritual is, in short, its mimetic dimension.[6]

However, my counterpointing of meaningless public ceremonies and meaningful domestic ones is not quite accurate. At least one exception is to be found among the former in the offering rites devoted to the Mountain Lords by Cancuc's *principales* at least twice a year, guided by the Mesoamerican calendar. These rites are performed in each hamlet, following a preordained itinerary that passes by springs, caves, and several other irregular features in the earth's surface that are marked by crosses, in front of which offerings are made of liquor, incense, candles, string music, rockets, and speeches. All these acts are conducted in exchange for the guarantee of a good harvest for the families of the hamlet. In this case, the end and the justification of the ritual manipulations are easily explained, undoubtedly because their basic scheme coincides with that of the healing ceremonies, insofar as they involve a reciprocal transaction, a relationship of give-and-take. For obvious reasons, these episodes did not figure among the ritual repertoire that the friars performed in the Indian communities. On the contrary, they are Amerindian offering rituals that must have been practiced secretly, taking full advantage, no doubt, of the fact that they were performed away from inhabited places, and therefore far from the inquisitorial gaze of the priests. How subtle the irony that these ceremonies—in reality, any type of offering to the Mountain Lords, in exchange for permission to hunt their "domestic" animals when they come out to the surface of the earth, for example—are called *mixa*, a borrowing of the Spanish word *misa*, "mass."

So the contrast we see taking shape is not strictly between public and private ritual, but between Christian ritual and Indian ritual—or, what amounts to the same dichotomy, between ritual performed in the square and ritual performed beyond it. Therein lies the difference: the space where the ritual is performed.

On several occasions, I have highlighted the dramatic contrast between the domestic units and the public square. Residential groups are constructed out of highly perishable materials and are scattered about the countryside extremely sparsely. On the other hand, the "square" is a perfect rectangle, two hundred meters by fifty, whose eastern perimeter is marked by the huge church, while the town hall dominates its western side, all built from durable materials (mortar, stone, and tile). It is easily visible from afar, thanks to the light color of the buildings that contrasts with the green of the surrounding vegetation in which the domestic groups are set. It is well known that Hispanic towns tend to branch out from this central portion, but in Cancuc, the square comes to an abrupt halt; it is radically self-contained.[7] This lends it a disproportionate appearance. It looks out of place, almost unreal in the mist. It is a piece of Castile sealed off in a bubble in the middle of an Indian landscape.

The square occupies a position analogous to the one assigned to the heart of the Tzeltal anatomy. It is what is "alien" in its own space; inside it replicates both what is outside Cancuc and what is Cancuc's past. And, of course, it is a predominantly "Castilian" outside and past. It is an inside space that puts Indian space into contact with the spheres of activity of other beings. The church and the town hall are the center of the community, and at the same time they submit to the outside powers to which the Tzeltal have been subject for four hundred and fifty years. There the parish priest and the delegates of the Mexican government took up residence; that was where strangers ended up for the night when the royal road crossed Cancuc and the Indians had to serve as bearers. In the 1930s, it was around the square that a few Ladino families in the business of selling liquor to Indians established themselves, only to be brutally murdered years later, women and children, too, by a group of Cancuqueros. Since then, no Ladino has attempted to settle in Cancuc again. And, in a different but significant sense, it is also the point of departure (via the cross in the atrium of the church) for the *ch'ulel* of the dead on their journey deep down into the earth. In a way, the square *is* the history of Cancuc, and as with the heart in the body, the past is to be found condensed within its space.

The Indian's own bodily posture changes once he enters this space, no doubt partly due to the fact that the business conducted here encourages the drinking of liquor. For example, men greet each other with a handshake instead of with the more conventional salute, appropriate in other contexts, where the younger person brings his forehead close to be touched by the elder person. In contrast, the airing of the personal grudges that arise every day is permitted, though it is deferred to a later meeting in the square, making the latter, especially during fiestas, a stage for confrontations—insults and shows of disrespect more than anything else—that have been slowly brewing, finally to overflow there.

The very name with which Tzeltal identifies the group of activities played out in this rectangle (official and religious activities) is revealing. It is known as *jtaleltik*, a term that may be translated as "our tradition," but whose literal meaning is, as we have seen, "that what comes to us as given," the same word (*talel*) that is employed to stress the hereditary, received, nature of the souls. The alternative term, perhaps used more frequently, is *kostúmbre*, plainly a borrowing from Spanish *costumbre*, or "custom." But, as a matter of fact, all Tzeltal practice some "custom." There is a Presbyterian custom, a Catholic custom; the bilingual teachers practice another custom; and so on.

All that explains why the Tzeltal see nothing strange in Mexican government officials, tourists, or anthropologists showing such keen interest in the "custom" of Indian villages. The same notion can be seen in other towns in the Chiapas highlands where tourists are even made to pay for a look around inside the church. That is to say, interest is expressed in everything performed within the perimeter of the square: the "officials" sitting on their seats, the festivals, the processions of saints, the string music, the uniforms of *mayordomos* and *capitanes*, and so on. It is logical that the aforementioned people are interested in this kind of thing, because they are things proper to Castilians; they are their own things. The *principal* Alonso K'aal was of the opinion that, as the Mexican president had recognized Cancuc's status as a free *municipio* (having risen a category from being an *agencia*), the *kostúmbre* was going to be financed by the government of Mexico City. Why? Because everybody knows the government (like the *ch'ulel*) is very fond of fiestas. Shortly after I was told this, a flyer was received in Cancuc asking for a "traditional music" group to enter a competition in aid of the preservation of Indian traditions in the state of Chiapas. Meanwhile, an enormously expensive (given the difficulty of access to the village) building project was in full swing, completely revamping Cancuc's square with money from the Mexican federal budget; a bandstand and the clock tower, which I mentioned earlier, were built. Two years later, in 1992, the church was refurbished.

Like so many other reciprocal ethnic images in the region of the Chiapas highlands, the understanding between "Castilians" and Indians on this point actually hinges on a misunderstanding: Both sides regard "custom" as something inherited, but to the former (us), tradition is a matter of what is their (or our) own, while in the Indian view of tradition, "what comes as given," is synonymous with what is alien, particularly European.

Let us return from this brief detour to public ritual. It would not be too daring to compare the square with a theater, a large stage set by the Dominican friars where, with some Indians among the cast and the majority as audience, they could wheel out their imposing didactic scenery. The distrust with which the friars viewed religious instruction through texts is well known, just as is their predilection for dramatization, iconographic illustration, and liturgical solemnity. An example would be the Jesuit José de Acosta, who thought that "[the Indians] could only be converted by the extensive use of ritual, for ritual is, no doubt, another form of language, but one that requires less rational understanding than language" (Pagden 1982, 230). The very way a symbol is interpreted (the Catholic way, at least since the Council of Trent) may have a bearing here: The efficacy of the sacrament resides, regardless of whether its meaning is understood or not by those who receive it, in its performance, in its staging. The religious ceremony is effective in itself.

The Tzeltal have continued this representation on their own. And ritual still preserves its theatrical quality: a pantomime of the Christian drama. It is a sort of ongoing imitation of the strange ceremonies conducted by Castilian priests that bring close together, and sometimes even fuse, interior space with the world outside from which the priests came and to which they returned. In fact, there is no communion between the congregation at public ceremonies, nor a genuine exchange, unlike in the rituals of Amerindian origin; there are just some players acting a role: *mayordomos* and other religious officers who are just expected to faithfully stick to the script. Yet, just as the traces of Castilian conduct and culture are confined to the heart, to be periodically "acted out" and thereby distinguished from "Indian" culture, so the Catholic rituals are enclosed within the rectangle of the heart of town, acted out collectively and thus distinguished from the Amerindian domestic rituals.

It is far from my wish to imply that they are false. Quite the contrary: The Tzeltal who participate in them, first under priestly compulsion, then obliged by the Indian authorities themselves, take it very seriously. If the representation is faulty, at the very least the participants will be the object of gossip, a very severe fate in itself, but they may also fall ill and even die. Matters reach such an extreme that almost all prayers uttered at public ceremonies (to be more precise, just before them, at each participant's household altar) are really private in intention, aimed at guaranteeing a performance that is correct and not fuel for mockery. Nonetheless, these Christian rituals are semantically empty, so to speak. There is nothing in them to be understood. For the most part, they form a myriad of arbitrary signs, things, and acts that apparently float blissfully free of "concordances"; they do not "represent" anything because they have no underlying meaning. Thus, it is possible to interpret the usual covert conflict that pitted Indians against friars as a struggle not over the meaning of the ritual but for the monopoly of its performance (or the monopoly of the means of imitation). Hence, when the priests left Cancuc, the festivals went on being celebrated in basically the same way. Roland Barthes, writing about Japanese Bunraku puppet theater, says: "Here we find that exemption from meaning that does indeed illumine so many works from the East and that we are scarcely able to comprehend, since for us to attack meaning is to conceal or oppose it, never to absent it" (Barthes 1982b, 309).

It is plain to see that the Christian ceremonies did not exercise or impose the didactic function that the friars attributed to them. Rituals did not employ a common, natural language, nor could they even be translated easily. Viewed from this perspective, they constitute the antithesis of narrative, the very character of which makes it an expressive, highly contaminating medium; that is, it is easy for narratives from different cultural traditions to blend together. The Tzeltal appear to have been aware of this possibility, and nowadays the result is a body of narrative, including myths, tales, stories, and the like, that is certainly rather poor but also almost entirely Amerindian. It comes as a surprise to discover that there is barely a single tale, theme, or hagiography in Tzeltal narrative with an Old World origin. This absence is even more surprising when one considers that borrowings from Iberian narrative are common among many of Mexico's indigenous groups. One almost has the impression that it was preferable for narrative to be kept at such a low level of development that it would simply be unable to be mixed with European stories. In any case, both the narrative of the past and public ceremonies have remained neutral, the former by atrophying, the latter by developing and even being augmented.

Difficulties of Dialogue with the "Castilians"

The encounter between the Tzeltal and Castilians seems to be a case of double exclusion. On the one hand, there is a narrative of the past that is incapable of disputing its Western versions, due to its content and form. On the other, there is a public ceremony that is incapable of being robbed of any meaning, for it is permanently devoid of any acknowledged meaning. In my opinion, this is no accident. A strategy lies behind this attitude, one that could be called silence.

The reverse of silence is dialogue. One of the most refined examples of the latter in Mesoamerica is what Louise Burkhart (1989) has called "the moral Nahua-Christian dialogue," which took place during the first decades of the encounter in Central Mexico between the Nahua (mainly inhabitants of cities and often members of the elite) and the friars, at a time when evangelization was still intense. Burkhart shows how in the course of this dialogue, the Nahua were able to partly refashion Christian moral categories (formulated in absolute dichotomies such as good and evil, salvation and damnation, sin and purity), molding them into a more familiar shape in line with their own moral system and cosmological principles. A decisive role in this process was played by the very difficulty, to an extent a technical but fundamentally rhetorical one, of translation. The friars found they had no other recourse but to teach

Christian doctrine in the Nahuatl language, thus losing a good part of its subtlety in the conversion from one tongue to another. In Nahuatl, doctrinal formulas lost their metaphorical substance to reappear transformed into a conceptually native reality (Burkhart 1989, 4–45). This is the source of a "domesticated" Christianity. But the process also occurred in the opposite direction. By paying attention to the mythical and historical cosmography of the Nahua, the friars managed to build sufficient bridges between it and the European version of it that, as the dialogue intensified, the Nahua gradually and willingly modified their original myths to conform to Christian teachings (1989, 77–78). The outcome was an incipient reformulation of the past and a redistribution of space, including the birth of a heaven and hell, although these notions did not necessarily entail, at least in the sixteenth century, the acceptance of the doctrine of reward or punishment in the afterlife. In short, what arose was a mixed world.

Dialogue is only one of the potential options in the range of communication; war is another. Holding a discussion allowed the preservation of what was one's own through the refashioning of European Christian discourse. However, all dialogues, by necessity, demand something in exchange, and given the difference between the two forces in confrontation, resistance was bound to submit to the logical categories and, above all, the forms of that other discourse. The very process of constructing a "counterdiscourse" will, over a long period of time, inevitably end up dragging along with it fragments of whatever it is opposing.

There is some evidence that the Tzeltal had attempted to engage in this dialogue in the past. An inescapably hypothetical reconstruction would go something like this: In the early days, around the second half of the sixteenth century, exposure to Christianity cannot have been very intense, since the priests were few in number and the Indian relations with the Castilian world limited. However, as it became increasingly apparent there was no way of undoing the conquest—that is, domination was becoming consolidated instead of slowly "abating," losing strength, and finally dissolving, in line with the Tzeltal model of historical events—the Indians gradually began to test the channels of cultural conversation. The culmination and final moment of this attempt was probably marked by the 1712 rebellion, when the Indians sought a Christian miracle, the appearance of the Virgin Mary.[8] In fact, at the beginning, the rebellion's command structure, in the hands of Indians who had been close to ecclesiastical and/or administrative activity, was woven by reproducing the Castilian norms. For the Tzeltal, the warning implicit in this happening (the proof of how far open confrontation replicated what it resisted) was preserved for all time in the account of the events of 1712. Juan López, the Tzeltal "hero," who in an early skirmish delivered Cancuc from the invasion of the Guatemalan troops (Spaniards), later transformed himself into a Castilian of a sort, as if this were the basic lesson that the Indians derived from those events. At one point, he refuses to work the land, preferring to live from the tribute he demands from the Indians. In one version of the account, the words "Juan is already in the book" are heard, alluding to the final step in becoming the "other," for only Castilians write and read and are featured in books.

Despite all this, interest in the Chiapas highlands in integrating Christian forms and content never seems to have been very great, and certainly not as pronounced as in other parts of New Spain. No mass baptisms were recorded as having taken place, unlike in Central Mexico; nor, unlike in Yucatán, was there a zeal for carrying out hasty religious syntheses. In this regard, the Chiapas highlanders and the people of Yucatán may function as an example, for various reasons, of two opposing attitudes regarding "syncretism." They are both Indians that speak Mayan languages and are therefore both conventionally considered to belong to "Maya culture." Whereas among the Indian groups of the Chiapas highlands, public ritual reaches extraordinary levels of development, in Yucatán it is minor. Yet to turn things around a little, in Yucatán, narrative (tales, legends, and so on) are highly developed, as well as densely intertwined with Iberian narrative. Meanwhile, in Chiapas it seems to have atrophied. Between these two extremes, the Guatemala highlands may occupy an intermediate position.

In any case, in Chiapas neither friars nor Indians, at extremes from each other, seemed ready to give up enough to be able to establish mutually acceptable common denominators. The fact that evangelization and administration of doctrines long remained the responsibility of Dominicans must have had a hand in that standoff. This order was always stricter in matters of doctrine than others and less willing to make concessions that the Indians could have modified for their own benefit. The prompt disappearance of the Indian nobility, and the replacement of their authoritative functions with a rotating system of posts filled by commoners, must also have played a role. This process did not occur in the Quiché villages of Guatemala, for example, until the second half of the seventeenth century (Carmack 1983), or among the Maya of Yucatán until almost the very end of the eighteenth century (Farris 1984). So there was no permanent, unchallengeable group in society that could produce hybrid cultural forms by being accepted by the Spanish authorities, on the one hand, and by continuing to maintain a distance from the common Indian, on the other.

Any attempt at cultural conversation, however weak it may have been, was rudely interrupted in the wake of the suppression of the 1712 rebellion. After a hiatus, the friars stepped up the celebration of Christian ceremonies, and as if they no longer had any faith in the effectiveness of their symbols, topped that off with a renewed interest in sermons and confessions. The Indian response to this new Christianizing impulse seems to have been silence, an eloquent and at times subversive silence.

The interruption of that dialogue, which had been opened in such unfavorable circumstances and converted in fact into the classic European Christian monologue that monopolizes language, was always a perfectly logical possibility, given the Tzeltal way of conceiving the word. As words form part of the things of the world and of its vast network of commercial exchange, they can just as easily be put into circulation as they can be withdrawn from it. We may recall, at this point, Keith Basso's study on the transcendental role of silence in Apache culture. It is an absence of verbal communication that is produced by those very circumstances in the life of society when the status of the speakers is ambiguous, and when the expectations one has of a particular role are erased, along with the predictability of social interaction. In short, among the Apache, silence is the response to uncertain and unpredictable social relationships (Basso 1972).

These limitations might explain the fact that to counterbalance their refusal to integrate Christian meanings, the Tzeltal also had to sacrifice certain aspects of their own mythology and cosmology, presumably those that were in most open conflict with Christian discourse, to prevent any intermixing. In competition, on the one hand, was a narrative that progressed in time through the Creation, Redemption, and Last Judgment, not the tiniest vestige of which survives in the beliefs of the Tzeltal. On the other hand, there were moral issues linked with conceptions of time and space, expressed in this life and the afterlife, and in heaven and hell, notions that were equally ignored. In sum, the Tzeltal response to the intransigence of Dominican doctrine in the viceregal period was silence, the end result of which was the perpetuation of ritual acts carried down through generations severed from meaning contained in Christian doctrine, which disappeared along with the friars. This may explain the utter lack of concern among Cancuqueros for the

significance of public ritual today and the parallel indifference and refusal to engage in disputes over European visions of the past.

Crosses

Although the Tzeltal have an image of vertically ordered space, it differs
fundamentally from the Christian model, which presupposes an array
of Christian moral implications—chiefly heaven and the bowels of the
earth, where the glory of paradise and the torments of hell can be found;
this is another notion that does not seem to have made any impression
on the Indians at all. Instead, they envision the sky (*ch'ulchan*) as composed of thirteen superimposed layers (*oxlajun lam ch'ulchan*), resulting
in a total of twelve spaces. There is no doubt that the lowest layer is
occupied by the sun and the moon, envisioned to circle the earth in
their daily movement. Little is known about the rest, although it is not
beyond the realm of possibility that other beings inhabit them. For example, K'aal says other "Xut" might live there, their "work" now done,
having jumped to a higher level in some extenuated form, as in some
atomic theory. What is certain is that they have no relationship with
human beings.[9]

The interior of the earth (*yutil lumilal*) is in turn composed of nine
"hanging" layers (*balun pal lumilal*), whose levels, as indicated by their
numerical classifier (*pal*), are not arranged in an orderly, even way, but
are randomly lumped on top of each other. Deep down inside the earth
is the *k'atinbak* where the *ch'ulel* of those who have died live; it is a place
about which little is really known, except that it is dark down there
because the souls have to light their way, in the absence of any wood,
with the bones they pull down from beneath the graves. It is unclear
whether they also use the bones to light fires to keep themselves warm,
or whether the *ch'ulel* do not feel the cold. There, too, are the bases of
the four columns that hold up the surface of the earth.[10]

However, a word of caution regarding this discussion is in order before we proceed. The layout of the cosmos is not as straightforward as
my explanation might suggest. Heaven is not properly "above," nor the
underworld "below": These places have no clear time-space coordinates
and thus have no dimensional extension. Moreover, the Tzeltal descriptions about these places are laconic, vague, and contradictory.

In contrast, the relations between flesh-and-blood humans and their
"other" beings are played out horizontally on *balumilal*, "on the earth,"

or, to be more exact, on the "summit of the earth." As far as I understand it, *balumilal*, the surface of the earth, is not the third division of the cosmos, but rather an interstitial zone with somewhat vague vertical boundaries, that ambiguous interface that joins and separates the earthly levels from their "others," the celestial tiers. We should notice that the subterranean stratum contiguous with the surface, obviously including mountains, caves, and water courses, also belongs to this domain of *balumilal*, as well as the visible atmosphere. The "beyond" is to be found on the earth's surface, but the word must be interpreted fairly literally. The "beyond" covers environments inhabited by beings that are supernatural from a European viewpoint, such as *ch'ulel*, *lab*, etc., in addition to "real" places such as Mexico City, San Cristóbal de Las Casas, Guatemala, the jungle in the tropics, the ocean, Spain, and so on. In a way, the "beyond" is simply whatever lies beyond the horizon of the mountains that ring Cancuc, but not ordinary places beyond the reach of the sense. Communication with these places is conceived of as facilitated by the presence and intervention of crosses.

The whole floor of the valley of Cancuc, and in fact the entire region of the Chiapas highlands, is dotted with crosses (*kurus*). They may be found beside springs, near the entrance to certain deep caves, at the top and at the foot of the important mountains, and at crossroads. They are wooden crosses, more or less a meter high, that have to be replaced whenever the humidity rots them; as the old ones are not taken down, they end up forming groups, often half-hidden by the vegetation. There are also crosses on the paths around hamlets, inside the church, in the atrium, and, of course, on small domestic altars.

As in Mediterranean Christian communities, Indian crosses offer protection from the outside.[11] But any similarity stops there, because there is a distinct process of logic underlying them. Instead of blocking the way to what is outside, the Indian crosses are objects through which it is possible to establish an exchange with other beings. In return for something, offerings of certain sacred substances are made before them—incense, sugarcane liquor, tobacco, blood, formal words, and so on. The protection afforded by the crosses consists not of thwarting communication but rather of mastering it, taming it, subordinating it to Indian rules of exchange. As if they were ports of trade (perhaps not unlike the pre-Hispanic trading centers), they constitute the nodes of exchange in a vast network that trades in substances and fitting words.

In principle, any kind of cross, irrespective of where it is found, may be used to communicate with any kind of addressee. Even when a man is traveling at night and decides to pray to the angels of his lineage for protection, if there is no cross nearby, all he has to do is tie two twigs together with a reed, plant them vertically in the ground, and place a little tobacco before the makeshift cross. Nonetheless, there is a degree of specialization among the crosses, depending on their location. Those that are beside a spring or at the foot of a mountain communicate more easily with the lords of the corresponding mountain; those of domestic altars, with *ch'iibal* mountains or with the *lab* who kidnap the *ch'ulel*, or with the saints of Cancuc or other villages; wayside crosses and crosses at crossroads, with one's own *lab* and other inappropriate contacts; and the ones in the church, with Mexican political authorities. For example, one version of the *bik'tal ch'ab* ceremony aimed at weakening the resolution of Mexican authorities, which is sought when a delegation is sent to negotiate something, includes positioning four saints facedown in the shape of a cross in the center of the Cancuc church floor.

This system seems to owe its existence to the notion that relations with foreigners are considerably less dangerous if they are established in accord with Indian norms of exchange. There is no reason why such a relationship should necessarily be propitious for the Indians, but without doubt, it significantly reduces and mitigates the risks attached to contact. Similarly, it is preferable for Indians that any commercial transactions they conduct with Spanish-speaking people take place in the market, not outside of it.[12] Furthermore, who can survey the events in Cancuc's history—wars, epidemics, disasters, and so on—without seeing a collection of untimely intrusions that break utterly with the appropriate channels of exchange?

A particular kind of meeting with the Mountain Lords illustrates a relationship diametrically opposed to those that are established in front of a cross. As will be remembered, the majority of these beings are European in appearance and keep fabulous treasure troves that one could make off with if one visited them in their house inside the mountains, tricked them, and escaped with the loot. A few tales are told of Indians who have gotten rich in this way. However, things are not so straightforward, as it is much more likely that the attempt will end in the loss of one's own *ch'ulel* soul at the hands of these characters, who will forever hold it captive, working as a *mozo* (servant) on their underground estates. An enterprise of this type is characterized, in short, by the completely random nature of its outcome; no pattern or rule of exchange lessens the unpredictability of the meeting. And what is more, it is a meeting that generally bodes ill for the Indians, both in fiction and in ordinary life.

Thus, crosses facilitate communication with realms of otherworldly power, whether the realm of the souls or the Mexican government. Yet the whole notion of travel holds special interest for the Tzeltal. The earth's surface, *balumilal*, is broken up into different spaces and times, but they are not entirely unconnected, because the crosses put them into contact with each other. It is intriguing that when Tzeltal travel by foot, they do so in stages marked out by crosses on the ground, always the same crosses for the same route. For example, from Cancuc to San Cristóbal de Las Casas, there are four three-hour stages, each marked by three crosses, generally where a halt is made for a rest and a bite to eat. However, clearly this conception of space measured by crosses only applies to a limited radius within the Chiapas highlands. It is also possible to travel to more distant places, but this is a more complex matter, as is shown by the insistent concern of the Indians to find out with the greatest precision the exact number of days, form of transport, price of ticket for the trip to Spain, or any other detail for any other place. Why is there so much interest in the details of traveling?

Different locations do not seem to be governed by the same spatial and temporal coordinates. It is worth recalling that inside the *ch'iibal* mountains, souls are "contemporaneous," while they are also conferred with the title of "ancestors," and they possess replicas of goods that the people in Cancuc will not become familiar with until some time later. Other mountains inhabited by their own masters—the rain forest in the lowlands, the modern cities of Mexico, the United States, and any other different place—seem to have their own corresponding space and time, as if each one formed a world in itself where the ordinary coordinates of Cancuc do not apply. Instead of defining time by means of a constantly applied single scale, whether cyclically repeated or not, it might be preferable to imagine time as being intrinsically bound to each place, discontinuously. In other words, time is not a measurement unique to each space, which might be found here or there more advanced or behind, but rather as a kaleidoscope of different sorts of time, each with its own nature in tune with the place where it resides, qualitatively distinct in each location.

Considering the importance that the Tzeltal ascribe to differences of light and darkness, the description of space and time could be formulated (as a simple imaginative recourse) in photographic terms or in terms of perspective. It could, for example, be compared with Erwin Panofsky's description of pictorial space in Hellenistic and Roman works: an unstable space, inconsistent within itself, "conceived as an aggregate or composite of solids and hollows, both finite, not as a homogeneous system within which each point, regardless of its situation in a solid or a hollow, is determined by three coordinates that are perpendicular to each other and extend *ad infinitum* from a given 'focal point'" (1975, 185). In this type of composition, the objects are distributed "freely over vast expanses of land and sea; but space and the items within it are not fused into a unitary whole," and as a result, the image as a whole takes on "an unreal character, almost ghostly, as if the extracorporeal space might only declare itself at the expense of the solid bodies and, in the guise of a vampire, feed on their very substance" (Panofsky 1975, 184). The impression caused by the description of this kind of painting, which is simultaneously a form of imitation, vaguely recalls the "spectral" world of Indian souls that can only live at the expense of solid bodies. Crosses can thus be conceived of as channels allowing communication that breaks the traditional boundaries of time and space, connecting the world of the flesh-and-blood Indians with their soul world.

New Religious Identifications

Only recently, since some groups of Cancuqueros have begun to identify themselves as Catholic or evangelical, has the dialogue with Christian conceptions seemed to be timidly starting up again. However, independent of Catholic or evangelical religious authorities (with their inordinate concerns and interests, quite in keeping with the history of Cancuc: almost a diametrically opposed "structuralist" position of neat categories of opposition), there remains the same generalized lack of interest in Christian moral geography (that vertical heaven/hell axis), the same disregard for the salvation of the soul, and the same particular misunderstanding of biblical narratives.[13]

Small doses of "rationalization" over religious practices and conventions may be distilled from comments exchanged between different religious groups (Catholics, evangelicals, traditionalists practicing indigenous belief systems). For example, the idea of the resurrection of the flesh during the Last Judgment (that is, the very literal image of corpses rising to heaven with all their flesh) is so at odds with Tzeltal common sense that not only is it the object of mockery by the traditionalists, but the evangelicals themselves have an awkward time defending such an idea in public. On the other hand, Protestant evangelicals object to the veneration by Catholics and traditionalists of wooden dolls, that is, the images of the saints in the church, whose construction holds no more mystery than the hands of men. For their part, the Catholics reproach the traditionalists for performing (public) rituals without knowing why they do so, and doing it badly to boot. And so the crossfire of criticism continues.

However, the questions at stake are not exactly doctrinal. New religious affiliations are extremely precarious, given that they are adopted and abandoned with chameleon-like ease, while groups of worship are continually being formed and disbanded. The interest in them resides in the advantages they promise to their adherents of being able to "live better on earth," a promise that is not always kept. It would be no exaggeration to say that the better life begins as soon as individuals decide to abstain from drinking liquor. This is something on which all "converts" stubbornly insist: The traditionalists are called *yakubeletik*, "drunks," and they accept the name without qualms. As a Dominican missionary told me, it once happened that in a small Tzeltal hamlet, the Indians who had recently converted to Catholicism refused to take part in a mass when they found out that wine was consumed there. Both Catholics and evangelicals declare they are opposed to wife-battering, and their speeches on the matter are virtually indistinguishable: "Treat her like your mother, a wife is like a second mother." They also agree that children should be treated well and neighbors not be sinned against. Avoiding all this is the same as avoiding all those situations that encourage drunkenness. It is a concern that goes hand in hand with the not entirely explicit, but nonetheless evident, intention of breaking down the suffocating atmosphere of isolation and secrecy that smothers each domestic group. In the case of the Indians of Cancuc, the adherence to an ecclesiastical community does not entail a tendency toward individuality—in the conventional sense of the word, the opposite of "communitarianism"—but quite the contrary. It is a reduction of the almost "incestuous" domestic intimacy in favor of more communitarian relations. It makes itself felt in aspects like participation; communion; public religious ceremonies; the use of *kerman*, "brother" (Sp. *hermano*), as the only term used for addressing members of the same faith; or, among Catholics, in the creation of ties of ritual kinship, and so on.

The enormous social and personal cost of such a high level of alcohol consumption is certainly reason enough to account for the emphasis placed on giving it up entirely or on an abstinence respected for a short time, or at least intermittently. Nevertheless, although I lack ethnographic evidence to substantiate this argument and so I must confine myself to supposition, it would not be going too far to think that this zeal to abandon the consumption of cane liquor implies an impetus to rearrange the relations between the body and the inside of the heart (always eager to drink some liquor), to restore, perhaps, the dominion of the head over the heart. However, this is tantamount to an attempted remaking of interethnic cultural and political relations; the relationship, brought on by inebriation, that the Tzeltal enjoy with themselves, with their hearts, is analogous to the relationship they have with the Castilians.

When all is said and done, the group of beliefs about souls seems to preserve itself basically intact among Cancuc's new Catholics and evangelicals. On the whole, evangelicals and Catholics have no doubts about the existence of the Bird of the Heart, the *ch'ulel*, and the *lab*. Antonio K'oy, a Presbyterian, clarified things for me. There comes a time at chapel meetings when the congregation is asked to rid themselves of their *lab*, but, as is well known, this is virtually impossible. Some pastors (Tzeltal Indians, though not necessarily from Cancuc) claim that the *lab* are expelled at the moment of baptism, something even more unlikely. God must be prayed to in order to recover the *ch'ulel* or to intercede before the *ch'iibal* powers-that-be. Nevertheless, sometimes the requests are fruitless, and the shaman has to be called in, although the two procedures are not incompatible: one is carried out in the chapel, the other at home. Furthermore, K'oy seems to believe that the number of illnesses among evangelicals is greater than among the rest, because the *lab* of the latter give illness to the former to test whether their new identity really does make them invulnerable.

To compensate, evangelical ritual practices offer new forms of protection against illness, especially through access to the "word of God," the text of the Bible translated into Tzeltal and employed directly for therapeutic purposes. This may explain that feverish commitment among evangelicals and Catholics alike to fabricate and surround themselves with words, that veritable torrent of words that issues from sermons, Bible readings, hymns, and the like, and that saturates the confined space inside the Indian evangelical chapels during the long Sunday services. It is all unintelligible discourse, despite being uttered in Tzeltal, but it creates the sensation of a protective barrier, a therapeutic space that offers defense from the illness-producing words to which one is exposed on a day-to-day basis (the same principle may be applied to the insistence on incessant sound throughout the day; radio sets remain switched on all day, and no one seems to be disturbed by barking and other sounds made around or inside the house at night). In other words, what is fashioned in this space are alien words, words capable of protecting against the equally alien words of which illnesses are made. I now realize that this technique is none other than the one that forms the core of the argument in shamanic healing texts and ceremonies, as we shall see later. I met a Catholic who had replaced the conventional domestic protection ceremony that is performed two or three times a year (*muk'ul kuxlejal*) with the reading of the "evangelical Bible," which he did alone, sitting on a little chair, reading aloud with the utmost difficulty for hours at a time, over a period of three days. Yet the protection bestowed by the word of God is only partial, incomplete. It is said—but it is only hearsay—that if you move to live in other places, like the outskirts of the city of San Cristóbal or on lands settled in the Lacandon jungle, you will find the word of God is more powerful there. In Cancuc, there are so many souls, and human relations are so entangled, that the biblical texts turn out to be insufficient.

Possibly the only novelty that I could find among the Christian Tzeltal and the rest has to do with the final destiny of the soul, a question that different churches naturally expend considerable energy on. However, this question remains confusing and of little interest to the Christians in Cancuc. Marian Kaxtil, a youth who, until a short time ago, was a catechist and is still Catholic, answered me unhesitatingly that the *ch'ulel* goes to heaven if one has been good. And the *lab*? "The *lab*, they say, are passed on to the heirs." And the Bird of the Heart? "Well, perhaps our Bird of the Heart goes to live in Rome, they say." Rome is envisioned as an enigmatic place of uncertain location, perhaps somewhere on the other side of the ocean, reached by underground passages, and where the chief of the Catholic church lives, a being who is whiter-than-white by dint of not seeing the sun. If a moment's thought is given to the matter, the choice of this destiny is not so fanciful, for, it will be remembered, the *lab* priests cook/baptize the Bird of the Heart, and by means of this culinary process, not only make possible their ingestion of it, that is, their literal incorporation of it, but also its incorporation into the society of the church, whose center is Rome. It is not easy to escape the grasp of the logic imposed by the Tzeltal imagination of the person.

The four *alcaldes* of Cancuc, 1990

The plaza of Cancuc, 1992

Market scene, Cancuc, 1990

School in Cancuc, 1990

The church in
Cancuc, 1990

Saint Nombre of
Juan and Saint
Juan, 1990

Before Saint Juan, 1989

Festival of the Games, 1990; on the left, Lorenzo Lot as a feline

String musicians, 1992; Xun P'in in the center

Members of a sublineage making an offering to the dead, 1990

Visit of the state's governor, 1990

The hamlet of Nichte'el, 1992

A Tzeltal house, 1990

Xmal Ijk'al—a shaman—praying at her altar, 2003

A shaman's domestic altar, 2001

Manvela Max with her granddaughters, 1990

Making tortillas, 1990

A Tzeltal girl with a corn doll, 1990

CHAPTER 7

The Mirror in the Saints

In Cancuc, as in all Indian villages that were formerly under the rule of the Spanish Crown, there is a collection of images of "saints" inside the church. In the Tzeltal language, the generic name given to these sacred figures is *yosetik* (gods), a word borrowed from the Spanish word *dioses*, although they are also known as *k'anantik* (guardians). The actual physical image seen in the church is called *slok'omba* (image), a word we will return to later. The presence of these images is obviously a result of the imposition of Catholicism. However, the fact that they are almost automatically recognizable as Catholic saints tends to obscure any understanding of the identity attributed to them by the Indians, begging the questions: What exactly are indigenous saints, and what sorts of beings are they?

My guess is that the saints are considered to be "reversed," with their inside out, so to speak. The figures of saints are the inverted images of normal human beings. Like the fetus in the womb, the inside is on the outside, and vice versa. The saints are able to show what in human beings is hidden in the heart, as if there were a skin turned out on itself; looking at a saint is like contemplating oneself in a mirror that reflects one's innermost being.

Saints clearly fall into the category (which basically defies classification) of beings that belong to the *ch'ul*, or sacred state. But unlike most of these—souls, spirits, the dead, etc.—saints have a permanent image to represent them in an ordinary state, even though the image stops short of being exactly like a human body. Saints are considered to be "complete beings" in the sense that they have thirteen *lab* souls. These are not contained in the heart, however, but are found instead outside the body, which is not fully folded. In any case, images of saints are not thought of as residing entirely in an ordinary state; in the Tzeltal language, the church is called *ch'ul na*, meaning "sacred house" or "house of the other." The church, in turn, is situated in the village square, which, as we have seen, is considered to be the heart, in an analogy with the human body: *yo'tan lum*, the "heart of the village." The center of the square contains whatever is alien—the colonial and Mexican institutions within which the images of saints are found.

Taking the door of the church in Cancuc as a starting point and proceeding in a counterclockwise direction, we see two large and four small crosses (decked in a white cloth) and the following saints: Pasko (Spanish "Pascua"); Sebastián; Rosario (the child she holds in her arms is Rosa); Pirti Santo (Spanish "Espíritu Santo"—Holy Spirit); Juan; Antonio; Rosa (in her version as "older sister"); Lucía (although her identity is uncertain); the Upper Canvas (a painting commissioned by the president of the High Court of Guatemala to commemorate the defeat of the native uprising of 1712); María (holding the child Isabela in her arms); Vicente (whose body is reduced to just a head placed on the altar); Alonso; the Lower Canvas (a painting of the Virgin of Guadalupe, although this particular dedication is not recognized); Santa Cruz (a cross draped in white with colored ribbons hanging from its arms); Jesus; Nombre de San Miguel; Miguel; Manojel (an image of the Holy Burial); Sorirat (possibly the Spanish "Soledad"—Solitude); Candelaria; Sacramento; Esteban; Lorenzo; Nombre de San Juan; Diego.

According to the Tzeltal, the use of "Castilian" names for the images goes back to the distant past. It was the Castilians who knew the proper way to attend to the saints, which left the indigenous community at a disadvantage. For example, the saints liked to hear mass, but this was something the Indians were unable to provide for them. The same applied to Castilian music, which was aimed at pleasing the saints (and the human heart), but was considered to be of inferior quality when played on native stringed instruments, such as the guitar, violin, and harp. From an ethnic point of view, saints are thought of as being Europeans, something easily deduced from their names. This association is explicit in Cancuc, where mention is made of their beards and the paleness of their skin. In the Tzotzil village of Chamula, the tutelary saint is referred to in prayers as *muk'ta kaxlan* and *muk'ta patron*, meaning "Great Castilian" and "Great Patron" (Gossen 1993). Nevertheless, as we shall see, there is still some ambiguity attached to identifying the saints as Europeans.

The Body of the Saints

Let us first consider physical appearance. Their garments are unfamiliar. They usually wear several layers of clothes, mostly red with a flowery print, although the color is often faded as a result of the elaborate washing ceremony that takes place annually in a stream near the church. The cloth, of a commercial type, was probably bought in the city of San Cristóbal de Las Casas; what is beyond doubt is that it was not woven on the backstrap loom that the Indians use to make their own tunics. The most important saints also wear chasubles, stoles, and red felt ponchos edged with gold thread that probably formed part of the liturgical vestments of the last priests to officiate in Cancuc toward the end of the nineteenth century. Their heads are usually covered with red head scarves or sometimes with a cap, also red. Soledad and Candelaria (two images of Virgins) wear metal crowns on their heads. San Juan, the titular saint of Cancuc, and his double, Nombre de San Juan, have necklaces and bracelets fashioned from silver coins that are worn when they are paraded in processions in front of the church. The coins are made of Spanish or Mexican silver from the eighteenth and nineteenth centuries, and the Tzeltal place an enormous value on them because the economic well-being of the community depends in part on their existence (they are threatened by the greed of those who would try to steal them through their *lab*). The money-counting ceremony of San Juan—where it must be demonstrated that none of the coins have disappeared—is a ritual event of great importance; responsibility for them lies with the so-called Steward of San Juan, who keeps them in a small metal coffer at his home.

This sort of clothing, with garments from different sources and in various combinations, seems even more bizarre when compared to Indian dress, which is practically uniform, apart from differences between men's and women's clothing. However, it should be noted that although the saints wear Castilian clothes and accessories, these do not represent ordinary Castilian clothing. The choice of colors, types of garments, and, above all, the weird mixtures, give an odd overall effect; the clothes may be Castilian, but the combinations are not.

This recombining of categories also extends to the saints' sexual characterization. In general, the Tzeltal have no difficulty distinguishing the gender of saints, who are either masculine or feminine. Nevertheless, the genitals are absent, which has to do with the fact that they cannot reproduce sexually. Likewise, several saints, among them San Juan, have a long plait of natural hair down their backs, despite plaited hair being associated with women, particularly Castilian women, and the style of some garments and the way they are worn is more feminine than masculine. In other words, what these details reveal is a double transvestitism in the saints that is both ethnic and sexual.

As for the bodies, some are made out of plaster and were probably bought some time in the nineteenth century or the beginning of the twentieth. They have a fair complexion, the color of the cheeks ranging from ivory to pink, and European features that sometimes include a thick beard. There is little in their appearance that is Amerindian. Other saints are carved from wood and are often in poor condition. It is not unusual for the arms or legs to be missing, having broken off at some time in the past. Their facial features, damaged over the centuries by the great humidity that pervades the inside of the church, have become indistinguishable and have taken on a grotesque appearance. Some of the saints have no body as such, either because only the head or torso remains or else because there is only a cross-shaped structure beneath their clothing, something that is of great significance to the Tzeltal. It is said that diseases the saints have suffered, such as leprosy and smallpox, have left their mark on their skin in the shape of tumors. One Indian compared the saints' skin to that of the jaguar, that is, skin that was spotted and affected by a process of decay leading to illness and death.

This bodily decrepitude is obviously the result of the passage of time and the state of conservation. Far from being a disadvantage, however, it is considered an appropriate state for the saints to be in. The condition of sacredness plays against corporeal conservation because the carnal body (*bak'etal*), made during ordinary life in the here and now, is what ultimately defines human beings. Among saints, erosion of the flesh forms part of their sacred identity; the power of their souls overwhelms and consumes the body.

In fact, the worship of deformed saints was a constant feature in Chiapas during the colonial period, to the extent that some bishops ordered these images removed, for they judged them to be "tantamount to idols" (Viqueira 1997, 403). In 1687, Bishop Núñez de la Vega (1988, 67) discovered two "idols" inside the church of the Tzeltal town of Oxchuc. One, called Poxlon, was a "fireball" painted on a panel; the other, Hicalahau (*ijk'alajaw*, "Black Lord"), was apparently a sculpture of a human body, albeit deformed, blackened, and accompanied by several carrion birds and owls. Could it be that the Indians introduced these idols into the church so that they might enjoy the Christian liturgy together with the saints?

On the other hand, saints have to be fed by humans, as they are unable to provide food for themselves. Unlike the saints of Mediterranean Catholicism, who seem to enjoy access to unlimited provisions, the Tzeltal saints are characterized by scarcity. Their favorite diet includes candles, *copalli* incense, tobacco, and assorted liquors, such as that made from sugarcane. Nevertheless, the saints "see" the food given to them as if it were human food. For example, *copalli* incense is the equivalent of corn, and for this reason it is sold in markets wrapped in a sort of spathe resembling a corncob (López García 1994, 252). In reality, what they consume is not these products as such but the smoke of the incense, the aroma of the candle, the alcoholic vapor of the liquor, in other words, the *ch'ul*, or "other," of these substances. This also explains why saints have no anus, as they have no need to defecate. What all these "hot" substances have in common is that they are the result of the elimination of the physical body (candlewax, tobacco leaves, etc.) in favor of the volatile material, a process brought about by the application of heat. Seen from this viewpoint, they function rather like the saints themselves, whose heart power, as we have seen, has an erosive effect on the body. The volatility and subtlety of these substances represent an inverse state of the food formed from the "dense material"—basically corn and beans—that human beings consume.

For humans, interaction with the images of saints is not without risk if certain precautions are not taken, and this is why the saints are wrapped in different types of cloth. For example, the image of Manojel is kept in a horizontal position in a wooden box, with his body completely covered by thirteen garments, because Manojel is the most powerful of all the saints in the church. Whenever they are transported, the saints are wrapped in straw matting and are also placed on matting during processions. Any vegetable material that has been in contact with them during ceremonies must be buried, together with the matting, away from inhabited areas and at a specified depth. The most important images remain inside the church in wooden boxes placed in a vertical position. The front openings of these are covered with cloth similar to that used for dressing the saints.

The use of these cloths lessens the extent to which the power of the saints reaches humans, but an opposite procedure can also be resorted to: to get closer to the saints, talk to them and handle them, it is necessary to renounce the use of ordinary gestures, at least in part. The Stewards of the Saints, who are entrusted with their care for a year at a time, must therefore attain a state of slight drunkenness if they are to carry out their ceremonial functions with a certain degree of security; drunkenness befuddles the senses and leads to some loss of bodily control, which in turn reveals the inside of the heart. The stewards and captains also dress up for the ceremony in vivid red jackets and trousers in the old Castilian style and wear bright red scarves on their heads. In other words, they place themselves in a state similar to that of the saints, a state that facilitates relations with them and at the same time protects these ritual specialists from their power.

This complex folding and unfolding between the inside and the outside of the body was revealed with particular clarity during the Indian Rebellion of 1712. During the few months it lasted, the Indians put themselves in various ways in the role of Europeans, and with this attitude, deployed themselves corporeally, from what can be deduced from a series of case studies by Viqueira (1997). For example, in their speeches and proclamations, the rebel leaders of Cancuc exhorted "all who were witches and healers" to "come forward and use their art to kill Spaniards"; this was what God had given them this ability for (ibid., 431). The "power" of these witches was in their naguals, in other words, their souls. Among the rebels, military authority was given to people to whom these powers were attributed. One important leader said that a twelve-year-old boy had been made a captain because of "his reputation as a witch" (ibid., 433). A Spanish sergeant reported that the reason captains were chosen was governed by "the nagual of each one and their reputations as witches; those that have none are taught." No explanation is given as to how this was achieved, but outside ritual practices, inciting someone to bare their soul was in any case a transgression. To fight the Spaniards effectively, it was necessary to lose the Tzeltal corporeally correct condition.

Incidentally, Viqueira's study (1997) makes plain the difficulties that beset the Spanish investigation's attempt to discover, once the uprising had been crushed, what it was that the rebels worshipped in the hermitage: The image of a Catholic Virgin? An earthenware idol? A human being? An animal? It was difficult to find out, since whatever it was had been hidden behind a straw mat, and only a select group of leaders had access to it. The inquiries undoubtedly encountered technical hitches, as well as problems of cultural translation. In fact, the descriptions in Indian testimonies are typically piecemeal and consequently seem to contradict one other. If, on their part, the Spaniards were interested in determining a real or single identity of what was kept within the hermitage, the Indians, on theirs, responded, appropriately enough, with disparate details intended not to clarify the profile of that being but rather to suggest concordances between it and other beings, domains, and societies. As was to be expected, the Spaniards were never able to figure out what was in the hermitage.

What is even more compelling is that it seems this altered state could be induced by the donning of certain garments. During the battle of Huixtán, the Spaniards reported seeing among those attacking them "Indians wearing what seemed to be the clothes of Our Father Santo Domingo, who were giving the blessing to the others" (Viqueira 1997, 406). And a young girl, María de la Candelaria, to whom the Virgin had appeared, used to come to the masses celebrated in the village of Cancuc "dressed in an amice, surplice, and stole with a cape used by San Juan Evangelista because it was so small" (ibid., 409). In other words, Indians who abandoned their ordinary state could exchange clothing with that of the saints, or, to be more exact, they could abandon their ordinary state precisely because they were enveloped in saints' clothing. This, in effect, is what Stewards of the Saints do during present-day ceremonies: partially turn their second skin inside out. In this respect, one of the most revealing episodes of the 1712 rebellion was that of the "witches" carried on shoulders. When the Spanish militia finally occupied the town of Cancuc, the rebels who had fled called on four women, together with a blind man who called himself "the king of witches," so as to use their "powers," consisting of wind and lightning bolts, to drive out the Spanish. The women were taken to a certain place on the riverbank overlooking the town, accompanied by four hundred Indians. They were then covered with straw mats and blankets so they could not be seen and carried on chairs raised onto shoulders. However, when it was realized "they had not achieved what was expected of them, they were pulled to the ground, the chairs were thrown away, and they were forced to return on foot" (Ximénez 1931, 7:307).

Enveloping oneself in the "other"—or divesting the self—is what ultimately permits identification with, and therefore relation to, the sacred. As Alfredo López Austin explains: the ancient Nahua idea of *nahualli*, which "in a general sense is someone who has the power to transform either himself or the person or animal into which he is transformed," can be translated as "what my clothing is" or "what I wear outside on my skin or around me" (1973, 118).

Saints in Narrative

As happens with spirits and sacred figures in general, stories in which saints are the main characters are notably rare. This was something already observed by Garrett Cook in Momostenango, where "saints lack a developed mythology and are more important in Momostecan religion as *sacra* (power objects) than as supernatural persons" (1986, 148). Among the Tzeltal, saints do not have a narrative identity, an exception being San Juan, the patron saint, about whom two stories were told.

One of these was told to me by Sebastián K'aal in response to a question of mine about whether saints have souls and, if so, which ones. It relates how San Juan saved the village of San Bartolomé de los Llanos from flooding. A long time ago, the course of the Grijalva River became obstructed, and the water was threatening to flood the village. Its patron saint had few *lab* souls and therefore very little power, so he decided to call in other saints from nearby villages: San Juan (of Chamula), San Alonso (Tenejapa), and Santo Tomás (Oxchuc). Their efforts to save the village were going nowhere until Bartolomé remembered San Juan Cancuc, the youngest brother. Not without some reluctance, San Juan traveled to San Bartolomé by mule, carrying with him a metal box of tools. On arrival, he opened the box and commanded the tools (a pick, a spade, a machete, and a saw) to unblock the river. By demonstrating that he was the most powerful of the brothers, San Juan became the dominant saint.

The narrator himself pointed out to me that the tools with metal heads were snake *lab*. The story explains why this type of soul is very common among the Cancuc Tzeltal, and the idea that Cancuqueros have this kind of soul is also accepted by Indians in other villages. But, as Sebastián K'aal went on to say, this is not the only type of soul San Juan possesses: "The mule is his soul because he has to travel all over the world; that is why he doesn't want to take a wife. He's always weary, always on the move. He has many souls. All the *lab* there are in the world, San Juan has all of them, and he was able to demonstrate this in San Bartolomé." San Juan has all the types of *lab* souls the Cancuc Tzeltal have. But the story reveals a telling detail: he does not carry the souls within his heart but outside himself—in a box of tools or as the mule he travels around on (a sterile animal, we may recall), something that is impossible for ordinary human beings.

The second story takes place even further back in time—"four hundred years ago"—and tells of the pilgrimage of the saints from the

East to where they are today. The saints were living in another place, a place in the East, when they decided to spread out all over the world and found villages. San Juan opted to go the center of the world (Cancuc), while other saints chose villages like Chamula, Tenejapa, Oxchuc, and Guaquitepec. They set out on their journey, crossed the ocean, and took the steamship from the Tabasco coast to Salto de Agua in the foothills of the Chiapas Mountains. There they disembarked and continued on foot. For some years, San Juan stayed in Bachajón, a village to the east of Cancuc, where he grew chili peppers, sapote, cotton, and sugarcane. He then decided to emigrate to the place where Cancuc is situated nowadays. The patron saints of Chamula, Tenejapa, Oxchuc, and other villages were also settled around this time. Other "saints" that accompanied the present patron saints were unable to find places to settle and were obliged to become Mountain Lords, the beings that govern the hinterland.

These events inevitably bring to mind the episode in the book by Popol Vuh in which the ancestors of the Quiché left the city of Tulán-Zuyua. Carrying the tutelary gods Tohil, Auilix, and Hacauitz, who were assigned to the three main lineages, the Quiché crossed the sea (possibly the swampy region of the Tabasco coast) until, after stopping off at several places on the way, they founded the Quiché capital in the Guatemalan highlands. However, there is a difference between the two stories. In the Popol Vuh migration, the human ancestors of the Quiché play a part, together with their tutelary gods (they are humans who carry their gods), while in the Tzeltal story, there are no humans, only saints. It is likely, however, that in the Tzeltal story the presence of humans is implicit in the telling. The genre the story belongs to is that of "words spoken by the first mothers-fathers" (*sk'op yayej nail me'el mamaletik*), which refers to an ancient time in which there was no differentiation between different types of beings. Animals and spirits, human beings and saints, Mountains Lords, and stars all formed part of a single community of creatures of similar appearance, behavior, and abilities. In all probability, it was a time when the sun had not yet appeared. Although the cultivation of fruits and vegetables is mentioned in these stories, the indigenous crops par excellence—corn and beans—did not yet exist, and without these food products it was impossible to fabricate a proper human body, an Indian body.

In other words, in these ancient times the collective "folding" that gave rise to human beings had not yet taken place. It is likely this did not happen until the sun emerged with its light and heat and dried out what until then had been a cold, damp world. A closer look at this process reveals a parallel with individual birth. For the Tzeltal, the fetus in the mother's womb finds itself in cold, damp, inhospitable surroundings; only with birth does it become warm and dry. In the time before the folding that gave rise to modern humanity, there would be no difference between saints and humans, and the ancestors of today's Tzeltal would already be present in San Juan.

As we have seen in Chapter 6, in the story about the "second war"—the 1712 Tzeltal uprising—Cancuc was under threat from the president of Guatemala's army. At that moment, two small boys, Juan López and Juan García, appeared and introduced themselves as "sons" of San Juan. They went on to inflict defeat on the Spanish soldiers. After the victory, their presence was too great a burden for the village to bear, and they were put to death by the town leaders in what could only be described as ritual sacrifice. Nowadays, the Tzeltal consider the two brothers as heroes and avatars of San Juan; in Tzeltal, it is said that they have "come out" of San Juan; in other words, they embody themselves and their own father.

From time to time, there is an implosion, so to speak, of these ancient times into the present time. Incidents describing a casual encounter with San Juan or one of his avatars are not uncommon. One example is that of a woman who saw somebody bathing in the river whom she took at first sight to be a *kirinko*, a "gringo" or foreigner, but it was really San Juan, who then disappeared. In 1992, two years before the Zapatista rebellion, an elderly man came across a child on the road who told him that the people of Cancuc need not fear the war because he, San Juan, would protect them; again, he immediately disappeared. A much-talked-about incident concerned an old man with a long white beard and ragged clothes, a "Castilian," who entered the church and vanished in front of the image of San Juan. Saints effectively have the power to manifest themselves many times over in the human domain; they reproduce through partial images of themselves. San Juan is found in many different places at the same time (much as souls are present in different spaces simultaneously), and he sometimes intervenes in the ordinary world by appearing as a child, an old beggar, or a "gringo."

Narrative does not give the saints any consistent identity, however, and even less are they endowed with individualized features that identify each one as unique. The stories do not create a real figure; they leave the saints incomplete and in suspension. To come into existence, characters require some sort of narrative plot in which the structuring principle is configuration of the action in time (Ricoeur 1987, 174). But any temporal configuration is extremely weak in these stories; not only are they few in number but the narrative is poorly developed. Saints appear in a time that is practically a place, a space in which different types of beings, among them those that in present times are the equivalent of humans and saints, are jumbled together with no differentiation between them. Under rules of composition such as these, it is impossible to create a character that is minimally recognizable. But in my opinion, this is the effect that was intended. Both as a visual representation and in narrative (and in shamanic songs, as we shall see in the next chapter), this profile adopted by the Tzeltal saints is sufficiently piecemeal and precarious as to be appropriate.

Images of Origins in the Mirror

The images of saints found in the church constitute a reversal, albeit partial, of the Tzeltal representation of the outer face of a human being. Their bodies are fragmented; their soul powers are so intense that they overflow and pour out all over to the extent that they erode the body. The anomalous appearance of their clothing and adornments means that their gender and ethnicity cannot be readily distinguished, but at the same time neither is there complete confusion in this respect. In other words, the image of the saints is the opposite of the correct model for the human body. Nevertheless, their nature coincides perfectly with the souls that human beings carry in their hearts.

We have at least one direct piece of evidence on this identity between saints and souls. The *lab* called "name"—described as holding a book and a writing quill with which to transmit illness—coincides exactly with the visual representation of two of the saints in the church; the Nombre de San Juan and the Nombre de San Miguel. It is possible that these were originally images of evangelists. Each holds a book in one hand and a quill in the other because they are the respective secretaries of San Juan and San Miguel and are frequently described as their doubles. There are other cases where certain accessories associated with the saints are often repeated in the souls. For example, some of the *lab* of the *pále* group are described as having the same type of clothing and the tonsure of the saints in the church. We also know that among the saints who became more popular throughout the Maya region in the colonial period were those represented in Catholic hagiography with animals or atmospheric phenomena (Ruz 1997, 55), in other words, those with their souls on the outside.

When the Tzeltal stand before a saint, they are looking into their own interior, their heart. This reversed relationship between humans and saints is expressed with great feeling in shamanic songs:

> *ayukbal bit'il sut awelaw*   Can you give me your face?
> *ayukbal bit'il sut asit*   Can you give me your gaze?

In other words, the shaman asks the image in front of him to return the reflection of himself once it has crossed the sacred "other side." I suspect this is why saints in the indigenous churches of the Chiapas highlands usually carry a mirror at chest level (where the heart is), an object that not only reflects our image but also multiplies and fragments it.

Apparitions of saints in the ordinary world, which we have already mentioned, are known as *slok'omba*, the same term used to designate the figures of the saints found in the church. We have seen how the word is conventionally translated as "image," and its literal meaning is "what is taken out of itself." The root of the word—*lok'*—also means "to remove or change one's clothes" (or skin). The images of the saints and their unexpected apparitions in the ordinary world seem to be interpreted either as a change or an envelopment of clothing. The saints come out of themselves, as it were, and partially fold themselves to be able to communicate with humans (although not sufficiently to take on the appearance of an appropriately clothed adult Indian), much the same way that humans temporarily unfold themselves through the consumption of liquor and tobacco and the donning of certain garments in order to manipulate the saints' images.

In fact, this theme of folding and unfolding seems to dominate all relations between human beings and the *ch'ul* sacred state. One of the best-known pieces of advice for protecting oneself against *lab* souls or spirits, or any other being originating from a sacred state, consists of removing all one's clothes, turning them inside out, and putting them back on again. This way, the spirits cannot attack. The effectiveness of this action probably lies in the relationship between the skin and clothing in both similarity and contiguity: one "turns oneself inside out" like a glove to reveal what is on the inside, in other words, one's other self. With this act of unfolding, so to speak, the human abandons the ordinary state and enters a state analogous to that of the attacking spirit, which, ipso facto, loses its power. The significance of this was explained to me by a friend: on seeing a human with his clothes turned inside out, "the spirit feels ashamed [*kexlal*] of itself." This is also why spirits do not attack humans who go around in a state of drunkenness; it is said they are able to recognize a sort of inner luminescence in the look of the inebriated.

The Tzeltal assert that when the fetus is still in the womb, when it has not yet completely abandoned the *ch'ul* state and entered the ordinary human world, it actually has the souls outside its body, very much as saints do. Before birth, the human being is unfolded; only by being born does the body become folded. One way to identify the type of *lab* a newborn has is to examine the surface of the placenta: the souls are "outside" the body, pressing on the placenta, and this leaves prints or marks on it according to which figure is involved. Moreover, during gestation, the fetus feeds on its mother's blood, the same substance that is consumed by the spirits and sacred beings in general.

In short, in the images of the saints, the Tzeltal see their inner selves, their other side. But at the same time they also see their origins and their future. The saints are a reflection of times long past when they made the pilgrimage from the East to Cancuc to found the village, when bodies that were culturally human had not yet been formed and humans and saints belonged to the same kind of beings. They are also a reflection of the origin of individual life, of the prenatal state before the human body is folded. In this case, ontogeny recapitulates phylogeny. The saints and the souls that human beings trap inside their hearts pertain to the same ontological state, the *ch'ul*. It is a state of being that predates the emergence of humanity and the birth of individuals, and even when each human dies or humanity disappears—something that is for sure—the *ch'ul* will remain there.

CHAPTER 8

A Case of Healing: Text and Ritual

Being Indian, or rather, not yielding to the regressive condition of being "Castilian," is a burdensome task. From the viewpoint traced here, namely that of the person, that exceptional loyalty to Amerindian culture displayed by the Tzeltal has devastating consequences in terms of individuals. In exchange for the ongoing effort to distinguish and affirm cultural difference, the Tzeltal seem forced to carry the burden, quite literally, both of their "others" and of their history. It is not easy to be an Indian.

One of the consequences of this state of being seems to be an intense anxiety over illness. In a rare moment of philosophical abstraction, Xun P'in defined life as an endless healing ceremony (*ch'abajel*). It is not by chance, he said, that so many curing ceremonies are performed. In fact, he imagines the world would be a much less difficult place if the *ch'iibal* mountain were sufficiently distant that it would be unable to affect those here, and if the "Christians" from here did not have so many powers (that is to say, *lab*). This is not to mention, I would add, the Bird of the Heart, an almost atrophied soul, a fragile being whose temptation by the siren song of liturgy seems to reduce its very reason to exist to being simply a decoy that draws the priests who come to devour/baptize it.

It is not uncommon to pay a visit to a household in Cancuc and to find it either carrying out or preparing for a ceremony at the domestic altar aimed at curing or preventing illness, or else to notice signs that one had been performed only a short time before. In all of this, I think I detect something a little different from a normal, understandable concern for incurable illness on the part of a rural population. Instead, it is more of an obsession with illness, with its origins, with its symptoms, with the alternatives for its treatment. The practice is a form of self-absorption (in both senses) that can at times verge on what one might call utter wallowing.

In the following pages, I describe a healing ceremony in Cancuc as a practical recapitulation of certain themes that have already been treated.

The Ceremony

One day in September 1990, Xun P'in is teaching me about souls in his house, when a man arrives to ask whether Xun can have a look at his son, who is sick. Xun says he can, and the man leaves, returning about an hour later with his wife and his son in his arms. It is more or less two o'clock in the afternoon.

The boy, Manuel, is about twelve years old. Since the previous night, the father explains to Xun, he has been complaining of a severe pain (he points to the approximate location of the appendix, but the Tzeltal do not identify such an organ, and the boy's parents speak of pain in the stomach-intestinal region as a whole). Xun, helped by the mother, gets Manuel to lie down, faceup, with his head pointing south and his arms held tight against his body on a straw mat in the middle of the earth floor in the house-bedroom (a rectangle measuring about seven by four meters). Once he is lying down, Xun covers him with a garnet-colored cloth called *kaxlan pak'*, "piece of Castile." Xun sits on a small chair in the eastern part of the room, leaning toward the child and thus with his back to the household altar. The parents sit on the other side on some raised boards that act as a bed. I am a little more withdrawn, in the southern part of the house.

Xun repeatedly takes Manuel's pulse with great care, first the right wrist, then the left. A good diagnostician must feel with the pad of his fingertips the blood, not of the main arteries, which tends to be more misleading, but of the finer ones. Xun tells me the boy is very sick; his pulse is very irregular. Then he decides to make a *poxil* ("remedy" or "medicine"), a type of cure that essentially consists of chants also called *poxil*, cane liquor, and some herb specially recommended to cure affliction in some part of the body (internal pains, wounds, complicated births, and so on). Such a decision presupposes that no soul entity has been affected, at least not up to that moment.

Xun asks me to prepare a measure of liquor (from a half-liter bottle the father had brought with him) in a white, enamel cup, where I have to dissolve the tobacco from one of my cigarettes, as we have been doing in other healings (even though what is common is to add *may*, wild tobacco leaves ground with lime). The child is given part of the mixture, and Xun drinks another part while spurting some from his mouth, forcing it out through the gaps between his teeth and over the patient's body. He does this three consecutive times. Outside, a fine drizzle has begun to fall, and a turkey and some chickens waddle in; I take charge of shooing them out, more than anything else so that their noise won't prevent me from recording the ceremony.

Xun utters the first *poxil* song, which lasts some ten minutes. He does it by talking directly to the patient's body, as the medicine is none other than the text he recites. Then for two or three minutes he takes the child's pulse at his wrists again to feel the effect of the song on the patient; it seems to be taking effect. Xun turns to me and says he is going to defeat the illness.

He utters a second song (each one consists of a different text, but a Tzeltal only has to hear a brief snatch to know it is a song of this type). He takes the pulse again and says that the boy is still getting better, but now he does not seem to be so confident. Manuel continues to cry and complain. In addition to giving him some liquor, Xun wafts incense over him. The blood, he says, is better now; it is more regular and slower than when he first took the pulse. I ask him how many songs he is going to say, and he replies, three or four . . . as many as it takes.

A third song is said. While Xun prays, he holds the child's wrist between his fingertips so that he may detect the immediate effect produced by his words on the patient's blood. However, Manuel does not seem to find any relief. Quite the contrary, he moans, writhes in pain, and vomits several times. Nobody says a word, but it is becoming apparent to everyone that the *poxil* is not having the desired effect. In spite of her best efforts to control herself, the mother begins to sob silently. I am now convinced that the boy has appendicitis and that he is going to die.

Though still serene, Xun also looks more worried. He now takes the pulse for several minutes at the boy's wrists, ankles, and temples.

His wife, who is a relative of Manuel's parents and who has heard the boy's groans from the kitchen, comes in. (She, too, knows how to diagnose using the pulse, but she does not do it anymore so as not to have to drink liquor.) She strips the boy down to the waist and squeezes his stomach while asking him directly about his pain (something Xun has not done and must not do, as it is improper for the *ch'abajom*, for whom a "reading" of the symptoms should suffice; however, he now seems to show more interest in the site of the pain). Hesitantly but with a mother's common sense, she suggests that it might be constipation, and returns to the kitchen to prepare the herb *chikin buro*, "donkey ear," which has to be cooked and then dissolved in liquor.

Xun prays a fourth *poxil* song. He keeps taking the boy's pulse; the pulse, he says, is now too slow in the right hand and very fast in the left; nevertheless, Manuel seems to be complaining less. A little desperate, I suggest adding three "Mejoral" (aspirin) tablets that I carry with me; it does not seem a bad idea to Xun, but he says they have no strength compared with the alcohol and the tobacco. At this point, the pain makes the boy sit up, and he leans back between his father's legs. Xun continues to take his pulse.

He utters a fifth song. Manuel has fallen silent and hardly moves; he must have ingested about a fifth of a liter of sugarcane liquor by now. When he stops praying, Xun addresses the parents with some gravity, finally explaining to them that the pulse says the boy has been affected by the *lab me'tiktatik*, that is, they have captured his *ch'ulel*. How does he know? On this occasion, he says nothing, but from what he has told me on others, he notes a certain number of "drunk" words in the patient's blood, one of the symptoms produced by these *lab*.

These are the *lab* known as "earth." They bear the appearance of elderly people with gray hair and beards, but they are invisible; they are the ones who set themselves up to eat and drink in the middle of the pathways, and previously I have attempted to relate them to the modern cultivation of coffee. The boy or his *ch'ulel*, while it was roaming through the night, must have knocked over their table of food, and they have kidnapped his soul in reprisal. What is certain is that Xun P'in has a predilection for this type of diagnosis. He belongs to a generation of more modern shamans (though not necessarily younger) who began to exercise their power about three decades ago and who are distinguished by their recognition of the symptoms that this kind of *lab* generates, and by their knowledge of the necessary powers (chants) needed to deal with them.

Three hours have elapsed since the patient's arrival at Xun's house. The initial diagnosis was wrong, because it is not, as Xun originally assumed, the body that is affected, but rather the soul; the body is suffering from the absence of the *ch'ulel*. But this kind of "mistake" in diagnosis is fairly common; the range of possible illnesses (that is, of their origins) is enormous. Furthermore, the causes change with time, or several causes blend together, and to complicate matters even more, the traces that the agents causing the illness leave may be deliberately false in order to hinder the diagnosis. Diagnosis and treatment are not consecutive but rather alternative, each one coming into play depending on the other throughout the entire course of the medical treatment. It is not rare for Xun P'in, after several days of ceremonies and the patient's recovery, not to know for sure which of the different exchanges (with which beings) has been the truly decisive one. In this particular case, however, the *poxil* have not been completely useless, because they have soothed the pain, and thus the *ch'ulel* will find a more welcoming body upon its return, if it does indeed return.

To recover the *ch'ulel*, a different kind of ceremony (*ch'abajel*) is needed, one that has to be carried out at the household altar, preferably at night. There are still some hours to go before dusk.

Meanwhile, the price of the ceremony is settled between Xun and Manuel's father. Healings have no fixed price. The truth is that Xun's fees are a mystery to me. Sometimes they seem disproportionately high, sometimes too low; I can never see any reason to justify them, be it a matter of resources, kinship, friendship, or type of illness. As the boy's father has no money or foodstuffs, it is agreed that he must work in Xun's cornfields for a few days in the approaching season. The precise number of days is subject to haggling, though discreet haggling, because the power of curing is a sacred gift that Xun has received, so although he has every right to be given some compensation for his work (work universally considered to be highly risky), it would not be right to overcharge.

Like most shamans (*ch'abajometik*) in Cancuc, Xun began to practice relatively late in life, when his children were already grown up. He started when his eldest daughter became ill. At that time he had a series of consecutive dreams, fairly stereotyped in their overall content, but necessary in order to be able to practice, because they are a sign of the "sacred license" (*ch'ul lisénsia*). In his dreams, there appeared before him (in images that Xun compared with those of a film for cinema, so that I could get a better idea) a man resembling a European, with white skin and a beard, on a wide path. Without exchanging a word, the man gave Xun a thick volume with a red cover containing all the texts of the healing prayers—not a single one was missing—together with diagnostic techniques and some recipes for the preparation of medicinal herbs. Shortly afterward, Xun attempted to cure his daughter and he was successful. So he saw that his dream was true; he knew the prayer texts thanks to the dream.

Xun P'in's household altar is no different from that in any other house, except perhaps for usually having a larger store of ritual substances. Placed halfway along the east wall of the house, it is composed of a small, very plain table, about twenty centimeters high, measuring thirty centimeters by forty on top. A crude pinewood cross, blackened by incense smoke and about thirty centimeters tall, stands on it, leaning against the wall. These are the altar's basic elements, but there is also on the table a transparent plastic bag with incense (a mixture of resin from the copal tree and cheaper pine resin), a clay censer, a three-quarters-full bottle of sugarcane liquor (low-quality stuff, dressed up in the prayer as good liquor, by telling the *lab* it is tequila or *comiteco*, a liquor made by Ladinos from the agave of Chiapas and rarely drunk in Cancuc), and a store-bought bottle of hot chili sauce (that I recently brought as a present and which has now ended up here). Unlike altars I have seen in one or two other Indian communities, Cancuc's have no statues or prints representing saints or any other assorted objects of the kind typical of household altars of Spanish-speaking curers.

I prepare the altar as on previous occasions. With two small, recently cut branches of green pine to replace earlier branches that have now dried out, I arrange an arch above the cross. The green branches are said to open the cross as if it were a door. At Xun's instructions, in front of the altar I also place six thirty-centimeter white candles in a row on a strip of wood with notches to hold them (altogether there are thirteen holes, for a maximum of thirteen candles). Later, once the ceremony has begun, Xun's wife will bring three eggs and place them on the altar, and a big black live hen, its feet tied, which is set on the ground beneath an inverted gourd, so that, according to Xun's explanation, its clucking will not disturb the songs.

The purpose of the cross is to transport the words of the text, together with the fragrance of the substances (all of them catalogued as "hot") found on the tabletop. Obviously, what passes through the cross is the *ch'ul* of these substances: the glow of the candle, the smoke of the incense, the vapor of the alcohol, and most likely the "meaning" of the words uttered. What Xun P'in is preparing to do with all of this is to negotiate with the *lab me'tiktatik* the return of the kidnapped *ch'ulel*. In this particular case, the substances are understood to represent a reparation (*selol*) equivalent to what the boy knocked off the table where the *me'tiktatik* were eating.

The ceremony starts at dusk and therefore by candlelight. Manuel, who should actually be lying on the straw mat on the floor, is sitting on his father's lap, motionless and quiet, almost without complaint, but aware of what is happening around him. Xun P'in has his back to the patient and is sitting on a small chair, leaning toward the altar, his elbows resting on the tops of his thighs and a rosary tied around his two wrists and hung over one hand, although he does nothing more with it. It is a conventional Catholic rosary, which can be bought in the city of San Cristóbal; most Tzeltal shamans and religious office holders have one.

During the ceremony, six long songs are addressed specifically to the *me'tiktatik*. It is said that these songs first started to be used by shamans in Tenejapa some decades ago, and were unknown before then. It is a preestablished series of texts, each one lasting about ten minutes: *alan me'tiktatik* (mothers-fathers of the lower section), *ajk'ol me'tiktatik* (mothers-fathers of the upper section), *jamalal me'tiktatik* (mothers-fathers of the open space), *chukel me'tiktatik* (jail of the mothers-fathers), *chukel ta yantik lum* (jail in other places), and *jelwe'el ch'ulelal* (exchange of food for souls).

Before he starts each song, I serve two small glasses of liquor to Xun, the first of which he spurts out of his mouth over the cross, making it pass (if he is on target) through the flame of the candle, causing it to hiss softly, and the second he drinks, sometimes asking for more; but I must not allow him more, because if he drinks too much, there is a risk that he may not make it to the end of the ceremony. Then I offer another glass to the other people present: the boy's father and mother, just enough to the boy to wet his lips, and if they happen to be present, to Xun's adult children; I am the last one to drink. After every round of liquor, Xun perfumes the cross by blowing over it the censer that contains smoldering embers (that I have taken from the kitchen, after ceremoniously asking Xun's wife's permission) on top of which he drops little balls of incense. A candle is lit for each one of the songs, which is why there are six. In fact, the recitation of each text should last as long as it takes for the candle to be spent, but this is rare; it is more usual to have to wait for the candle to be consumed unaccompanied, before the next song can be started.

Chicks and turkeys have settled down inside the house, filling it with a constant noise. Outside a hard rain is falling. The whole interior of the house is laden with a thick fog of incense smoke, the vapor of cane liquor, and the smell of burning wax, all of it heightened perhaps by the penetrating dampness. While Xun prays, the proper thing to do is sit in silence or talk by mouthing, to avoid allowing the impurities characteristic of ordinary speech from getting stuck to the fragrant words of the song as they pass through the cross. But people do talk in the intervals between songs; the children of the house go in and out. Naturally, the daily round is not interrupted; the house has no internal divisions, and while the ceremony is in progress, the different couples who live there lie on their beds in order to sleep; some actually do sleep, while others watch the ceremony from their rickety old beds or talk in whispers.

Each time Xun finishes a song, he turns around on his chair and, without getting up, takes a careful reading of the patient's pulse. Twice he gets Manuel to breathe in the incense smoke through his nostrils and then nonchalantly wafts incense over his body. Finally, just before the sixth and final song begins, I wring the hen's neck as delicately as I can, then place it on the altar and make a small wound in its neck, allowing two or three drops of blood (it must be warm) to trickle over the cross. This final song, called "food in exchange for soul," is the culmination of the treatment, for which the previous prayers, spoken ceremoniously and slowly and presented with the appropriate fragrant substances, have been preparing the way.

Two and a half hours have passed since nightfall. The child is sleeping. Xun, extremely inebriated by now, wakes him clumsily to take his pulse for the last time. Xun can barely articulate a single word, but by his brusque gestures of assent, he looks satisfied. This means that the *me'tiktatik* have accepted the exchange, the patient's *ch'ulel* has been released, and it has been reincorporated into the child's heart. Xun then says some garbled words in Spanish that I do not understand at all, except that there are a lot of "*nagualeros* in revolt," which he repeats twice.

It has stopped raining. Around midnight, almost in silence because of our weariness and sleepiness, we eat the sacrificed hen with tortillas and *petuul* tamales (made from corn dough and whole beans), which the women have been cooking outside the house (but not in the kitchen). Then we sleep on the floor on the straw mats.

The child will stay there two more days, so that Xun can continue to take his pulse and do any other chanting that might be needed.

In the early evening of the second day, Xun performs at the altar four *majtanil* (gift, offering) songs, addressed to the *ch'iibal* mountain of the boy's lineage: two for the current soul *cargos* (officials), two for the soul *cargos* of the past so they know they have not been forgotten. The aim is that they will take special pains to care for the boy's *ch'ulel*, because since it has encountered difficulties in the "open space," it may also feel the effects in the mountain, which would end up affecting Manuel's body as well, thereby adding an unexpected complication.

On the third day, Xun goes through the normal procedures for patients who are recuperating. Again at the altar, he speaks two lengthy prayers of protection for the following months, when the person is "shut up" inside a "fence" so that no ill may befall him. The first is a *kuxlejal ta naj ta lum* prayer that asks for protection of life in the *ch'iibal;* the second is a *kuxlejal ta jamalal* prayer that asks for protection of life on this side of existence.

The next morning, Manuel returns home with his mother, who has stayed with him all these days and shared in the cooking with the women of Xun's house. He is weak but apparently mended. That evening and the next, Xun sends him a potion in an enamel cup, a mixture of herbal infusion (again *chik'in buro*), liquor, and tobacco, over which he utters s short *poxil* song. Here again the most important part of the medicine is the text. Xun himself will continue to drink cane liquor and to sleep for three more days.

The following text is a complete transcription of the first prayer from the *poxil* ceremony. My reason for choosing this one is simply that it is the first. Like any healing prayer, whether a prayer of "remedy" or exchange, it is a long text; but there is no alternative to presenting it whole, since its form is as important, if not more so, than its content. It is uttered by Xun P'in in a monotone (*tojil*, "straight") and at breakneck speed, so fast at times that he skips words. As is formulary in any prayer, it opens and closes with making the sign of the cross over the face while uttering "Jesus, Mary . . ."

The Text

	jesús, maría	Jesus Mary
	tatil rios nich'anil	father god son
	sánta me' sus.	holy mother Jesus.
1	tat ch'ul páre tat	father sacred father father
	ch'ul san antónyo tat	sacred San Antonio father
	ch'ul san páre mikel	sacred father San Miguel
	obispo santiako, yo'tik	bishop San Diego, now
	kajkanan ch'ul winik	helper sacred man
	sánto san juan	holy San Juan
	jalame' ch'ul sánta maría, yo'tik	sacred godmother holy Mary, now

rios jesukrísto, yo'tik telek a	god Jesus Christ, now comes
bantikati tal ati'	where does your word come from?
bantikati tal awo'tan	where does your heart come from?
jtalel yo'tik	so I have been given, now
jun belta talemon yo'tik, xiatwan	once I come, now, you'll say
13 jun belta julon yo'tik, xiatwan	once I arrive, now, you'll say
oliltel be yo'tik, xiatwan	down the middle of a path, now, you'll say
oliltel kamíno yo'tik, xiatwan	down the middle of a lane, now, you'll say
ts'ujolontel yo'tik, xiatwan	dampness of dew I bring, now, you'll say
k'ajintabilontel yo'tik, xiatwan	I have been given in a song, you'll say
ya xk'ajintel jun pále, xiatwan	a priest has been singing, you'll say
ya xk'ajintel jun kériko, xiatwan	a clergyman has been singing, you'll say
la jetuntaytel oxeb be, xiatwan	I crossed three paths, you'll say
la jetuntaytel oxeb kamíno, xiatwan	I crossed three roads, you'll say
la jetuntaytel oxeb wa'ale, xiatwan	I crossed three headlands, you'll say
la jetuntaytel oxeb suklej, xiatwan	I crossed three ridges, you'll say
belta talemon, xiatwan	I have come again, you'll say
nakalon julel ta yolil yo'tan, xiatwan	I am settled in the center of his heart, you'll say
26 nakalon julel ta sejkub, xiatwan	I am settled in his liver, you'll say
nakalon julel ta skajonil, xiatwan	I am settled in his belly, you'll say
teyme ma tabatel jti', xiatwan	so my word cannot be found, you'll say
teyme ma tabatel ko'tan, xiatwan	so my heart cannot be found, you'll say
jun ko'tan chawaj, xiatwan	I produce madness of the heart, you'll say
k'ajk'al ti'awal chawaj, xiatwan	hot and biting madness, you'll say
chawaj julbakon, xiatwan	pain in the bones, you'll say

nakalon julel ta yolil yo'tan, xiatwan
I settled in the center of his heart, you'll say

nakalon julel ta sejkub, xiatwan
I settled in his liver, you'll say

nakalon julel ta ch'ich', xiatwan
I settled in the blood, you'll say

ma'uk stukel kerem
it cannot be, boy

sel ma taba ati'
I will sway your word

sakbet ati', yo'tik
I will find your word

39 oxlajuneb jti' tukel, yo'tik
I am thirteen words only, now

oxlajuneb may, yo'tik tukel
I am thirteen tobaccos only, now

oxlajuneb pilíko, yo'tik tukel
thirteen tobaccos only, now

rios jesukrísto tat
god Jesus Christ father

ch'ul sánta lusía
sacred Santa Lucía

asuséna maría, yo'tik
lily Mary, now

rios sánto san alónso tat
god holy San Alonso father,

rios sánto san alónso kajwal
god holy San Alonso lord

teuk te ma tabatel jti', xiatwan
my word cannot be swayed, you'll say

teuk te ma tabatel ko'tan, xiatwan
my heart cannot be swayed, you'll say

tek'elontel oxlajunebtel jti', xiatwan
I already raised the thirteen words, you'll say

tek'elontel oxlajunebtel ko'tan, xiatwan
I already raised thirteen hearts, you'll say

ma tabatel jti', xiatwan
you don't find the word, you'll say

52 ma tabatel ko'tan, xiatwan
you don't find my heart, you'll say

ma'uk, yo'tik
not now

sakbaal tabet ati', yo'tik kerem
I must discover the word, now, boy

ch'ajan julbakon, xiatwan
I am pain of wire, you'll say

ojtsel julbakon, xiatwan
I am pain of slingshot, you'll say

ti'awalon jun xch'ujt kawayui, xiatwan
I give pain of horse stomach, you'll say

ti'awalon jun xch'ujt misi, xiatwan
I give pain of cat stomach, you'll say

ti'awalon jun xch'ujt tentsun, xiatwan
I give pain of goat stomach, you'll say

pumel kawayu, xiatwan
horse indigestion, you'll say

jich atalon, xiatwan
that's how I came, you'll say

jich ajulon, xiatwan
that's how I arrived, you'll say

jich ajul jmey, xiatwan	that's how I came given out, you'll say
jich ajul k'ol, xiatwan yo'tik	that's how I came unwrapped, you'll say now
65 jun belta jun kérico	once I come from a clergyman
jun belta jun wíspo, xiatwan yo'tik	once I come from a bishop, you'll say perhaps now
jun belta jun pále, xiatwan yo'tik	once I come from a priest, you'll say perhaps now
jun belta jun kérico, xiatwan yo'tik	once I come from a clergyman, you'll say perhaps now
kaxlan ts'i', xiatwan	as a dog from Castile, you'll say
kaxlan bik'it, xiatwan	as a boy from Castile, you'll say
jich ajulon talel, xiatwan	that's how I've been given, you'll say
jich akuyon talel, xiatwan	that's how I've been given concealed, you'll say
k'ajinontalel, xiatwan	singing I came given, you'll say
bik'it bik'itik axuxubajontel, xiatwan	low, with a tenuous whistle I came, you'll say
bik'itik ak'ajinontel, xiatwan	low, with a tenuous song I came, you'll say
jichuk joyet atalon, xiatwan	I came spinning like that, you'll say
bit'il kaxlan janante'el, xiatwan	like a whipping top from Castile, you'll say
78 bit'il kaxlan trómpo, xiatwan	like a top from Castile, you'll say
jich asujtp'ejon, xiatwan	that's how I turn, you'll say
jich ajoyp'ejon, xiatwan	that's how I spin, you'll say
jich ajulon ta yolil chij, xiatwan	that's how I reached the center of the vein, you'll say
jich ajulon ta yolil bak'et, xiatwan	that's how I reached the center of the flesh, you'll say
jich ajulon ta yolil kajon, xiatwan	that's how I reached the center of the belly, you'll say
jich ajulon ta yolil chij, xiatwan	that's how I reached the center of the vein, you'll say
jich ajulon ta yolil sejkub, xiatwan	that's how I reached the center of the liver, you'll say
tabet ati', yo'tik	I will find your words, now
bit'il ma tabet ati'	how will I not find your word,

bit'il ma tabet awajtal	how will I not find your count,
sak jujchi'at, yo'tik	blowing you, I dislodge you, now
sakba jujch'iat, yo'tik	blowing you, I dislodge you, now
91 bik'it mákina, yo'tik	with a little machine, now
muk'ul mákina, yo'tik	with a big machine, now
cheba jnoyat, yo'tik stukel	with both I crush you, now alone
ik'ba nogat, yo'tik stukel	with strength I crush you, now alone
ta molíno, yo'tik	with a mill, now
ta bik'it molíno, yo'tik	with a little mill, now
sakba jlikat, yo'tik stukel	with ease I pick you up, alone
sakba wuyat, yo'tik stukel	with ease I smash you, alone
oxlajuneb kaxlan waréta, yo'tik	with thirteen skullcaps from Castile
oxlajuneb kaxlan píko, yo'tik	with thirteen picks from Castile
jun belta bak'et julbakon, xiatwan	once I am pain in the flesh, you'll say
jun belta nivel julbakon, xiatwan	once I am pain in the whole body, you'll say
ta yolil yo'tan, xiatwan	in the center of his heart, you'll say
104 ta yolil chij, xiatwan	in the center of the vein, you'll say
mabi awuybelon, xiatwan	you can't smash me, you'll say
mabi anakbelon, xiatwan	you can't extricate me, you'll say
ma'uk, sakba jk'oponati	he can't come out, we'll talk (we'll fight)
ta oxlajuneb kaxlan baréta	with thirteen skullcaps from Castile
ta oxlajuneb kaxlan dinamíta, yo'tik	with thirteen dynamites from Castile, now
ja'bal ma xwuy aton, yo'tik	not even a stone offers resistance, now
ja'bal ma xwuy aséro ton, yo'tik	not even stone of steel offers resistance, now
ja' jichat amene	that's what you're like
sakba jwuyat, yo'tik	you come out breaking yourself into pieces, now
sakba lilintesat yo'tik	you come out pulverizing yourself, now
ta oxlajuneb jti', yo'tik	with my thirteen words, now
oxlajuneb chikin búro wamal, yo'tik	with thirteen "donkey ear" herbs, now

117	oxlajuneb ch'aal wamal, yo'tik	with thirteen sour herbs, now
	oxlajuneb kaxlan payte', yo'tik	with thirteen *payte'* herbs from Castile, now
	oxlajuneb kaxlan asufre, yo'tik	with thirteen pieces of sulfur from Castile, now
	oxlajuneb kaxlan jos wamal	thirteen "vulture from Castile" herbs, now
	oxlajuneb kaxlan pérsa, yo'tik	thirteen forces from Castile, now
	bit'il lilinbilat, stukel	how I pulverize you, alone
	bit'il jwuyat, stukel	how I break you, alone
	maba tajbilontel, xiatwan	you can't find me, you'll say
	maba nikbilon, xiatwan	you can't displace me, you'll say
	melel xchawajilon ti', xiatwan	because I am truly mad words, you'll say
	melel xchawajilon yo'tani, xiatwan	because I am truly a mad heart, you'll say
	jun beeletike, xiatwan	some walkers, you'll say
	jun okeletike, xiatwan	some speakers, you'll say
130	jun kamíno, xiatwan	a path, you'll say
	tey yu'un ma taba jti'a, xiatwan	that's why my words are not found, you'll say
	tey yu'un ma taba jko'tanabi	that's why my heart is not found, you'll say
	bit'il ma jtabet ati'	how not to find the word
	bit'il ma jtabet skuyulil, yo'tik	how not to find his symptom, now
	ja' chikan stukel	it is visible, alone
	sánto san alónso, tat	holy San Alonso father
	jalame' ch'ul sánta maría, me'	sacred godmother holy Mary, mother
	ajk'ol liensa me'chun, yo'tik	upper canvas grandmother, now
	alan liensa me'chun, yo'tik	lower canvas grandmother, now
	rios ch'ul kuxul san mikel, tat	sacred god living San Miguel, father
	rios ch'ul kuxul san mikel kajwal	sacred god living San Miguel, lord
	jk'antik yutsikil ati', yo'tik	we desire the caress of your word, now
143	jk'antik yutsikil ak'op, yo'tik	we desire the caress of your speech, now
	ta yolil chij	inside the vein

ta yolil kajon, xiatwan yo'tik
binti kati ut'il, yo'tik xiatwan
ja wala xicho' manojel, yo'tik
ta yolil chij
ta yolil kajon
tey ma taba jti', xiatwan
    yo'tik
tey ma taba ko'tan, xiatwan
    yo'tik
melel jich melbilontel,
    xiatwan
melel jich albilontel,
    xiatwan
oxlajuneb kux o'tanil, xiatwan
oxlajuneb jetobabe,
    xiatwan
156 oxlajuneb kurva, xiatwan
talon ta yolil ch'iwich,
    xiatwan
talon ta yolil plása,
    xiatwan
talon jlo'o naraxil,
    xiatwan
tey ma tabatel jti',
    xiatwan
tey ma taba ko'tan,
    xiatwan
mabi tabelon kuyulil,
    xiatwan
jun belta xti'awanontel,
    xiatwan
jun belta talemon, xiatwan
k'alal ta yolil yo'tan,
    xiatwan
jun belta kich'otel ti'awal
    ajawchan, xiatwan
jun belta kich'otel ti'awal
    pakom, xiatwan
kich'otel tiawal ts'inte' chan,
    xiatwan

inside the belly, you'll say now
what can it be now, you'll say
you humble buyer, now
inside the vein
inside the belly
so it's not easy to find my word,
    you'll say
so it's not easy to find my heart,
    you'll say
in truth that is how they
    pronounced me, you'll say
in truth that is how I have been
    given, you'll say
thirteen resting places, you'll say
thirteen crosses on the path, you'll
    say
thirteen bends, you'll say
I came to the center of the market,
    you'll say
I came to the center of the plaza,
    you'll say
I came with eaten oranges, you'll
    say
it isn't easy to find my word there,
    you'll say
it isn't easy to find my heart there,
    you'll say
it isn't possible to find my signs,
    you'll say
once I am biting pain, you'll
    say
once I have come, you'll say
right to the center of his heart,
    you'll say
once I'm the bite of a rattlesnake,
    you'll say
once I'm the bite of the *nauyaca*
    snake, you'll say
I'm the bite of a coral snake, you'll
    say

169   kich'otel tiawal ch'ox chan,
      xiatwan

I'm the bite of a vine snake, you'll
      say

oxlajuneb kaxlan ts'ibon,
      xiatwan

I'm thirteen writings from Castile,
      you'll say

oxlajuneb kaxlan chup,
      xiatwan

I'm thirteen caterpillars from
      Castile, you'll say

spisil kilotel, xiatwan

I've seen it all, you'll say

oxlajuneb stsek, xiatwan.

thirteen scorpions, you'll say

ma'uk yo'tik kerem, yo'tik

it can't be boy, now

tsakat ta be, yo'tik

I chase you on the path, now

kilbatik ta be,
      yo'tik

on the path we meet face-to-face,
      now

ja' chikan jalame' ch'ul
      senyóra sorirat, yo'tik

make yourself visible, sacred
      godmother lady Sorirat, now

jalame' ch'ul sorirat sme'
      balumilal, yo'tik

godmother Sorirat mother of the
      world, now

muk'ul manojel tat, yo'tike

mighty Manojel father, now

muk'ul manojel kajwal,
      yo'tike

mighty Manojel father,
      now

sánto sakaraménto tat, yo'tike

holy Sacrament, father

182 sánto sakaraménto kajwal,
      yo'tike

holy Sacrament lord,
      now

rios jesukrísto stukel

god Jesus Christ, alone

tat ch'ul sánto san sebastian,
      yo'tike

sacred father holy San Sebastián,
      now

jalame' ch'ul ninya kantaláru,
      yo'tike

godmother sacred girl Candelaria,
      now

tat ch'ul sánto san lorénso,
      tat

sacred father holy San Lorenzo
      father

tat ch'ul sánto san lorénso,
      kajwal

sacred father holy San Lorenzo
      lord

tat ch'ul nómpere kajwal,
      yo'tik

sacred father Name lord,
      now

tat ch'ul apóstol, yo'tik

sacred father apostle, now

tek'elat, yo'tik

you are present, now

pajalat, yo'tik

you are raised, now

banti ma jk'antik yutsikil
      ati'

where we desire the caress of your
      word

banti ma jk'antik
      ak'op

where we desire the caress of your
      speech

	talel yo'tik stukel	it comes given, now alone
195	ta yolil kajon, yo'tik	to the center of the belly
	ta yolil jo'ben, yo'tik	to the center of the chest
	binti kati yo'tan, yo'tik	how much will his heart bear, now
	binti kati sti', yo'tik	how much will his word bear, now

	tey ma tabatel jti',
	    xiatwan
		you don't reach the word like that,
		    you'll say

	tey ma tabatel jk'op,
	    xiatwan
		you don't reach the word like that,
		    you'll say

	k'ajintabilontel, xiatwan	singing I found him, you'll say
	xuxubtabilontel, xiatwan	whistling I found him, you'll say
	jun atalon yo'tik, xiatwan	so I came, you'll say

	jo'on priméro ajulontel,
	    xiatwantel
		I got here first, you'll
		    say

	jul jk'opon jun micrófono,
	    xiatwantel
		I'm the word of a microphone,
		    you'll say

	jul jk'opon jun sínta,
	    xiatwantel
		I'm the word of a cassette, you'll
		    say

	ma tabatel jti' ko'tan,
	    xiatwantel
		He doesn't reach my word/heart,
		    you'll say

	[xujch'i]	[Xun P'in sprinkles liquor over the patient four times.]
208	rios ch'ul jesukrísto	sacred god Jesus Christ
	yo'tikat, tat	now, father
	sánto san nikolas, tat	holy San Nicolás father
	sánto san nikolas, kajwal	holy San Nicolás lord
	tat sánto san markos, tat	holy father San Marcos father
	tat sánto san markos, kajwal	holy father San Marcos lord
	jk'antik yutsikil ati'	we desire the caress of your word
	jk'antik yutsikil ak'op	we desire the caress of your word
	stukel ek ato	so I hope
	rios jesukrísto	god Jesus Christ
	rios sánto san jasínto, tat	holy god San Jacinto father
	jalame' ch'ul kantalaru	sacred godmother Candelaria

	ayat ta okutsinko ch'ul lum,
	    yo'tik
		you are in the sacred town of
		    Ocosingo

221	ayat ta okutsinko ch'ul k'inal,
	    yo'tik
		you are in the sacred land of
		    Ocosingo

ch'obontel awala lekil, yo'tik	grant me the kindness, now
ch'obontel awala utsil, yo'tik	grant me the caress, now
li' ta yolil kajon, yo'tik	here in the center of the belly, now
li' ta yolil chij, yo'tik	here in the center of the vein, now
binti kati yakal ta ti'aw, yo'tik	where pain is given, now
binti kati yakal juch'etel, yo'tik	where it grows sharper, now
chawajiwan jun me'eletik	maybe an old woman's disorder
chawajiwan jun karseletik	maybe a prisoner's disorder
chawajiwan jun soleletik	maybe a transient's disorder
ta olil bewan, yo'tik	in the middle of a path perhaps
ta olil kaminowan, yo'tik	in the middle of a road perhaps
ja'wan jich ayal sti'ik, yo'tik	maybe that's how they started to say, now
234 ja'wan jich ayal sk'op, yo'tik	maybe that's how they started to give the word
k'aalel pálewan, yo'tik	a diurnal father priest, now
k'aalel kelériko pálewan, yo'tik	a diurnal father clergyman, now
jich ajach ta jun spisil	that's how everything started
jich ajach talel spisil	that's how it started and everything was given
la smeyontel jun sakil k'u', xiatwan	someone dressed in a white tunic distributed me, you'll say
la smeyontel jun sakil pak', xiatwan	someone dressed in a white robe distributed me, you'll say
la smeyontel jun sakil k'u', xiatwan	someone dressed in a white tunic distributed me, you'll say
tey ma taba jti', xiatwan	my word can not be found, you'll say
tey ma taba ko'tan, xiatwan	my heart can not be found, you'll say
jich ajulon ta kámpo, xiatwan	that's how I came to the place, you'll say
jich ajulon ta lum, xiatwan	that's how I came to the town, you'll say
jich ajul jk'opon bak'et, xiatwan	that's how I came to talk to the flesh, you'll say
247 jich anakajontel, xiatwan	that's how I came and settled here, you'll say

jich apetsajontel, xiatwan	that's how I came hiding myself, you'll say
yolil kubéta, xiatwan	to the center of the chest, you'll say
yolil kajon, xiatwan	to the center of the box, you'll say
tey ma taba jti', xiatwan	my word can not be found, you'll say
tey ma taba jk'op, xiatwan	my word can not be found, you'll say
ma'uk yo'tik, kerem	not now, boy
bit'il ma yakubtesat, yo'tik	how I make you drunk, now
bit'il ma ch'ajubtesat, yo'tik	how I make you dopey, now
ta oxlajuneb wamal, yo'tik	with thirteen herbs, now
ta oxlajuneb wamal payte' yo'tik	with thirteen *payte'* herbs, now
jun ta muk'ul ton ch'ajte', yo'tik	together with the mighty *ton cha'jte* herb, now
jun ta bik'it ton ch'ajte', yo'tik	together with the small *ton cha'jte* herb, now
260 ta bik'it kaxlan búro wamal	with the small "donkey of Castile" herb
bit'il ma jnoyat, yo'tik stukel	how I crush you, now
bit'il ma juch'at, yo'tik stukel	how I grind you, now
bit'il bik'it tuyat, yo'tik	how I break you into little pieces, now
bit'il bik'it noyat, yo'tik	how I crush you into little pieces, now
bit'il lilinat, yo'tik	how I pulverize you, now
bik'it molíno, yo'tik	with a little mill, now
kaxlan molíno, yo'tik	with a mill from Castile, now
bit'il ma jnoyat ta kaxlan rapícha tak'in, yo'tik	I crush you with a metal sugar mill from Castile, now
bit'il molíno, yo'tik	like a mill, now
jich amiil talel, yo'tik	what is your number
banti tal awisim, yo'tik	where have you taken root, now
ma'uk, lonpimontel, xiatwan yo'tik	no, I am myriad, you'll say now
273 esmajemontel, xiatwan	I multiply myself, you'll say
chaxujkul smoch, xiatwan	rooted on both sides of his ribs, you'll say
yolil sejkub smoch, xiatwan	in the center of the side of the liver, you'll say

tey ma taba jti',
    xiatwan

that is why you can not find my
    word, you'll say

tey ma taba jk'op,
    xiatwan

that is why you can not find my
    language, you'll say

melel xchawajilontel,
    xiatwan

in truth I come as a disorder, you'll
    say

melel xchawajilontel,
    xiatwan

in truth I come as a disorder, you'll
    say

melel xchawajilontel mut,
    xiatwan

in truth I am a bird disorder, you'll
    say

melel xchawajilontel chitam,
    xiatwan

in truth I am a pig disorder, you'll
    say

yak'an k'atp'ojokon ta pumel
    kawáyu, xiatwan

I can transform myself into horse
    indigestion, you'll say

yak'an k'atp'ojokon ta pumel
    chanbalam, xiatwan

I can transform myself into animal
    indigestion, you'll say

melel jich la smeloniktel,
    xiatwan

in truth we came distributed, you'll
    say

melel jich la choloniktel,
    xiatwan

in truth we came lined up, you'll
    say

286 ma'uk kerem, xiatwan

no, boy, you'll say

talemon ta naj ta lum,
    xiatwan

I have come from the underground
    house, you'll say

talemon ta naj ta awil,
    xiatwan

I have come from the home, you'll
    say

talemon ta yol ch'iibal,
    xiatwan

I have come from the center of the
    ch'iibal, you'll say

ta muk'ul naj ta lum,
    xiatwan

from the great underground house,
    you'll say

ta muk'ul naj ta awil, xiatwan

from the great home, you'll say

bik'it naj ta lum,
    xiatwan

from the small underground house,
    you'll say

bik'it naj ta awil, xiatwan

from the small house, you'll say

ta xch'iib yantik lum,
    xiatwan

from the *ch'iibal* of other towns,
    you'll say

ta xch'iib ta yantik k'inal,
    xiatwan

from the *ch'iibal* of other lands,
    you'll say

tey ma taba jti' abi,
    xiatwan

that is why you can not find my
    word, you'll say

tey ma taba ko'tan abi,
    xiatwan

that is why you can not find my
    heart, you'll say

jun belta tilaon xiatwan	once I am from Tila, you'll say
299 jun belta k'ajol, xiatwan	once I am from Tumbalá, you'll say
jun belta latin xk'opojontel xiatwan	once I come speaking Latin, you'll say
jun belta krieko xiatwan	once Greek, you'll say
tey ma tabatel jti' abi, xiatwan	that is why you can not discover my word, you'll say
tey ma tabatel ko'tan abi, xiatwan	that is why you can not discover my heart, you'll say
jich ajul nakajokon, xiatwan	that's how I came unnoticed, you'll say
jich ajul pejtsajokon, xiatwan	that's how I came hidden, you'll say
ta yolil chij, xiatwan	to the center of the vein, you'll say
ta yolil kajon, xiatwan	to the center of the belly, you'll say
ma'uk, yo'tik	not now
juch'atix, yo'tik	I have ground you up already, now
noyatix, yo'tik	I have crushed you already, now
ta oxlajuneb kaxlan asúfre, yo'tik	with thirteen sulfurs from Castile, now
312 ta oxlajuneb kaxlan tumin, yo'tik	with thirteen cottons from Castile (wool), now
ta oxlajuneb kaxlan sansíbre, yo'tik	with thirteen gingers from Castile, now
lajuneb kaxlan wamal, yo'tik	ten herbs from Castile, now
lajuneb kaxlan jos wamal, yo'tik	ten "Castile vulture" herbs, now
bit'il jnoyat, yo'tik tukel	how I break you up, now alone
bit'il juch'at yo'tik, tukel	how I grind you up, now alone
ta teb ora, yo'tik	in a moment, now
ta xujt' ora, yo'tik	in an instant, now
ayuk bit'il xlametuk chij, yo'tik	how the aching veins will be soothed
ayuk bit'il xlametuk bak'et, yo'tik	how the aching flesh will be soothed
tejk'anbon aba, yo'tik	stand up for me, now
jalame' ch'ul sánto rominko, yo'tik	sacred godmother Santo Domingo, now
jalame' ch'ul guadalupe, yo'tik	sacred godmother Guadalupe, now
325 jalame' ch'ul sánta kurus	sacred godmother Santa Cruz
tat ch'ul sánta kurus	sacred father Santa Cruz

ayat ta tumbala, yo'tik

muk'ul manojel, yo'tik tat

tat ch'ul san pedro, yo'tik tat

ayat ta sabanílla

tat ch'ul san pablo ta xijtalja'

jalame' ch'ul sánta ana, yo'tik

jalame' ch'ul natiwirat

ayat ta ch'ul lum sti' witsil
k'inal, yo'tik

jalame' ch'ul sánta katarína,
yo'tik

jalame' ch'ul sánta sesília,
yo'tik

yutsil ati'ik, yo'tik

338 yutsikil ak'opik, yo'tik

ch'ojbontalel ach'ul bentision,
yo'tik

tsobon talel ch'ul, yo'tik

li'ta yolil jo'benal, yo'tik

li'ta yolil kajonal, yo'tik

ja ich'o manojel, yo'tik

ja ich'o ich'ojel, yo'tik

li' kati yak'oboniktel stukeli

talemon ta st'ojobil te',
xiatwan

talemon ta st'ojobil ak',
xiatwan

talemon yo'tik xaal, xiatwan

tojkesbil chanon, xiat bal

ma'uk yo'tik kerem

351 tsakbet ta be awajtalejel,
yo'tik

ma'uk yo'tik kerem

tsakbet jmesat lok'el, yo'tik

ik'ba noyat lok'el, yo'tik

ta teb ora, yo'tik

ta xujt' ora, yo'tik

ta yantik lum, yo'tik

ta yantik k'inal, yo'tik

ta sakil k'u', yo'tik

you are in Tumbalá, now

mighty Manojel, now, father

sacred father San Pedro, now, father

you are in Sabanilla

sacred father San Pablo in Sitalá

sacred godmother Santa Ana, now

sacred godmother Nativity

you are in the sacred town at the
edge of a mountain, now

sacred godmother Santa Catarina,
now

sacred godmother Santa Cecilia,
now

the caress of your words, now

the caress of your speech, now

unwrap a sacred blessing for me,
now

reunite me sacred, now

in the center of the chest, now

in the center of the belly, now

great buyer

great receiver

here they have given it to me only

I come from the dripping of a tree,
you'll say

I come from the dripping of a bush,
you'll say

I come again, you'll say

I arose as a worm, did you say?

now it cannot be, boy

by the path I will pursue your
numbers, now

now it cannot be, boy

sweeping you, I drive you out, now

smashing you, I drive you out, now

in a moment, now

in an instant, now

to other towns, now

to other lands, now

with the white tunic, now

ta sakil tokal, yo'tik	with the white cloud, now
jkuchat k'axel, yo'tik	carrying you, I shift you, now
kijkatsinat k'axel, yo'tik	holding you, I shift you, now
yantik lum, yo'tik	in other towns, now
364 yantik k'inal, yo'tik	in other lands, now
ja'xa tejk'anbon aba, yo'tik	you can give me help, now
tat ch'ul san mikel tat	sacred father San Miguel father
san pédro tat	San Pedro father
tat ch'ul san juan chamula	sacred father San Juan Chamula
san lorenso ta sinakantan	San Lorenzo of Zinacantán
muk'ul manojel ta istapa, yo'tik	mighty Manojel of Ixtapa, now
jk'antik yutsikil ak'op, yo'tik	we desire the caress of your word, now
jk'antik yutsikil ati', yo'tik	we desire the caress of your speech, now
lametukix stukel, yo'tik	it is now becoming soothed, now
lametukix bak'etal stukel	the flesh is now becoming soothed
lametukix siketul	the flesh is now becoming cooler
ba siketuk bak'et yo'tik stukel.	may the flesh get cool, now, alone
377 yan belta talemon xaal, xiatwan	once I come again, you'll say
yan belta t'ujbilontel xaal, xiatwan	once I return again more beautiful, you'll say
ti'kba sakbetel ati', yo'tik	I will find your word again, now
ti'kba sakbetel ak'op, yo'tik	I will find your speech again, now
tsakba jlilinatel, yo'tik	I pulverize you, now
me tsajal julbakat, yo'tik	may you be a red disorder, now
me p'ejk julbakat, yo'tik	may you be a sleeping disorder, now
me ojtsel julbakat, yo'tik	may you be a shrinking disorder, now
julbakel chanbalam, xiatwan yo'tik	an animal disorder, you'll say, now
julbak sikil tejon, xiatwan	a cold badger disorder, you'll say
yan chanbalam, xiatwan	of another animal, you'll say
ma'uk yo'tik ek a	not now
tabetel ati'	I'll find your word
390 tabetel awo'tan	I'll find your heart
ma'uk yo'tik	not now

sakba tabet awajtal	without difficulty I'll find your numbers
ik'ba tabet akuyulil	quickly I'll find your signs
stukel ek ato	in this way alone
ta oxlajuneb píko	with thirteen picks
ta oxlajuneb tsajub tesat lok'el	with thirteen incandescent picks I extract you
oxlajuneb kaxlan komitéko, yo'tik	with thirteen liquors from Castile, now
oxlajuneb kaxlan taráwo, yo'tik	with thirteen sugarcane liquors from Castile, now
bit'il jnoy ach'ujti	how to smash the end of your stomach
oxlajuneb kaxlan kakaan, yo'tik	with thirteen epazote herbs from Castile
oxlajuneb kaxlan kakaan ch'a ak', yo'tik	with thirteen sour epazote herbs from Castile, now
oxlajuneb kaxlan kakaan bak', yo'tik	with thirteen cores of epazote herbs from Castile, now
403 jmilat yo'tik tukel ek a	you are dead, now
jnoyat yo'tik tukel ek a	you are crushed, now
ma'uk yo'tik kerem	not now, boy
jun belta bik'it keremon, xiatwan	once I am a small boy, you'll say
jun belta bik'it xulemon, xiatwan	once I am a small vulture, you'll say
yak'an k'atp'ojokon, xiatwan	I can transform myself, you'll say
jun tsek chan, xiatwan	as a scorpion, you'll say
jun nap'ak, xiatwan	as a *nauyaca* snake, you'll say
ma'uk yo'tik ek a, xiatwan	not now, you'll say
tey tabet ati'	there your word is to be found
tey tabet awajtal	there your numbers are to be found
k'opojontalel, yo'tik	I bring my word, now
oxlajuneb chiilte', yo'tik	with thirteen ants, now
416 oxlajuneb yo'tik	thirteen, now
oxlajuneb kaxlan sinal, yo'tik	thirteen *sinal* trees from Castile
bit'il jmilat, yo'tik	how I can kill you, now
bit'il kulubtesat yo'tik	how I can destroy you, now
ch'ajubtesat, yo'tik	I exhaust you, now

ta mulawil jti', yo'tik	the bad word, now
ta mulawil k'op, yo'tik	the bad speech, now
oxlajuneb ti' rios	thirteen words of god
oxlajuneb koltayel	thirteen helps
ayuk bit'il sujt awelaw, yo'tik	how can you give me your face, now
ayuk bit'il sujt asit, yo'tik	how can you give me your gaze, now
ch'ul sánto san mexicáno, tat	sacred holy San Mexicano father
ch'ul sánto rominko, yo'tik	sacred Santo Domingo, now
429 ayat ta jo'bel, yo'tik	you are in San Cristóbal de Las Casas, now
jalame' ch'ul mersed, yo'tik	sacred godmother Merced, now
tat ch'ul san kristobal, yo'tik	in the sacred city of San Cristóbal, now
tey ajil stukel ek a	there only
ch'ul sánta lusía me'	sacred Santa Lucía mother
ch'ul san francísco tat	sacred San Francisco father
me'chunina guadalúpe	grandmother Guadalupe
yutsikil ati'	the caress of your word
yutsikil ak'op	the caress of your speech
sánto san antónyo tat	holy San Antonio father
sánto san antónyo kajwal	holy San Antonio lord
ch'ul san felípe tat	sacred San Felipe father
ch'ul san felípe kajwal	sacred San Felipe lord
442 yutsikil ati'	the caress of your word
yutsikil ak'op	the caress of your speech
xjamametuk chij	the vein is soothed
xjamametuk kajon, yo'tik	the belly is soothed, now
teyuk xlamet k'axel, yo'tik	there is relief there, now
k'alal xk'at swinkilel	when it arrives at his body
k'alal xk'at sjo'benal	when it arrives at his chest
jun may, yo'tik stukel	a tobacco, now alone
jun tabáko, yo'tik stukel	a tobacco, now alone
xicho' manojel,	great buyer
xicho' icho'jel	great receiver
sus maría	Jesus, Mary
tatil rios nich'anil	Father, God, Son
sánta . . .	Holy . . .

Commentary

According to the text of the song, some words have entered the patient. The words are determined according to a set formula, and they are applied as a function of the patient's illness origin within the healer's scheme, but the condition, age, sex, activity, and other characteristics of the individual are barely taken into consideration. Clearly they are not just any words, but rather words of illness; as we saw before, the words are in fact the illness itself. These words, which the shaman will question subtly or commandingly depending on the case, are forced to speak, and in this way, they are revealed. They also divulge that they have been uttered by a *lab* of the *pále* genre ("I come from a priest, I come from a clergyman"), apparently of the diurnal variety ("someone dressed in white distributed me"), whose ultimate objective, it is understood, is to kill the boy so it can eat his Bird of the Heart when it is released at the boy's death. It could be that they are sung words, for they say, "once I return again more beautiful" (*t'ujbil*). Just as they are presented, the word ailments are rattlesnake bite, *nauyaca* snake bite, thirteen writings, a book, a word from a microphone, a word from a tape, words in Latin, words in Greek, animal disorder, and so on. However, we should not be so naïve as to believe everything the words say about themselves, especially if they are spoken by a priest, because they are crafty (*ay mánya*, *mañoso* in Spanish), deceitful, and probably imparting a combination of truths and falsehoods. For instance, it is more than doubtful that the origin of the words, as the words would have us believe at some point, is a *ch'iibal* in Cancuc or any other village; they are plainly trying to assert some authority that they are clearly lacking.

The shaman's procedure consists of asking different questions so that the words speak and thus say something about themselves. Xun P'in is testing different possibilities; remember, this is only the first in a series of five similar songs, a series that is open by definition. This questioning will lead Xun to decide later on that this is not a case of some physical disorder, but an abduction of a soul, for which he will have to resort to another kind of ritual and text. In fact, he continually takes the pulse of his patient to measure the effect of his recitation. The information the words give him (their nature, the place where they have settled) allows him to "intervene" in the patient's body to extract the words that have taken root in his belly, digging in deep around the ribs and liver. He "uproots" them by crushing, grinding, and smashing them into smithereens with hand mills, sugar mills, picks, and dynamite, and extracts them with certain herbs and cane liquor, before finally sweeping them away. To that end, he solicits assistance from saints, both from Cancuc and elsewhere.

Thus, in synthesis, the prayer's argument is relatively straightforward, just one more of the odd alliances formed in Chiapas: An Indian shaman begs the favor of Castilian saints to help him combat the sermon of a Dominican priest.

Even the Tzeltal regard the prayers with a certain ambiguity; they find them beautiful and moving, but also extremely strange. On the other hand, ethnographic literature on the Tzotzil and the Tzeltal has, with a few notable exceptions—i.e., Köhler (1977); Breton and Becquelin-Monod (1989)—largely overlooked healing texts. The absence of meaning, that sensation of absurdity produced by hearing a song and even more so by translating it from one language to another and one culture to another, may account in part for this lack of interest on the part of anthropologists; quite the opposite occurs with tales and narratives. Given that ethnographers mainly channel their energies into the search for meaning, the prayers represent more of an obstacle than a contribution. But it is still a serious oversight, especially when one considers the decisive role played by the chants in native life, as well as their complex and precise typology and the frequency with which they are uttered. In terms of "quantity of text," the prayers must be by far the most copious genre. To paraphrase Xun P'in, life is not a myth, a tale, or a biography; it is an endless healing text.

As for me, I make no pretense of offering a complete explanation of the text. Even so, not only is it possible, it is even useful to point out some particular aspects of the chant that are directly related to questions regarding the representation of personhood discussed so far. First, I would like to examine the content of the prayer and then its form.

With respect to content, one is immediately aware of a marked emphasis on movement: displacements, horizontal journeys through and between points. To begin with, there is the illness, displacing itself from the periphery of Cancuc to its center, indirectly in the form of the priest or, later, directly as his words. In its intermittent sinuous, zigzag movement, the illness crosses geographical features like paths, promontories, hollow places, crossroads, bends in the road, and so forth. The text seems to be highlighting not so much the places passed en route as the very sensation of movement: Its onward progress is as if the text were a camera adopting the point of view of the person, or thing, in motion. As a matter of fact, the whole text seems to me to possess a deeply cinematic style. At one point it even says, "dampness of dew I bring," thereby letting us know that the illness has brushed up against the dew-laden vegetation on the side of the path; more than sensual, it is a palpable expression of movement.

What is more, illness seems to move around stealthily. For instance, the healer has a hunch that it may have hidden itself for some time in the market ("I came to the center of the market, I came to the center of the square"). It is certainly the ideal hiding place, because although words may be found all over the airwaves in the market, illness may easily be confused with the words habitually uttered there, which the Tzeltal know as *woch' woch' k'op*, referring to the characteristic noise produced by the confluence of all conversations. Last of all, the illness advances as far as the victim's body (we do not know from the text whether it has been designated beforehand; it probably was not in this case), which it penetrates as words do, in a rotating, clockwise movement ("I came spinning like that, like a spinning top from Castile, like a whipping top from Castile")—a type of motion that tears, that opens—that ends up by embedding itself inside the victim ("that's how I reached the center of the vein, that's how I reached the center of the flesh, that's how I reached the center of the belly, that's how I reached the center of the vein, that's how I reached the center of the liver"). The image sometimes used is that of taking root within.

As for the shaman, his words also produce a movement to counteract the illness, but it is a movement of another sort. Repeatedly he invokes the help of "saints," whom he asks not so much to cure his patient, but rather to bestow upon him a certain type of words (no doubt many of those he cites) so that he himself may do the healing. The shaman usually addresses the saints as follows:

> grant me your kindness
> grant me your caress
> we desire the caress of the word from your lips
> we desire the caress of the word from your heart
> grant me the sacred blessing
> reunite me with the sacred blessing
> can you let me have your face?
> can you let me have your gaze?

The "sacred blessing" consists of words provided by the saints in their role as shamanic assistants, words that must be "opened out," something that appears to tie in with the central theme of folding and unfolding that characterizes the relationship between saints and human beings. This does not mean that the words of the saints are intrinsically "good," but instead that they are effective because they are "other" (after all, they are in Spanish), so they are tools that are capable, in a shaman's mouth, of expelling the illness. The repeated use of the number thirteen, a "methodical" number and thus a more efficacious one, seems to be along the same lines. "Illness-giving" *lab* are also believed to utter an incantation composed of thirteen words, whose exact content is a secret, but one that many Tzeltal are privy to.

The saints invoked fall into two groups, or rather, they occupy two distinct positions. Until the pause when he sprinkles the patient with liquor (before line 208), the chanter names only sacred figures inside Cancuc's church, and he names them in the same order as they are to be found there, starting with the first one next to the church's door and proceeding counterclockwise. After this pause, the figures named correspond to the patron saints of villages near Cancuc, none more than a one- or two-day walk away. Here again, the direction of the itinerary is counterclockwise, as it starts out from the center of Cancuc toward a point in the east, which is Ocosingo (on an imaginary Tzeltal map, it would be "up"), describing from there a semicircle toward the north (to the "left"), then descending toward the west of Cancuc ("down"). In sharp contrast to the priest's words that travel from outside to inside Cancuc in an erratic movement, the chanter reels off the patron saints of Indian villages in an orderly circuit of Cancuc's periphery, passing from Tzeltal to Chol and then on to Tzotzil speakers, before ending up with the patron saints of the different barrios of San Cristóbal de Las Casas (San Cristóbal, San Mexicano, Santo Domingo, Santa Merced, Santa Lucía, San Francisco, San Felipe). Today, these are all Spanish-speaking barrios, but in the past, other Indian languages (Nahua, Quiché) could be heard there, as they were the permanent bases for the Spaniards' auxiliary Indian troops during the conquest of the region.

In the *poxil*-genre songs, like the one we are commenting on, it seems that any movement described is only semicircular, whereas in other types of songs, the circle around Cancuc is completely closed by mentioning other towns. Based on Gossen's (1974) analysis of ritual movements of Chamula, we know that this counterclockwise movement "closes off" space, separating what is outside from what remains inside. Among the criteria used to judge the quality of a shamanic song is that of the number of saints cited, in other words, the towns included. The greater the diameter of the circumference and the denser the "dotting," so to speak, the more effective the text is considered to be.

It seems clear that saints are not invoked in chants by virtue of their individual competencies (as in the case of Catholic saints); their value resides in the position they occupy in Indian geography, a geographical route that at the same time is also a journey back into time. In reality, the fact that the tutelary saint of the village of Sabanilla, for example, may be male or female, San Pablo or San Felipe, does not affect its therapeutic function in the slightest, a function understood to be that of a donor of words of healing who operates from the vantage point afforded by a particular position in time and space. From this point of view, the role of the Tzeltal saints in therapeutic rituals is equivalent to that of the specialist "auxiliary spirits" invoked in Siberian or classical American shamanic ceremonies. In a way, the saints can be thought of as milestones with which the person who is singing delimits the surface area of known space, the here and now, characteristic of the ordinary state of existence. In any case, there is some significance in the fact that saints mentioned in songs are found both in the main square of Cancuc, "the heart of the village," and on the outer limits of known space, at the limits of its body, so to speak. This is precisely what happens with souls with respect to the human body: they are found at the geographical edge, in the past and, simultaneously, in the heart.

Every illness may be said to be the result of a movement in space on the part of beings who abandon the place corresponding to them. As long as they stay in the spots Tzeltal cartography has assigned them, they are simply considered to be in counterpoint to the ordinary world of Cancuc. But when they start traveling and leave *their* place, they enter into contradiction, and illness is the outcome. This chain of cause and effect is relatively clear in the movements made from the periphery of Cancuc's valley toward the inhabited nuclei (for example, in the case of the *lab* "illness-givers") and is paralleled in the events of Tzeltal history: the intrusion of epidemics, wars, and other disasters. However, it is equally true of displacement produced from within, from the heart, and the physical environment of everyday life—for example, when the *ch'ulel* leaves the heart during sleep, or when the *lab* emerge in their inner version.

In addition to what may be surmised from the song's content, it is perhaps in song form that the text behaves more dramatically. More specifically, its composition appears to be an extreme case of the principles guiding the so-called "dialogic" narrative, as defined by Ricoeur (1987, 172–175) in his elaboration of Mikhail Bakhtin's analysis.

In the first place, the polyphony is taken to such extremes in this song that not only does the chanter enter into a dialogue with its characters on equal terms, but there are times when it is virtually impossible to identify who is saying what. In general, in Tzeltal narrative, it is not easy to recognize the identity of the voice of what has just been said; and even in everyday conversation, paraphrasing is a common resource. But when it comes to shamanic songs, this becomes a greater problem. In my experience, this is one of the principal difficulties in the transcription and translation of a healing text. In certain songs, the shaman may speak for, or with, six or seven characters at the same time; not even the Tzeltal I worked with from 1991 to 1993 on a selection of texts I had previously transcribed were always able to identify who was the speaker of what had been uttered.

Nevertheless, in this particular song, only two voices may be identified: the voice of the shaman and the voice of the very words of the illness. The voice of the illness corresponds to lines 14–38, 58–88, 104–109, 127–135, 153–176, 202–210, 242–255, 275–310, 349–352, 380–381, 388–390, 409–414, and the rest of the text corresponds to the voice of the healer, incorporating words from the "saints" as well.

The voice of the illness is distinguished from the shaman's by the apposition of the formulaic *xi-at-wan*, which means something like "perhaps you say," or "you'll say." Yet reliance on this marker of direct speech is most unusual in Xun P'in's recitations, and I do not know why he uses it in this particular case. When employed in a narrative context, the verb *xi* is introduced immediately after the direct quotation so as to reduce the degree of certainty in the information, as it implies the speaker was not a witness to what he is recounting. According to Brian Stross (1974, 14), it seems to be an irregularly conjugated intransitive verb that uses no particle or element to signal its verb tense. I believe this is of great significance, because it means that it may be used to express an action in the past, present, or future. Thus, in our text, we have no way of knowing whether the voice of the illness is talking right now, has spoken some time in the past, or means to speak some time in the future. Either all three alternatives exist at the same time, or the dimension of time proper to ordinary verbs is irrelevant in this (con)text. In the third person, *xi* is also, for example, the verb used to refer to what the *ch'ulel* saw and heard on its nocturnal ramblings.

Second, it is evident that the outlines of these characters are blurred, for they have not completely jelled; as soon as they start to talk and therefore to identify themselves, a sudden change of voice prevents them from gathering a momentum of their own, leaving them only half set. The text's ambiguous shifts in identity result in the meandering progress of its narrative, and this explains in part why it appears to be so disjointed.

Third and finally, the prayer lacks an ending, a closure in the strict narrative sense. Having reached a certain point, it simply stops suddenly, creating an unmistakable impression of inconclusiveness.

Following Paul Ricoeur, these three features go against the grain of what one expects in the narrative genre. Behind them lurks a plot that surrenders to interaction; they are the hallmark of a form in which "space tends to supplant time" (Ricoeur 1987, 174). This impression seems to be reinforced both by the vertiginous speed at which the text is uttered and its microtonal intonation, which generates a characteristic sensation of monotony. In shamanic songs, the structuring principle is not time but space, and it is in this dialogic space that narrative fiction yields in the interests of coexistence and interaction between those taking part, both humans and spirits.

In short, both the text's content and its form appear to lead in the same direction, in that they both favor deployment in space over development through time. The onward march of time is transformed into a circular journey through the landscape. If my understanding is correct, one consequence of this transformation will be that the public face of personal identity, in other words, cultural identity (the identity that evolves through time, in the course of a lifetime's education—education in the broad sense of formation and upbringing) tends to be eclipsed. And in being eclipsed, it exposes the other, interior identities, those identities that are *not* formed as time goes by, because they were given at or before birth (*talel:* what comes given), at which moment they were already fully formed, and because they are basically immutable throughout the course of one's life. The strange world in which the songs operate and build, then, reveals the world of the souls. In fact, several of this study's themes that we have gone to considerable lengths to trace and explain are presented in the prayer, if not more systematically, then at least in much more dense, magnified detail. For example, it can be seen that the types of identities that the text conjures before our eyes are not individual identities in any strict sense, but formal attributes, details, perceptible qualities of things and people.

Among these qualities of the soul, difference expressed in terms of ethnic difference is what stands out the most. In an understated way, almost easy to overlook, the text refers to qualities that in turn refer us to other Indian townships. For example, mention is made of the Chol language spoken in the villages of Tila and Tumbalá. On occasion, the shaman uses expressions that the Cancuqueros can easily recognize as belonging to other dialects of Tzeltal heard in municipalities such as Chanal or Amatenango del Valle. In other prayers (not in this one, as far as I can tell), Tzotzil words are spoken.

Yet over and above every other form of alienation, we find European objects, techniques, qualities. The greater part of this text (and the text of any other song) revolves around this axis in endless repetition. Practically everything that defines the illness is Castilian: Castilian spinning tops; Castilian songs and whistles; disorders in Castilian hens, pigs, horses, and other animals; Castilian dogs; Castilian children; Castilian writings, books, microphones, cassettes; Castilian caterpillars, scorpions, ants; Castilian trees; and so forth. However, what works the cure is not "Indian" but European objects and qualities that the healer manipulates. Thus the shaman fights the illness with a variety of Castilian herbs—and it is obvious that they are selected not for any chemical properties they may have but for the analogical reference of their names (the Tzeltal have a wide knowledge of curative herbs [Berlin et al. 1974], but in most cases, they use them in the text of songs and not in actual healing ceremonies)—pickaxes; Castilian skullcaps, machines, hand mills; metal Castilian sugar mills; Castilian liquor and tequila; Castilian sulfur, wool, and ginger; Castilian "strength" (*pérsa*, or *fuerza* in Spanish); and the like.

As a matter of fact, not only are the medicine words not Indian, the shaman is not either. Xun P'in is no longer himself but rather the inside of his heart, above all his true *ch'ulel*, but perhaps his *lab*, too, given that a good shaman ought to have thirteen of them, including, in all likelihood, a jaguar. Not only is the shaman manipulating the Castilian world; he is also identifying himself with it. Within the space of the text, the shaman is going about his work in the *ch'ul* sacred state of existence. To borrow Michael Taussig's (1987) forceful image, he is in a state of walking through "a colonial space of death." The healing texts refer to a long period of time and a disturbing historical experience, as it has been and is being interpreted and experienced by the Tzeltal. In a way, this healing prayer is an Indian historical text, a voyage of exploration through the body and memory.

However that may be, the healing rituals and the chants recited in them reveal the indissoluble link that binds the experience of illness together with the exploration of ethnic difference, the exploration of the distinction between what is one's own (Indian) and what is alien (European). In a way, the fixation of the Tzeltal on their illnesses is equivalent to an exploration of "the other side," of the "other." Self-absorption is also a way of relating to the rest of the world.

CONCLUSION

The Fold

A person is a fold, or an imprint, of the outside. On being born, the future human being folds in on him- or herself, capturing fragments of the "other" world and the presolar past—that is, souls—that will in turn form part of this new being until, with the body's demise, the moment of unfolding, these fragments are restored to the outside. In the prenatal state, these fragments, which will fuse to form a new person, are immersed in a distinct form of existence that in Tzeltal is known as the *ch'ul*.

The *ch'ul* state is not so much another place but rather another sort of reality or form of existence—perhaps we could call it "virtual"—that develops in a time and space distinct from ordinary understandings of these dimensions. It is the cosmos in its original state before the sun appeared with its light and heat to establish the coordinates of time and space and, with them, the present world—*jamalal*—where opaque bodies that cast shadows dwell. This world must be carved out of the sacred dimension, which constitutes the definitive underlying plan, the state on which existence is based. But even now, when the sun permits life as we know it—albeit provisionally—the *ch'ul* state envelops this world it has formed and is permanently present as the other side of existence, "the other face of being," the blank face, vacuity, to quote from Octavio Paz. This "other side" has no clearly defined limits: during the day it contracts, giving way to sunlight (and is present only in shadows, that other way of calling souls); at night, it expands and trickles down into the ordinary world, only respecting houses where the hearth is permanently lit because moonlight is not strong enough to create the necessary stability.

The *ch'ul* state is more unstable than day-to-day reality and has a tendency to mix or blur time and space. Perhaps the most characteristic aspect of this realm is that the basic categories that order the ordinary world of beings of flesh and blood become difficult to distinguish. No boundary or division is clear-cut or transparent in this world; rather, they are always in an indeterminate state or in ambiguity, that is, in the state of neither separation nor mixture. Such basic opposites for ordinary life as present and past, near and far, life and death, heat and cold, animal and human, masculine and feminine, older and younger, Indian and European, and so on intertwine here. It is this instability that characterizes the divinities, the saints, the spirits, the life of the dead or times past, referred to in the "ancient words" that we know as "myths," and the souls.

While the fetus remains in the mother's womb, it is still immersed in the *ch'ul* existence, where it feeds on the mother's blood. But the future body is inside out; its "souls" are on the "outside," in contact with the placenta (in some senses, the fetus is still not distinguishable from the placenta until after the birth, when it is buried, thus allowing the body to live). On being born, the body folds in on itself and the souls are encapsulated within the heart in such a way that the body drags fragments belonging to this other virtual form of existence into "this world." With the death of the body, the contents of the heart are restored to the *ch'ul* world, and the self disintegrates.

This fold—life—is a precarious achievement, since it is always at the point of coming undone. Souls can abandon the body and not return (although, to be more exact, souls are often taken by those spirits to whose community they belong; what we usually describe in ethnography as abduction is actually closer to restitution). Sleep, when the *ch'ulel* soul abandons the body, or drunkenness, when the body is partially won over by the heart, represents episodes of fleeting unfolding—dreams, illness, drunkenness—during which the nature of the *ch'ul* world is revealed. Human beings contain this other form of existence within themselves. Nonetheless, the souls are double. What is dragged from the *ch'ul* world is not so much the original but rather the copies. (The character of this process is not entirely clear to me, but one of the characteristics of the *ch'ul* world appears to be its ability to duplicate or copy itself in such a way that it turns into an avatar.) The connection between the soul confined within the body and the original *ch'ul* world is not broken during an individual's life. We have seen how the heart's *ch'ulel* soul is a double of the *ch'ulel* that can be found inside a magic mountain, which is a community of souls, meaning ourselves as well, that have a life completely distinct from the ordinary one, a life dominated by endless fiestas, music, and liquor. We not only have alternative lives within our hearts—as occurs when we dream—but we also live simultaneous lives as other sorts of beings: in a mountain of souls (*ch'ulel*) or as animals and other extraordinary creatures (*lab*).

Becoming is a process of extracting from this original and undifferentiated *ch'ul* state. But what in the end makes this possible is the existence of the body. In contrast to the souls, the body can and must be "invented." The body, that part of the person made of visible dense material (flesh and blood), which exists in ordinary time and space, is considered—and here we include the head, where the ability to learn and reason resides—to be the result of a continual process of making from the moment of birth. Only at an advanced age, over forty perhaps, when a person is already a grandparent, can they be considered to have acquired sufficient maturity to be considered a "correct" body. Now, this maturing of the body is, at the same time, a process of moral maturing: one is a condition for the other. Without physical development, there is no moral development and vice versa (Pitarch 2008). It is a process that involves both feeding as well as bodily etiquette. On the one hand, body postures, gestures, talking, and clothing are all subject to an extraordinary control. On the other, the body becomes literally what it eats. Eating too much meat, for example, produces an immoral body. If Indian schoolteachers start to use Spanish words too frequently, it is because they have eaten too much meat; it is the habit of eating meat that makes them schoolteachers. In other words, a body that behaves itself correctly is not a sign of morality, it is morality itself.

This making of the body starts at birth and stops with death or, to be more precise, a little before, with the decline of the physical faculties, when the moment of optimal corporal maturity has passed. The Tzeltal term that denotes that a person is morally correct, *k'otem* (from the verb *k'ot*, "to arrive"), means "finished, complete," in other words, with the body well formed. I believe that the "ethnonym" with which the Tzeltal describe themselves, *bats'il winik* (genuine people) should be interpreted in this sense, as beings that have managed to become authentic human beings, owing to the fact that their body behaves itself in a morally appropriate fashion. In this respect, children and adolescents are not truly "indigenous" and many adults may not be entirely considered "genuine people." Similarly, it possibly explains the fear that the elderly provoke, as if their ideal physical state has already passed and their person has started to enter into a *ch'ul* state.

In short, one is not born indigenous—it is not an inherited condition—one *becomes* indigenous, or at least this is the ideal goal. For the same reason, from a Tzeltal point of view, if the Europeans are different, it is because of the way their bodies are made: their social habits, what they eat, how they talk and what they talk about, the way they move, the way they dress and carry their clothes. In spite of my interest during fieldwork in souls, the Tzeltal never showed much interest in mine or in those of people in my country. They took it for granted that they were basically identical to theirs. In contrast, they always showed great interest in the body and in what I and the Spaniards ate. I asked about souls, and the Tzeltal asked me about the body.

If the body must be constructed, the soul, in contrast, is the given aspect of a person. The term *talel*, which denotes the heart's interior—the various soul entities—is literally "what is given." They derive from the *ch'ul* state completely formed and do not suffer any type of change or development during an individual life. Personal (corporeal) morality cannot affect them in any way; they are simply there, independent of the character of the body. If personal maturity is a slow and laborious process of bodily construction, the souls remain inside the body and only a slight relaxing of the body is sufficient for them to immediately break out.

Expressed in a schematic fashion, the Tzeltal conceive of the human being as a relatively homogeneous entity as far as its external appearance is concerned, but completely heterogeneous internally. The body and its visible quality—what other people see of oneself—should ideally be homogeneous, a well-articulated and integrated whole. However, above all, a body should be minimally distinguishable from the rest; ideally, the body's movements and postures, clothing, and speaking manner should be almost uniform. Native culture invests an enormous effort into suppressing individual features, as far as possible, to benefit the outside identity of bodies. Inversely, the person's interior—the heart—is characterized by its heterogeneity: a multicolored and unequal composite of souls. Souls are heterogeneous, given, and incomplete; the body, on the other hand, should be homogeneous, constructed, and complete: It is the part of the person that tends toward the whole, and probably from there derives the importance given to the fact that the human body—unlike souls, spirits, or saint bodies—should always appear, such as in photographs, complete.

Person, History, and Memory

The fold, as an internalized part of the outside, also drags history into the person. The past is found in the present within the body in the form of souls; the heart literally contains the past. It is not that Indians remember the past; they simply live with it; they are born with it, so they keep it within them. It might be easier to think of Indian souls not so much as beings but as the personification of past events. Therefore, if memory is subjectivized time, we are dealing here with an integral memory in which the past literally forms part of the person. A bit like in psychoanalysis, it seems to be an unconscious memory in which what appeared to be forgetfulness actually hides a much greater and deeper memory. The consequence is the inability to forget. Frequently, it is assumed that indigenous people, representing a syncretic culture, no longer distinguish historically between what is European and what is indigenous, nor are they concerned about such a distinction. But we have seen, particularly in the case of the shamanic healing chants, how after the more than four hundred and fifty years since the conquest, the Tzeltal recognize—and painstakingly separate—every object, force, action, and concept of European origin. The souls make up a complex means of storing and transmitting the accumulated historical experience. They condense a far-reaching memory.

In a certain way, they also make up a more faithful memory of the indigenous past. If the knowledge that the Tzeltal possess of their past depended entirely on narratives, this would have been lost irretrievably, or rather it would have merged with European versions of history to become something distinct. But to the extent that it is relevant to life now, the souls' memory is permanently up-to-date, remade according to current circumstances. We have seen that we are dealing with what is essentially a political memory, one that is particularly sensitive to colonial procedures regarding the reconstruction of the person and the body. In this field, a hard battle is fought between the European need to assign identity and the indigenous impulse to evade European identity categories. The Tzeltal lack a simple stereotype of themselves, and it is not easy for them to define themselves through a group of positive features (rather, they tend to define themselves with reference to what they lack). This attitude makes itself manifest in their reluctance to participate in censuses or be registered or nominated. But, above all, it can be seen in a broader and more radical opposition to internalizing the categories of European identity ("subjects of Castile," "Jews of the lost tribes," "Indians," "peasants," "Maya," etc.).

The scheme for personal identity repeats itself at the level of collective identity. If the souls, which come from the past, represent "oneself as 'other,'" and the body, which must be invented from the very beginning, represents "self as oneself," in collective terms the past is also something distant, alien. However strange it may seem, "tradition" is equivalent to the alien. What in the Tzeltal language is called *jtaletik* (the same term used to denote a group of souls in the heart)—"that which comes to us given," and that can be translated as "tradition" or by the Spanish term *costumbre*—is what comes to us from the past and is, in reality, "foreign." We are evidently dealing with a relationship between individual and history that is very different to the Western notion. If for the Europeans, identity is defined by reference to continuity—individual or social—between the past and the present, the Tzeltal construct their identity, if not exactly *against* the past, then *in spite of* their past, a past from which one can only extract an identity in its negative form. Just as it occurs at an individual level, in social terms the indigenous condition is characterized by the fact that inherited features should be overcome in order to be.

This perspective regarding the past alters the terms with which we conventionally interpret identity ethnographically: tradition, limits, origins, territory, etc. If we think about the category of the "indigenous community," in ethnography it is common that ethnic identification and the very idea of "Indianness" depend upon the existence of a local community, a territory, a set of religious and civic responsibilities (*cargos*), a system of fiestas, etc. But from an indigenous perspective, the "community" is positioned on the side of tradition, and thus with the Castilian. In this sense, indigenous memory perhaps finds itself better established with regard to history than ethnography itself. It radically recognizes the notion of collective identity—the "republic of neighbors"—that resulted from the policy imposed by Dominican friars in the sixteenth century, which grouped indigenous people together and has been continued up to the present day under the legal category of the municipality. But this is a type of identification that can be replaced by others, as perhaps indigenous people who have migrated to the cities are beginning to discover. The Amerindian culture is to a large degree independent of a territorial community, of an exclusive economic activity, and of a "tradition."

The Counterpoint between the Indigenous and the European

The indigenous conception of the person shows, conversely, how we cannot really talk of syncretism or cultural mixing. It is true that the

Tzeltal employ both Amerindian and European forms, but they do it in a differentiated manner and, on occasion, try to underline their respective differences. On the level of the person, the ethnic identification alternates between the body—along with all that with which it is associated, the "corporeal field"—which is culturally indigenous, and the heart's interior, where the soul constellation is found, which is culturally Castilian. These two very extreme positions reappear in the topological arrangement of the village. The dispersed settlement, where the domestic groups are found, is indigenous in character, while the enclosed rectangle of the village square—the plaza where the church and its saints are found, the municipal administrative building, the school, and other agencies of the Mexican state (as before, the authorities of the Spanish Crown)—refers to the Castilian world. The outside is also in the inside, or, if one prefers, the inside—as occurs with the heart within the body—is an extension of the outside. The square was founded by the Catholic priests themselves, those who live in the indigenous heart.

Asserting that syncretism does not exist, however, is by no means the same as suggesting the existence of a "pure Indian tradition." Cultural mixing is only one of the ways different traditions can coexist. Instead, the formation of personal and collective identity among the Tzeltal is, to borrow a phrase from Taussig (1993, 129), an activity "in which the issue is not so much staying the same, but maintaining sameness through alterity," by alternating both. For instance, the nonindigenous Spanish-speaking population from the Chiapas highlands also makes use of the Amerindian tradition. But although this population has various indigenous cultural features, the use to which they are put is very different. In contrast to indigenous people, "mestizos" actively mix both traditions without distinguishing the historical origins of each practice. The cuisine may serve as example. Indigenous people consume European products, but they always do their best not to mix them with indigenous ones, making, in fact, a simple cuisine in terms of the combination of ingredients. But the regional nonindigenous cuisine mixes up all the ingredients to the point where it is impossible, and unnecessary, to identify it as something singular.

However, in Tzeltal terms, these indigenous-European extremes are not found on the same level. What is "indigenous"—the body, the houses—makes up the ordinary state of things, easily appropriated. The "Castilian" state, in contrast, tends to be circumscribed and fleeting (perhaps particularly among the women, who, because they participate less in the public domain, have fewer opportunities to play at being

"Castilians" except while dreaming or day-dreaming). The identification with the Castilian world is to be found on the side of imitation, of mimesis. In getting drunk and thus discovering the heart's interior, the Tzeltal not only liberate themselves from the strict cultural dominion of the body, but also, and above all, play at being Mexicans and Europeans, interpreting the stereotype of the "Castilian," as they do in the lavish public ceremonies carried out in the village square. It is an extreme expression of identity, which is taken up and abandoned with little difficulty. The massive conversions to the Catholic faith or to evangelical churches represent an example of this game of fleeting identifications. Undoubtedly, indigenous people who join a new church try, as far as possible, to be fervent and faithful members, and the new identifications are experienced with great hope and enthusiasm. However, they seldom last. The result is rather a sort of "religious nomadism" in which natives "convert" a number of times to different churches in the span of a few years. But the same happens with electoral choices, political affiliations, ideological views, and so on. Loyalty (be it religious, political, ideological) is, in the best of cases, a transitory exercise.

In this regard, it is tempting to speculate as to whether the moral function given to the body among indigenous people might explain why they do not easily accept European foodstuffs and other products associated with bodily construction, while they apparently show much more curiosity in European rituals and ideologies—despite the fact that such interest does not last long. It is as if the latter were only cultural accessories, and the former, essential. This would seem to be almost the opposite case to the European attitude: an interest and rapid acceptance of indigenous products and a rejection and disinterest in indigenous ideas.

In any case, if the interpretation of the "Castilian" pole marks the difference between the indigenous and the European, it is possible that it also reveals an urge to communicate with the latter. In this counterpoint exercise, not only is a contrast produced but also a "contact" (Taussig 1993). It is as if the exercise to turn oneself, if only briefly, into the other sought not a genuine exchange—which is extremely difficult in indigenous experience—but dealings with the Spanish-speaking world in which the effect of the mimesis worked as a kind of guarantee of safe conduct. The agitated climate that many sectors of the indigenous population in Chiapas are experiencing in their adoption of roles belonging to the wider Mexican social context might be interpreted as if, through this type of identification, they were testing distinct possibilities and new ways of communicating with the nonindigenous world.

In this indigenous interest in others we can see the concern for symmetry and reciprocity. It is possible that the extraordinary and, at the same time, disconcerting ability of indigenous populations from the Chiapas highlands to accommodate themselves to the modern world—increasingly heterogeneous and immersed in a rapid transformation—and at the same time remain Amerindians can be explained by their capacity to alternate between poles of personal and ethnic identification. It seems that they have the logical capacity to *use* both, without confusing them, and to *be* both, without becoming confused. We have here a conception of a person, possibly originating from a culture of nomadic hunters, that has persisted through time thanks to its capacity to coexist alongside new conditions that gave rise to a sedentary agricultural life, the forces of European colonial government, capitalist relations, etc. It is as if in the initial blueprint for the person there existed a categorical space that allows for the internalization of those new conditions while maintaining a sense of their external origin.

The human being is, in the end, an entity made up of various nodes of consciousness, intention, and emotion, distributed in time and space, that interact with each other in a complex way and are determined by alien forces with which it is necessary to negotiate constantly. (One is tempted to say that we are dealing with a fragmented entity here, but in reality we cannot be sure if they are actually fragments because we may not know what it is or how it can be a whole from a Tzeltal perspective.) This constellation is provisionally and unstably united by a focal point that I have called a "fold," which is what permits individual life. While it lasts, souls continue to belong to the outside and to the past, and the heart's interior copies the other form of existence and history. The most intimate part of oneself is in reality the most altered, the most distant. It is precisely the existence of the "other" in the core of one's self that allows an indigenous person to come to constitute him- or herself. A human being is simultaneously Self and Other: human and animal, living and dead, ordinary and sacred, and, above all, Indian and European. To truly *become*, indigenous people need, almost by definition, their omnipresent historical antagonists: the Castilians, the Europeans.

What basically seems to underlie this Indian fascination with souls—with its mixture of attraction and repulsion—is the theme of the double and of differentiation. But, as Deleuze observes, the question of the double is not a projection of what is inside, but an interiorizing of what is outside. The double "is not a doubling up of the One, it is a redoubling of the Other. . . . It is not the emanation of a "Self" but the immanence of a permanent other or "Non-self." In the redoubling, "the other is never a double; it is I who lives as a double of the other. I am not on the outside; I find the other in myself" (Deleuze 1986, 129). Therefore, Rimbaud's famous poetic phrase—"I is an other"—is transformed in Indian terms into "the other is I." For the Tzeltal, it is self-evident, almost to the point of being tautological, that there is no "self" that is not alien to oneself. In this respect, they do not allow themselves to be deceived by the illusion of identity.

Here I bring the discussion to a close. But the text could go on indefinitely, a little like the souls, through a process of *slok'omba*, extracting itself through duplicates or doubles, showing its inside, which consists of folds of other folds, and thus other meanings, and so on. This study is perhaps nothing but that: a Castilian ethnography of indigenous people that deals with an indigenous ethnography of Castilians, in which indigenous people adopt the identity of the Castilians, who in turn—a disturbing image of the *lab* priests and scribes still haunts me—invent themselves (we invent ourselves) from the core of the indigenous heart.

An Outline of Tzeltal Souls

In addition to the body, the person is made up of three "souls":

1. The Bird of the Heart

This is a hen (in women) and a rooster (in men); in other accounts, it is a pigeon or a grackle. It dwells permanently in the heart, and the body cannot be without it for more than a few hours. However, some *lab* are able to extract it. As the bird is identical in every person, it plays no role in distinguishing one individual from another. When the body dies, the bird is set free, only to be devoured by wild animals or the *lab*.

2. The *ch'ulel*

The *ch'ulel* is a small shadow with human form. From the outset, it has different degrees of emotions, and as a result, it provides each human being with a distinctive temperament. It is the source of language, and its experiences are those of dreams.

It exists simultaneously in two places:

2.1. Inside the *ch'iibal* Mountains

These are four mountains, one for each of Cancuc's four major lineages. The *ch'ulel* of children grow up inside these hills, where they are attended by the rest of the souls. There is also an assembly of *ch'ulel* authorities who judge souls that misbehave. Their punishment brings about illness and even death in the person's body.

2.2. Inside the Heart

The *ch'ulel* escapes from the heart, either during sleep (as a matter of habit) or as a result of some misfortune. In the course of its wanderings outside the heart, it may be kidnapped by some *lab* or other, or be held by one of the Mountain Lords. In both cases, the body of flesh back in Cancuc feels the effects and ultimately succumbs if the *ch'ulel* does not return within a reasonable, albeit variable, amount of time. After death, the *ch'ulel* find their way to a certain place deep inside the earth. Nevertheless, there are other destinations possible, depending on the circumstances of a person's death.

3. The *lab*

A highly diversified group of beings: (a) animals of every species; (b) water snakes with metal tools for heads; (c) meteors (lightning bolts, winds, etc.); (d) "illness-givers" (Catholic priests, scribes, schoolteachers, cattle ranchers, goats, sheep, owls, evangelical musicians, "mothers-fathers," etc.).

One may possess a minimum of one and a maximum of thirteen *lab*. Some of their particular abilities are evident in the person as a whole. *Lab* may bestow power to an individual, but because power is a double-edged weapon, it can mean considerable additional risks for the person.

Lab also exist simultaneously in two domains:

3.1. *Lab* may be scattered all over the face of the earth, wherever it is appropriate, depending on the habits of their species.

In this version, they may suffer injuries that have repercussions on their human body counterpart. Moreover, some *lab* inflict illness on the Indians, whether directly on the body, or by kidnapping the *ch'ulel*, or by stealing the Bird of the Heart.

3.2. Within the Heart (as a Shadow)

From here they may leave (generally to no good end) while the body sleeps, but this is not frequent. Once outside, they act just as their external version does. In truly exceptional cases, some people make conscious use of the abilities of their *lab*.

At the moment of one's death, the *lab* are ceded to an unborn boy or girl belonging to the same major lineage as the donor and in the grandfather's generation. In this way, the *lab* act as a bond through time, joining together the members of a single exogamic group, just as the *ch'ulel*, shut away in a mountain, bind them together in space.

Notes

Chapter 1

1. The obligatory reference on the fold is, of course, Deleuze (1988).

2. From the functionalist perspective of the decades between 1950 and 1970, the belief system of souls was justified, to quote Alfonso Villa Rojas (1947, 583), by "its efficacy as a means of social control, making the continued acceptance of traditional customs possible, and sanctioning the collective moral code." Perhaps the exceptions to this generalization are the essays by Julian Pitt-Rivers (1970, 1971), who examines nagualism from a certain "totemic" point of view, and the studies by Evon Vogt (1970), who also employs a "structuralist" focus. Incidentally, it is to this period that we owe numerous and detailed studies on indigenous souls in Chiapas, for example: Foster 1944; Guiteras 1946, 1965; Villa Rojas 1947, 1963; Metzger and Williams 1963; Silver 1966; Vogt 1969, 1970; Hermitte 1970; Nash 1970; Fábrega and Silver 1973; Gossen 1975; Pozas 1977; Holland 1978; and Linn 1989. The ethnographies of the Nahua, Tepehua, Totonaco, and Otomí peoples of the eastern Sierra Madre have also underscored the role of souls in the socialization process, which is frequently related to the giving of names and personal destiny: Williams García (1963); Ichon (1973); Signorini and Lupo (1989); Galinier (1990); Sandstrom (1991); Lupo (1995).

From the most recent studies carried out, two authors can be quoted. John Watanabe (1989, 1992) argues that in the community of Santiago Chimaltenango, to be in possession of a soul means to behave in a culturally appropriate way. He compares the Chimalteco idea of the soul with the concept of "having soul" found in black culture in the United States: more than an inner life force, it is an elusive element of identity and solidarity that articulates a shared experience. The two distinct kinds of souls in Chimaltenango—*naab'l* and *aanma*—belong to the province of decorum in feeling, thinking, behavior, and prayer; in short, to a way of life in accordance with local Indian rules, so that community identity is thus seen to be nurtured by means of one particular "form of being" stored in the soul. For his part, Edward Fischer (2002)—in the chapter titled "Souls, Socialization, and the Kaqchikel Self"—maintains that for the

Kaqchikel of Tecpán and Patzún, personal socialization depends to a large extent on the formation during early childhood of a heart-soul (*k'u'x*) that represents a mechanism of cultural commonality. The expression *ruk'u'x anima*, that is, "the heart-soul-essence of one's being," means the very center or essence of individual identity, an identity that in turn is related to the acceptance of communal rules.

3. In this study, I have translated *kaxlan* as "Castilian," "European," or "Mexican" and have tried to avoid using the term "mestizo," which is more commonly found in the ethnographic literature.

4. Tristan Platt's study (2001) on the "aggressive fetus" is an example of Indian history internalized in the self. For the Quechua of the Macha canton in Bolivia, the fetus is conceived as a pre-Christian ancestral soul that lives underground and has to enter the maternal womb for gestation to take place. It is an aggressive soul, greedy for blood, so that the mother has to fight not to lose her life right up to the moment it is expelled at birth. Thus, the reincarnation of pagan ancestors as Christian babies recapitulates the process of conversion to Christianity in Andean societies in the sixteenth century.

5. For a study of the transformation of indigenous society in the region in recent decades, see Jan Rus (1995).

Chapter 2

1. In the ethnography of the Chiapas highlands, reports of the Bird of the Heart are few and far between, but some do exist. In Yochib, a village in the Tzeltal municipality of Oxchuc, near Cancuc, someone explained to Villa Rojas that "the soul that the *nagual* [sorcerer-shaman] eats is like a little chicken if it's a child's, like a hen if it's a woman's, and like a rooster if it's a man's. Sometimes this soul goes for a walk by itself and without noticing, comes upon the place where *naguales* meet; then they eat it all up, and the person it belongs to stops living" (Villa Rojas 1963, 255). Roberta Montagu, on the souls of Tzeltal who lived as peons on the Ocosingo cattle ranches, writes: "Another is a soul in the form of a small bird that lives in the heart" (1970, 361). Guiteras, on Chenalhó, a Tzotzil municipality neighboring Cancuc, also makes a brief reference: "Once, Manuel described the soul that is eaten like a bird or fowl" (1965, 244).

2. But their name and exact location are unknown to many Cancuqueros (no one is supposed to know about them, although many are, in fact, suspected of having such knowledge), and few hazard a guess as to any specific place, always referring to the location of another lineage, never one's own. Nevertheless, those names and places that one may occasionally hear about tend to coincide. The first of these mountains is *ajk'abalnaj* (dark/night house) near the Tzeltal community of Yajalón, about a day's walk northward; it can be seen from several vantage points in Cancuc. The identity of the second is more uncertain, but sometimes it is located toward the east and sometimes it is thought of as the mountain at the foot of which lies the city of Tuxtla Gutiérrez, in what was formerly a Zoque-language area but is now the Spanish-speaking capital of the state of Chiapas, and located two days' walk toward the west of Cancuc.

Another possibility is Chiapa de Corzo, a former Nahuatl-speaking town, two days' walk toward the south. The third mountain is *yalanch'en* (low cave), on the slope of which lies the Tzotzil town of Venustiano Carranza, about two days' walk south, along the path that leads to the Pacific coast coffee plantations, which is why it is known to some elderly Cancuqueros. The fourth and last, *ijk'alwitz* (black mountain), is in the Tzeltal municipality of Oxchuc, where it is known as *ijk'alajaw*, no more than six hours to the southeast. These mountains are not necessarily very high, but they are all alike in having a pyramidal shape that makes them stand out plainly from the surrounding landscape.

3. The discrepancy whereby flesh-and-blood Cancuqueros are divided into three main lineages and their *ch'ulel* into four is explained in the following terms. Forty-eight years ago, the *ch'ulel* of the *boj* joined the *ijk'a*, because their *ch'iibal* mountain flooded (in other accounts, its interior was overrun by ants or its roof, a kind of dome, fell in), so their authorities asked the *ijk'a* for permission to move into their mountain. The fusion is alleged to have taken place at some time between forty to eighty years ago, that is to say, at a time on the fringes of narrative memory. Guiteras, whose Cancuc fieldwork was conducted in 1944, was told that the clans had fused "thirty years ago" (1992, 142). Nevertheless, in baptism records for the years 1771 to 1777, which are kept in the Diocesan Archive of San Cristóbal de Las Casas, some priest made a note of the neighborhood to which each newborn child belonged, and there were three: *chejeb*, the name of a contemporary lineage; *chichijun* (perhaps the *ch'ijk* of today); and *saquichen*. It is therefore possible that at some date as early as 1771, the Cancuqueros divided themselves into only three lineages, and it cannot be ruled out that these were localized. From that time, the *boj* clans are *bojil-ijk'a*, and there can be no marriage between members of both main lineages, as they are relatives. I don't know whether the difference merely expresses a tension of a "structural" sort, that is to say, the presence of only three lineages in conflict with the preference to perceive and occupy space in groups of fours, or whether there is a historical explanation and the fusion of the two kin groups actually happened in the past. In any case, for matrimonial purposes, the *boj* and the *ijk'a* constitute one single lineage, but in healing ceremonies, the shamans regard them as distinct groups and make separate offerings to their respective *ch'iibal*, for there is a suspicion that their *ch'ulel* "don't get on at all well, don't like living together." (Flesh-and-blood Cancuqueros are divided into lineages because their souls dwell in separate mountains, not the other way around.)

4. Many of these details coincide with Esther Hermitte's ethnography of Pinola (1970), a Tzeltal-speaking community like Cancuc, but a long way from it and, in terms of conventional ethnographic canons, much more "acculturated." In her description of the soul components (the term that most closely coincides with what I learned in Cancuc), she translates *ch'ulel* as "spirit" and describes it as being "just like the person, except that it gets around in the air" (1970, 51). She adds, "The spirit is in the heart or the throat, and at the same time dwells in caves" (1970, 49). This cave, *muk' nah* (which means "big house"), "is the seat of the 'government.' Dwelling there are the *me'iltatiles*, who have their own secretary, policemen, and a judge to decide the fate of their subjects and frighten off evil that comes from outside. In Muk' Nah, no tiger lives, no

hens, nor monkeys" (1970, 49). But a few pages earlier, the author also identified this cave as the place where Pinola's legendary ancestors live.

5. These are conventional "generations," each encompassing twenty years. At the age of twenty, a man is probably already a father, and by forty, a grandfather. However, in the *ch'iibal*, the distinction between "real" age groups is far from being a banal matter, as Rominko Extul pointed out to me. He was neither a shaman nor a *principal*, he had never occupied any office of note, and he did not speak a word of Spanish, but he may well have been more than sixty years old. He gave a lot of weight to the fact that in *ch'iibal* the sanctioned age divisions were, and had to be, respected, whereas in Cancuc, people younger than he behaved as if they were his elder. In fact, the age principle is the top rung in the ladder of distinctions into which the social hierarchy is divided, even if, in practice, much liberty is taken with it. In a world where no one keeps track of the years, there are some who shift positions in the pecking order by adding on to their age or by taking it from others. There are some young men who will not shave the down (if it grows at all) on their chins or upper lip, as beards or mustaches are a privilege of the eldest; or on greeting someone they will address him inappropriately; or, as if they were old men, they will not lean over to kiss the nose or cheek of their elders. According to Rominko Extul, none of this happens in the *ch'iibal*.

6. Definitions of the term *ch'ibal* as found in the *Diccionario Maya Cordomex* (Barrera Vásquez 1980), cited by Hopkins (1988): 1. *Diccionario de Motul* (Maya-Spanish): "caste, lineage, direct descent." 2. *Diccionario de Motul* (Spanish-Maya): "caste, lineage, nation." 3. Vienna: "generation or lineage on the father's side; caste, generally by lineage"; (*Ah*) *ch'ibal*, "noble by lineage or reputation." 4. San Francisco (Pío Pérez): "direct descent or lineage on the father's side; offspring on the male side."

7. In ritual idiom, in relation to its role as soul council, the *ch'iibal* bears the titles of *muk'ul naj*, "big house"; *naj-ta-lum*, "house on earth"; *komento witz*, "mountain-convent"; and *kolibal*, a possibly archaic term whose meaning, unknown to many, seems to be "altar of the group of kins."

8. The few Cancuqueros who emigrate to other places (other municipal districts like Pantelhó or new zones of colonization that have opened up in the Lacandon jungle) still retain their *ch'ulel* in the *ch'iibal* of their respective lineage. That is also what happened around 1920, when many Cancuqueros had to emigrate to avoid the consequences of the Mexican revolutionary war that was underway in the heart of Chiapas. It seems that while living in Indian villages like Chilón or Sitalá, they preserved their clan name and continued praying to their *ch'iibal*. To this day, their descendants are considered "relatives" by Cancuqueros, and it is said that if someone migrates to those places, they must help anyone belonging to their lineage, though not necessarily those of the other Cancuc lineages. One consequence of this is that the criterion of municipality (that is, neighborhood or physical-geographical location, as opposed to kinship) is not the only way to define the general identity of the Cancuqueros.

9. This expression is obviously a contradiction. With it, I try to reconcile the idea that the *lab* is akin to a gas or a vapor, while at the same time possessing a given form.

10. There is one important exception. Animals owned by the Mountain Lords (also known as "Animal Lords") cannot be *lab*. These animals live in pens inside the hills and are sometimes let loose to roam the surface of the earth. They include most reptiles, especially ground snakes that occasionally take on the form of another animal when they remain inside the hill (a dog, for example, to keep its lord company); armadillos; frogs and toads, which also forecast rain; bulls and cows; deer and rabbits who, no matter how much you chase them, "don't let themselves get caught" unless the lord has given the hunter permission, which is sought in a special ceremony (*mixa*) at the household altar; crocodiles and iguanas; and all the river and lake fish that live inside the mountains and only come out during the rainy season and return with the onset of the dry season. All these animals are frequently described as "relatives" of the Mountain Lords, occasionally as the lords themselves in altered form. The mermaid (upper half woman, lower half fish), and the *tzotzk'ab* (hairy hand) monster are also the alter egos of the Mountain Lords.

11. Eugenio Maurer (1983, 401) briefly mentions this type of *lab* in his ethnography of Guaquitepec.

12. The region's ethnography yields a few references to "priests." Concerning *naguales* (wizards) of Yochib, Villa Rojas points out, "In most cases the *nagual* is thought of as an animal, a dog, a lizard or a hawk. But some *naguales* assume diminutive human form, dwarfs not three feet high, dressed all in black, in the vestments of Catholic bishops or clergymen. These are dangerous and very powerful" (Villa Rojas 1947, 583). Also Maurer on the Guaquitepec community: ". . . a little father, one meter tall that, wearing a little soutane, strolls the village streets at night working great mischief among the people" (1983, 403). However, in her 1944 ethnography of Cancuc, Guiteras provides us with the most detailed description: "The *pále* is always described as a little creature, about 50 centimeters tall, like a doll. Miguel says that it is like 'the father who baptizes'; with his 'little black gown like a long, little smock and his little black shoes.' Others say 'he's little, with his little hat and his little shoes.' The *wispa* gives orders to the *pále*. The *pále* has his little wife and his mother. Sometimes the mother with her little white head has been spotted spinning thread on a hilltop" (1990, 227–228). Some pages earlier it is stated: "The common or garden *pále* is the one that goes looking from house to house, reporting his observations to the *wispa*, who in turn gives orders to the *pále* 'seated in his house' . . . The *me'el pále* is also *saquil-cú* (because she is dressed in white). She is the wife of the *pále*, 'because the bastard has his little woman.' She is the one who wanders about by day, and he, 'because he's a man, wanders by night.' . . . The *pále* has a little dog that eats up the bones thrown to it by the *pále* when he's eating the *ch'ulel*" (italics and translation mine; Guiteras 1990, 219).

13. The title *provisor* may come from Provisor, a Spanish church official whose job is to prosecute misdeeds. I thank Mario H. Ruz for calling this to my attention.

14. Brent Berlin defines the numerical classifier *kun* as "large piles of individuated objects with maximal horizontal extension" (1978, 201).

15. I must confess to not finding in Cancuc such an immediate correlation between social status and *lab* category as that frequently emphasized in ethnog-

raphies of the area. Unlike (perhaps in opposition to) the *ch'iibal*, where everything is a matter of normative authority, the world of the *lab* is concerned with the exercise of power, of raw power. Nevertheless, as the attribution of *lab* is fraught with uncertainties, it is a remarkably contingent power.

16. There is a chance that a "transformation" might take place that has nothing to do with any of the soul components. It concerns the *yalem bak'et*, somebody who during the night goes to a cross beside a path or spring, strips off his flesh down to his bare bones, and then wanders around causing damage (without flesh, bones are dangerous). Nevertheless, his action is "magic," as he achieves the shedding and later restoration of the flesh by saying some special words that have an effect over the body; no soul type has any part in this. If you find some flesh lying next to a cross, all you have to do to prevent the bones from getting back together with it again is to sprinkle it with a little salt.

17. In a healing case undertaken by Xun P'in, the sick person, an old man, not only did not get better, but actually got worse. After several days had passed, another shaman friend of Xun (unusual indeed, given that there is a certain rivalry for prestige and very little cooperation among shamans) stated his opinion that there was no possible cure. He then hazarded the guess that if the sick person had not yet died, it was because he had not yet found a suitable woman to deposit his *lab* in. Then he asked the sick man's sons, who were present, if their wives were pregnant. None was, which seemed to confirm his suspicion. Nevertheless, a few days later, the patient recovered.

18. One final aspect of souls remains to be mentioned, although it may be regarded as a rather tangential detail, for it is not directly related to the heart or to the rest of life on the plane of souls. The Tzeltal conceive of a rectangular platform located up in the air where myriad white candles are set up, one for the life of each and every human on earth, whether Indian or not. Some say that the candles are in the care of an enigmatic *jtatik velarol* (Our Father Watchman). Just at the very moment a person is born, and not before, one of these candles is lit, gradually burning itself down, slowly, until at last it goes out, and with it the span of that person's life comes to an end as well. The candle is referred to as *orail* (from the Spanish *hora*, "hour"), or "span of life." This feature coincides substantially with Gossen's description (1975) of it in the Tzotzil community of Chamula.

19. This third class of relationship may be the one that has been preserved or elaborated in certain Tzotzil communities. I am thinking of Holland's information concerning San Andrés Larráinzar: "On each step of the holy mountain (*chebal*) there is a room where the ancestral gods judge the behavior of their animal companions" (1978, 115). Additionally, Vogt's information suggests that in Zinacantán the "ancestral gods" that live in a mountain keep the animal spirits in "pens," where they look after them and punish them (1969, 383–385).

Chapter 3

1. Brian Stross (1974) records in the following list the different "speech event factors" by means of which the Tzeltal of Tenejapa assess a given form of

speech: personality of the speaker, physical condition of the speaker, emotional state of the speaker, posture of the speaker's body, location of the speaker, the speaker's social identity, voice quality, volubility, number of participants, spatial distribution of participants, kind of place where they are speaking, sounds and gestures that accompany words, length and sequence of communication, degree of truth, subject at hand, and verbal genre to which what is said corresponds.

2. Nicknames are a good way of pinpointing the kind of detail that stands out most to Cancuqueros. Virtually all children have a nickname, given to them by their own parents in order to ward off any harm that may come to them through the use of their real name. Examples are "Big Ears," "Little Squirrel" (someone who hoards all he finds), "Peach" (for the fuzz on his skin), "Duck" (for someone's gait), "Anthony the Loafer" (like the character in a tale, this one does nothing but sleep). If children's nicknames are used beyond the limits of the domestic group, they may become a fixture for adulthood. However, it is not uncommon for more nicknames to be given in the course of life. For example: *mamal isim*, "Mr. Mustache" (for someone who had a mustache from his youth and did not shave it off); *me'k'ajk'*, "Mother Fire" (although a man's nickname, because he boasted of having a meteor *lab*); *ajk'*, "Tortoise" (for a sluggish gait); *me'el manta*, after the texture of a blanket, Spanish *manta* (something woven too coarsely); *mal kuin*, "María Cramp" (someone with an ungainly way of walking). Other nicknames have to do with some former activity: someone is nicknamed *pinka* because as a young man he worked on the coffee plantations (Sp. *fincas*). From time to time, nicknames are passed on to the following generation, but when this happens, the detail for which it was given to the father is assumed to be present in the son. On nicknames in the Tzotzil community of Zinacantán, see Collier and Bricker (1970).

3. For example, Hermitte (1970), Laughlin (1966, 1988), Tedlock (1981), Garza (1990).

4. Both Slocum and Gerdel in their Tzeltal vocabulary of Bachajón (1981) and Laughlin in his Tzotzil dictionary of Zinacantán (1975) distinguish *nop* in its meanings of "to learn" and "proximity." Even so, it is plain to me that in Tzeltal, both meanings form part of the same conceptual area: something like learning by contiguity.

5. Recently, Philippe Descola (2005) has drawn extensively and intensively on this relationship, calling it "analogical mode of identification," or "analogical ontology."

6. Roland Barthes (1982a) distinguishes between at least three possible ways of imagining the sign: symbolically, paradigmatically, and syntagmatically. The symbolic conscience conceives of the sign as existing in a sort of vertical relationship between the signifier and the signified. For example, the group of beliefs and practices that make up Christianity are symbolized under the cross. This vertical nature entails two consequences: (a) the relationship tends to be solitary, because the symbol is self-sustaining in the world; and (b) what is of interest in the sign is the signified, the signifier being a fixed element.

The sign may also be understood as forming part of a paradigm or system. This system implies that for each sign there is a pool of forms from which it is distinguished by the minimum difference that is necessary and sufficient to bring about a change of meaning. The color red means "forbidden" insofar as it is opposed to green, yellow, or the absence of color. In the system, the relationship of bilaterality characteristic of the symbolic relationship is substituted with a quadrilateral relationship. This is the relationship of Greimas's semiotic square or the relationship of "homology" between two or more series that, according to Levi-Strauss, gives meaning to totemism.

In the third, syntagmatical kind of relationship (which is of most interest for my purposes, as it comes closest to what I wish to say about the Tzeltal), the sign, according to Barthes, is no longer situated in relation to its (virtual) "brothers," but to its (present) "neighbors." Its job is to create between two aspects a relationship of meaning analogous to that which joins words within a phrase; the sign is thus related to others on the strength of its antecedents or its successors. It may be thought of as being a "functional" relationship, in the two senses of the word: "variable" and "of use." In an observation that I find most interesting, Barthes asserts that of the three kinds of relationship, the syntagmatic is the one that shuns the signified most easily.

7. I am also thinking here of Carlo Ginzburg's observations regarding what he calls the "elastic rigor" of the "evidential paradigm" in his essay "Clues: Roots of an Evidential Paradigm." He finds it to be an attitude "directed toward the analysis of individual cases, which can only be reconstructed by means of traces, symbols, signs" (1989, 146); those forms of knowledge that are "more tightly bound to everyday experience or, more precisely, to every situation in which the uniqueness of the data and the impossibility of substituting them are, as far as the people involved are concerned, decisive" (1989, 163). I also have in mind the remarks of Peter Mason regarding "fragmentary writing" (1993).

8. Ruz notes that in Domingo de Ara's Tzeltal vocabulary, "Next to the translation for 'to divine by book' appear more faintly the words *tococ tazcab*, apparently in connection with *cabui*, 'to see as from afar'; *tac*, 'to beseech'; and *oc*, 'scrutinize.' However, another possible, but less probable, reading would be *tacoc, ta zcab*, which could be translated as '/to divine/ in the foot, in the hand'. . ." (1985, 232). Personally, I favor the second interpretation.

9. As John Haviland says in his study of gossip in the community of Zinacantán, "Gossip alludes to otherwise inaccessible beliefs about 'hot' and 'cold', foods and diseases, about fertility and luck, about buried treasure and supernatural means to gain wealth, about the medicinal efficacy of various herbs and preparation, and so on. I call these beliefs inaccessible because they are infrequently expounded in other contexts; gossip, as the most common form of narrative, is almost uniquely responsible for keeping alive speculation about such matters" (1977, 57).

Chapter 4

1. There is a direct similitude between the Tzeltal *ch'iibal* mountains and the pre-Hispanic Quiché "big houses" in Guatemala. According to Robert Car-

mack's study (1979), the major lineages in Utatlán, the ancient Quiché capital, identified themselves with particular buildings, known as *nim já*, "big houses." These were centers with ritual functions, such as the storage of sacred bundles that the family's ancestors had acquired in the mythical city of Tulán, from where they had set forth in the distant past. Basically, they were buildings where the office holders related to the lineage's political and administrative affairs (including the administration of justice) gathered. Historical sources seem to underscore (perhaps echoing their Quiché informants' repeated descriptions of these places that had been destroyed by the Spaniards only shortly before) the fact that the *principales* of the lineages held audience in the "big house." Here, they sat on low, short-legged chairs covered with straw mats (a traditional symbol of authority), arranged on long daises joined to the wall (a detail confirmed by later excavation of the city). Furthermore, in a pictograph in the *Título de Totonicapán* (Carmack 1979, 189) that schematically represents the city of Utatlán, four of these "big houses" are drawn, one for each of the major lineages—Ajaw Q'uiché, Nimá Rajob Achij, K'alel Nijayib, and Q'uikab Ajpop Cawek—that made up Quiché society. Each building occupies one corner of the rectangle that formed the city plan, and they were drawn in the shape of a truncated pyramid topped by a kind of cupola.

It even seems as if the extraordinarily elaborate system of souls among the Tzeltal is in some way an attempt to compensate for the imbalance resulting from the lack of a scheme of "real" indigenous institutional relations, for reasons of historical privation.

2. Some meanings for *loc* (*lok'*), the root of *slok'omba*, as given in Fray Domingo de Ara's sixteenth-century Tzeltal vocabulary (1986, 322) are as follows: *loc:* "to set free"; *loc:* "to be born, as corn, a plant, etc."; *loquel:* "birth, as that of the sun"; *loc:* "to redeem a captive or prisoner"; *loctay:* "to resemble one's own father"; *loctay:* "to substitute"; *loctay:* "to transfer"; *locombahil:* "statue like of a saint."

3. It cannot be ruled out completely that in past configurations of the details of the *ch'iibal*, Christian descriptions of heaven and hell and, perhaps, purgatory, might have played a part, just as modern skyscrapers show up in today's descriptions. According to Le Goff (1984), the mountain is a geographical element fundamental to the location of purgatory, as in Dante.

4. As reflected in Haviland's (1989) article "They Had a Very Great Many Photographs," what apparently most attracted the attention of a Tzotzil Indian from Zinacantán about the life of the American anthropologists, when he visited them at Harvard in the 1960s, was the large quantity of photographs they had, particularly of Zinacantán, both in their homes, and at the university, everywhere for that matter, and the fact that, between drinks, they would project them (slides) on any occasion, to visiting friends, for example.

5. In this world of unlimited resources, there appears to be only one deficiency: the *ch'ulel* chronically suffer from a shortage of certain kinds of sustenance, especially liquor. To obtain this, they depend on periodic offerings provided to them by the bodily originals at the household altar (what passes through the cross is the immaterial substance of the foodstuffs, their *ch'ul*).

This detail (hunger and above all the unquenchable thirst for liquor) is undoubtedly another manifestation of the typical and almost universal "thirst of the dead" (Eliade 1958); but for the Tzeltal people, the role of radical alterity, which in other cultural traditions is played by the dead, falls to the souls.

6. This type of soul existed in the distant Mesoamerican past. After all, the nomadic bands of hunters who crossed the Bering Strait to America from Siberia could not have carried with them very different ideas. As for the Classic period of Maya civilization, which has not so far supplied abundant evidence regarding this kind of belief, Stephen Houston and David Stuart (1989) have argued that Maya writing and some artistic representations are documentary proof of the existence of the phenomenon of the relationship with "companion beings," as it is known in contemporary ethnography, and they go on to suggest that this concept was central to Classic Maya religion. The evidence rests on the assumption that the glyph read phonetically as *way* (which, as they point out, is the root in many modern languages of "to sleep" and "to dream," but which in addition frequently covers the notion of "companion animal," shaman, sorcerer, etc.) is the sign that indicates the relationship of co-essence between a historical figure—usually a member of the elite classes as represented in ceramics, lintels, stelae, and the like—and a "supernatural" being. If the hypothesis is correct, the authors observe that the current view of Classic Maya religion will have to be modified, given that many of the figures previously considered to be gods or inhabitants of the "underworld" would no longer be so; they would be the "souls," co-essential forms of living human beings. See also Justeson and Kaufman (1993).

7. The Tzeltal meal basically consists of corn and beans, prepared and combined in many ways, sometimes accompanied by cooked wild greens. There is no mixing with Castilian food. In contrast, "Castilian" foodstuffs are the basics of the meals of religious office holders, often mixed with autochthonous foods. The most common meal would be a bowl of broth made with chili, squash seeds, peppers, and small bits of meat (depending on the kind of ceremony, chicken, pork, or beef), all covered with the meat's fat (from an Indian perspective, greasy food is typical of "Castilian cooking"); instead of meat, hard-boiled eggs or boiled potatoes may be added. In addition, if the *mayordomo* so permits, wheat bread rolls may be served. There are usually stacks of tortillas that are torn apart and dipped into the broth. During the meal, liquor and sometimes coffee is consumed as well. It is, in short, a mixed repast.

8. It is a detail that Brian Stross has also observed in the Tzeltal community of Tenejapa (1973).

9. In contrast, in the city of San Cristóbal de Las Casas, drunk Indians usually fall on sidewalks, perhaps in an effort to avoid the risk of being run over by cars. Or is it because, until a few decades ago, Indians were forbidden to walk on pavements?

10. Ruth Bunzel (1940) describes alcoholic conduct in Chamula in detail during the 1930s in a way that ties in exactly with what I was able to observe in Cancuc six decades later. My observations also coincide in essence with the classic study by Christine Eber (1995) on liquor consumption and alcoholic

conduct and their effect on community and domestic life in a village in the Chiapas highlands.

11. This fact also occurs in the Andean region, in both colonial and contemporary times; see, for example, Thierry Saignes (1993).

12. This raises the thorny issue of "responsibility" and how it is distributed among the different intentionalities. In principle, the body has no responsibility (in relation to other flesh-and-blood Tzeltal) for what its *ch'ulel* or its outside *lab* do, nor for the actions of its internal versions, for example, the *ch'ulel* or the *lab* who abandon the body while it is sleeping, or for what they do while the body is intoxicated. However, if the body is on its feet and sober, it has full responsibility. In trials in Cancuc's town hall, when a woman accuses her husband of having beaten her (as they do frequently), what the court is chiefly interested in ascertaining is whether the husband was drunk or sober. (A different case would be if the situation were recurrent, in which case the wife would accuse the husband of getting drunk too often, not of beating her.) In fact, the most common trials in Cancuc deal with problems of conjugal responsibility and, to a lesser extent, disputes over farmland and thefts. Problems involving "feelings" are better judged in the *ch'iibal* mountain, where justice is enacted on the *ch'ulel*. As for the *lab*, it is doubtful they are judged at all (if they are restrained, it is, as with any animal, so that they do not put themselves in danger). Nevertheless, there are situations in which these distinct planes partially depend upon each other. An example would be when a man of flesh and blood decides to take it into his own hands to settle matters (maybe when he suspects there has been an "illness given," for example), even though he has no right to do so. I was told that some years before, in the neighboring community of Tenejapa, the authorities had executed some recognized "illness-givers," but comments on the case were all disapproving. In Cancuc, too, apparently in the 1920s, the people took advantage of violent factional conflicts and many men who were suspected of being "complete men" were killed.

13. "The transcultural diffusion of myths and rites revolving around physiological asymmetry," says Ginzburg (1991, 241–242), "most probably has its psychological roots in this minimal, elementary perception that the human species has of itself, of its bodily image. Anything that modifies this image on a literal or metaphorical plane, therefore, seems particularly suited to express an experience that exceeds the limits of what is human." This "minimal perception" is, according to Ginzburg, based in turn on Rodney Needham's work, that of being a living, two-legged (that is, upright), and symmetrical being.

Chapter 5

1. The turkey resembles the hen in many respects, except in its indigenous origin. Significantly, it is never conceived of as a Bird of the Heart, nor is it ever used in healing ceremonies.

2. In one Guatemalan account, the nagual of the Spanish conqueror Pedro de

Alvarado was a pigeon. On the battlefield where Spanish troops fought against those of the Quiché chieftain Tecún Umán, Alvarado's pigeon-nagual attacked the quetzal-nagual of Tecún Umán while in flight. As the story goes, once the latter was dead, the Spaniards were able to conquer the Quiché kingdom.

3. With an alimentary logic fundamentally mirroring that of the contemporary Tzeltal, but in another time (1558) and in another place (Central Mexico), Juan Tetón, an indigenous leader of a nativist cult, warned other Nahua:

> Listen, all of you! . . . Do you know what our grandfathers are saying? That when it is time for us to bind the years [at the end of the "century"], utter darkness will fall, the *tzitzime* will descend upon us, they will eat us and there will be a transformation. Those who were baptized, those who believed in God, will change into something else. He who eats cow's meat will become a cow; he who eats pig's meat will become a pig; he who eats lamb will become a lamb and will be dressed in its fleece; he who eats rooster will become a rooster. Everyone will turn into their food . . . (León-Portilla 1978, 155–169)

4. On the other hand, the pig, an animal that is occasionally bred in Cancuc and is not considered offensive, seems to have been assimilated with relative ease. In fact, it is given the same name as the indigenous wild pig (*chitam*). Meanwhile, bulls and cows have not been transformed into souls, but rather into companions of Mountain Lords. Quite the contrary occurs in Pinola, a Tzeltal village to the south, which for many years has had a much closer relationship with the cattle ranches in the region of Los Llanos; in Pinola, they are nagual, a *lab* (Hermitte 1970).

5. Long after Remesal's time, in 1797, the gold medal of the province's patriotic society was awarded to Matías de Córdova, a liberal friar who supported the independence movement and later established the Economic Society of Chiapas, for his dissertation entitled "Utilidad de que todos los indios y ladinos calcen a la española, y medios de conseguirlo sin violencia, coacción ni mandato" (García de León 1985, 1:132), a text on the usefulness for all Indians and Ladinos to model themselves as Spaniards and how this could be achieved without violence, coercion, or mandate.

6. To cite only a few of these works: Klein (1970); Bricker (1981); Gosner (1992); Martínez Peláez (n.d.).

7. The course of events, as presented by Viqueira (1997), seems to show how the Indians cast off Christian religious practices as the rebellion stumbled from one failure to the next, resorting instead to other practices that the chronicles call "witchcraft" or "superstitions." When all is said and done, these practices have much to do with the soul entities. Nevertheless, from an Indian viewpoint, the rebels began to make use of fringe practices (that is, Christian practices) in order to move backward to more central, more culturally familiar "religious forms" related to "soul power." This development probably goes hand in hand with the progressive loss among rebel leadership of people connected to the colonial institutions, their positions being filled by others much more distant socially from those institutions.

Chapter 6

1. For example, see the "Leyenda de los soles," as it appears in León-Portilla (1959, 110–114), on successive destructions of the world. Regarding the Nahua conception of history, Louise Burkhart notes that "crisis in history could be represented as an encroachment of the periphery onto the center. The most striking example is the famine of 1450–54. Wild animals invaded the cities, seeking human prey. People left home to sell themselves as slaves to the morally inferior Totonacs and Huaxtecs . . ." (1989, 76).

2. There are five or six short tales that illustrate the misfortunes resulting from incorrect behavior and conclude with a small "moral." The woman who refused to accept the husband proposed by the elders of the lineage died; the man who swapped identity with a vulture to get out of working in the cornfield was forced to eat carrion the rest of his life; the child who wanted to count all the stars in the sky died in the attempt; the man whose wife died had to follow her to the world of the dead.

3. The divide between the festival calendar and the Tzeltal calendar is bridged only once: The final day of the three that constitute the fiesta of San Juan (St. John the Evangelist), Cancuc's patron saint, coincides with the first day of the month after the only five-day month, referred to as *ch'ay k'in*.

4. That must explain why the "Carnivals" in the Indian communities of Chiapas have been the subject of considerable symbolic interpretations, while analysis of the other celebrations in the municipal head towns is noticeably absent. I agree that Carnival or equivalent humorous festivals represent an important exception within the norm represented by other festivals in the Chiapas highlands (Bricker 1981; Gossen 1986).

5. For some years, the group of Cancuc Catholics has built a second nativity, this time on the high altar and not in the south side of the church, in which images of the Christ Child are placed in a manger, along with the Virgin and Joseph, all representations of relatively recent acquisition. In this case, some Catholics do detect a relationship between the scene represented and some other story contained in "the word of God," the Bible. However, their notion of the story is muddled: a young woman married to an old man, unable to beget children because of his age, is made pregnant by a pigeon (*palóma-mut*), which angers the old man . . .

6. There may be a direct connection in the ethnography of the Chiapas highlands between the difficulty of seeing public ceremonies, fiestas, as an imitation (a useless excess) and the bewilderment caused among anthropologists by the expense (superfluous, useless, especially from the perspective of economic utilitarianism) of public ceremonies, the system of *cargos* (public offices), etc.

7. In some Indian communities of the Chiapas highlands, one can see that the square is spilling over the limits that contained it for centuries and is beginning to contaminate the layout of the Amerindian spaces with the slow appearance of streets, straight lines and corners, houses in rows, and a change in building materials: tiles replacing thatch, brick for adobe, and so on.

8. Not only the marvel but even the account of it reproduce with uncanny

fidelity the Spanish narrative genre of miraculous apparitions of local patron saints and virgins. The Virgin Mary appears before a young girl (María de la Candelaria) beside a spring and asks for a house (a hermitage) to be built for her, whereupon the girl informs the village's civil authorities, who verify the miracle and then lead the image of the Virgin in solemn procession to the village or its outskirts, where they build a small sanctuary.

9. It is odd that although the sun (perhaps the only Cancuc "deity" in the most conventional sense of the word), together with the moon, is a being that something is known about, since it is met with in the story of Xut, where the younger brother killed his older brother, went up to the sky, and became the sun. It nevertheless lacks any perceptible representation in ritual and therefore receives no attention in protocol. In contrast, the Tzeltal can tell very little about Jesus Christ and the other saints, but they are the object of ceremonial attention on any occasion throughout the year. The sun and Jesus Christ are not the same figure (contrary, it seems, to what some Tzotzil communities believe [Gossen 1974; Holland 1978], and perhaps some Tzeltal ones, too [Nash 1970]): The sun exists as a personage in mythology; Jesus Christ is more a nonpersonage whose exclusive existence is in ritual. One is spoken about, the other is looked after. On this level, it looks like the unsolvable paradox of a bifurcated, but not mixed, representation of the world.

10. According to one brief story, there was a man who descended to the deepest reaches of the earth and saw that there the *suk it* (literally, "plugged orifice") had their dwelling place. They were sexless and anusless (hence their name) albino dwarves, whose only sustenance was the odors given off by food, and who sported large hats to protect them from the sun whenever it passed through the underworld when it was night on earth. However, of all the people I consulted for accounts, this tale was only known to one family; and no one else recognized it when I specifically asked about it. In this and other similar cases, it is as if some vestige of ancient knowledge survived, closeted away somewhere and out of context, only to be transmitted within the heart of domestic groups, as if that knowledge itself, of little import socially but never falling so low as to disintegrate completely, remained in a latent state, awaiting better times when it might be resurrected.

11. According to Evon Vogt, the crosses surrounding the Tzotzil village of Zinacantán are decorated with green pine branches on their "outer" side, while their "inner" side (the side facing toward the houses) is adorned with geraniums. In several publications (e.g., 1976, 263), the author interprets this distinction between wild plants (the pine) and cultivated plants (the geranium) as marking the difference between the "natural," wild space, and the human, socialized space.

12. However, this is not the case for the region's Spanish speakers, namely Ladinos, who prefer to trade with the Indians away from the markets, as is to be inferred from the common noun given to some women, "interceptors" (*atajadoras*, a name made notorious by Rosario Castellanos in her novel *Oficio de tinieblas*), because they "intercept" the Indians on the pathways before they can reach the market at San Cristóbal de Las Casas to sell their goods.

13. In other words, in Cancuc, no true "conversion" is ever produced. There

is nothing similar to the procedures for the reconstruction of one's being that Jorge Klor de Alva (1988) identifies in Christian penitential practices ("with its sacramental confession and, more important still, its imposition of intro-spective tactics for self-training, its diffusion of an awareness of new ways of acting perversely, and its insistence on autobiographical discourse aimed at the divulging of an individual's innermost thoughts and actions, which contributed to the transformation of the Nahua into the Other, not only of the Europeans, but also of themselves" [1988, 74]) established by the priests among the Nahua in Central Mexico shortly after the conquest to shape a self-consciousness that permitted colonial domination.

Glossary

ak'chamel   Illness-giver, a type of *lab* soul.

ajaw   Mountain Lord; lightning.

bak'etal   The carnal body.

cabildo (Sp.)   The municipal corporation; the township building.

Cancuquero (Sp.)   Person from the municipality of Cancuc.

ch'abajel   To silence; healing ceremony and song to recover a lost or abducted soul.

ch'abajom   Shaman; specialist on *ch'abajel* ceremonies.

chajpan   Group; kinship group.

chanbalam   Snake-jaguar; animals.

ch'iibal   "The place to grow"; every mountain interior inhabited by the *ch'ulel* souls of the members of each major lineage.

chukel   Jail, imprisonment; also imprisonment of the souls.

ch'ul   Sacred; that which is "other"; the other dimension of being.

ch'ulchan   Sky; the other of the earth.

ch'ulel   One of the types of souls, with the same figure of the human body, that is housed in the heart.

ch'ulelal   Soul of a dead person.

ch'ulna   The church building.

jamalal   Open space; the space warmed and illuminated by the sun, as opposed to the *ch'ul*, or "sacred" state.

jun kuil mamil   "One grandmother-grandfather"; sublineage.

kawilto   Elder trustee of the community, also know as a *principal*.

kaxlan   Nonindigenous Spanish-speaking person; European; Mexican; foreign product.

kexlal   Shame; disease caused by shame.

k'op   Word, language; conflict, war.

lab   One of the types of souls, an animal, meteor, or human figure; similar to what is known in the literature as a nagual.

Ladino (Sp.)   Spanish-speaking person in Chiapas and Guatemala.

mam   Grandfather; grandson.

may   Ground wild tobacco mixed with lime (a ritual substance).

mayordomo (Sp.)   A ritual post in a sodality for the care of the saints.

me'tiktatik   A hostile type of *lab* soul with the appearance of elderly women and men.

mutil o'tan   Bird of the Heart, one of the souls that is a bird.

nagual   In Mesoamerican studies, a spirit companion, usually an animal.

nop   To learn and think through the head, as opposed to the heart.

o'tan   Heart.

pále   A very hostile class of *lab* soul with the appearance of a Catholic priest.

pik'abal   Diagnostician through the pulse.

poxil   Medicine; healing ceremony and song addressed to remove a pathogenic intrusive object.

poxtaywanej   Ritual specialist on *poxil* ceremonies.

principal (Sp.)   Elder trustee of the community.

San Cristóbal de Las Casas   The urban center of highland Chiapas.

slok'omba   Image, photograph; any of the statues of saints in the church.

talel   "That which comes as given"; the innate; personal character; tradition; the souls.

winik   Human being.

Bibliography

Aguirre Beltrán, Gonzalo. 1963. *Medicina y magia: El proceso de aculturación en la estructura colonial.* Mexico City: Instituto Nacional Indigenista.

Ara, Domingo de. 1986. *Vocabulario de lengua tzeldal según el orden de Copana-bastla.* Ed. Mario H. Ruz. Mexico City: Universidad Nacional Autónoma de México.

Aramoni, Dolores. 1992. *Los refugios de lo sagrado: Religiosidad, conflicto y resistencia entre los zoques de Chiapas.* Mexico City: Consejo Nacional para la Cultura y las Artes.

Barrera Vásquez, Alfredo (dir.). 1980. *Diccionario Maya Cordomex; Maya-Español, Español-Maya.* Mérida, Yucatán, Mexico: Cordomex.

Barthes, Roland. 1982a. "The Imagination of the Sign." In *A Barthes Reader,* ed. Susan Sontag, pp. 211–217. New York: Noonday Press.

———. 1982b. "Lesson in Writing." In *A Barthes Reader,* ed. Susan Sontag, pp. 305–316. New York: Noonday Press.

Basso, Keith. 1972. "To Give Up on Words: Silence in Western Apache Culture." In *Language and Social Context,* ed. Pier Paolo Giglioli, pp. 67–86. Middlesex: Penguin Education.

Benjamin, Thomas L. 1990. *El camino a Leviatán: Chiapas y el Estado mexicano 1891–1947.* Mexico City: Consejo Nacional para la Cultura y las Artes.

Berlin, Brent. 1978. *Tzeltal Numeral Classifiers.* The Hague: Mouton.

Berlin, Brent, Dennis E. Breedlove, and Paul Raven. 1974. *Principles of Tzeltal Plant Classification: An Introduction to the Botanical Ethnography of Mayan-Speaking People of Highland Chiapas.* New York: Academic Press.

Berlin, Brent, and Terrence Kaufman (with the assistance of Luisa Maffi). 1990. *Un Diccionario Básico del Tzeltal de Tenejapa, Chiapas, México.* San Cristóbal de las Casas, Chiapas, Mexico: PROCOMITH.

Breton, Alain, and Aurore Becquelin-Monod. 1989. "'Mais j'ai transmis l'espérance . . .' . Étude d'une priere de guérison tzeltal." *Amerindia* 14 (supplement, 113 pp.).

Bricker, Victoria. 1981. *The Indian Christ, the Indian King: The Historical Substrate of Maya Myth and Ritual.* Austin: University of Texas Press.

Bunzel, Ruth. 1940. "The Role of Alcoholism in Two Central American Cultures." *Psychiatry* 3: 361–387.

Burkhart, Louise M. 1989. *The Slippery Earth: Nahua-Christian Moral Dialogue in Sixteenth-Century Mexico.* Tucson: University of Arizona Press.

Carmack, Robert M. 1979. *Evolución del reino quiché.* Guatemala City: Piedra Santa.

———. 1983. "Spanish-Indian Relations in Highland Guatemala, 1800–1944." In *Spaniards and Indians in Southeastern Mesoamerica: Essays on the History of Ethnic Relations,* ed. Murdo Macleod and Robert Wasserstrom, pp. 215–252. Lincoln: University of Nebraska Press.

Castaneda, Carlos. 1987. *The Power of Silence.* New York: Simon and Schuster.

Chapin, Norman M. 1983. "Curing among the San Blas Kuna of Panama." Ph.D. diss., Dept. of Anthropology, University of Arizona.

Chiapas: XI Censo General de Población y Vivienda. 1991. *Chiapas: XI Censo General de Población y Vivienda, 1990: Resultados definitivos.* Aguascalientes, Ag., Mexico: Instituto Nacional de Estadística, Geografía e Informática.

Collier, George A., and Victoria R. Bricker. 1970. "Nicknames and Social Structure in Zinacantan." *American Anthropologist* 70: 289–302.

Collier, Jane. 1973. *Law and Social Change in Zinacantán.* Stanford: Stanford University Press.

Comaroff, Jean, and John Comaroff. 1991. *Of Revelation and Revolution: Christianity, Colonialism and Consciousness in South Africa.* Vol. 1. Chicago: University of Chicago Press.

Cook, Garrett. 1986. "Quichean Folk Theology and Southern Maya Supernaturalism." In *Symbol and Meaning Beyond the Closed Community,* ed. Gary Gossen, pp. 139–155. Albany, N.Y.: Institute for Mesoamerican Studies.

Corominas, Joan. 1961. *Breve diccionario etimológico de la lengua castellana.* Madrid: Gredos.

Deleuze, Gilles. 1986. *Foucault.* Paris: Les Editions de Minuit.

———. 1988. *Le pli: Leibniz et le Baroque.* Paris: Les Editions de Minuit.

Descola, Philippe. 2005. *Par-delà nature et culture.* Paris: Gallimard.

Eber, Christine. 1995. *Women and Alcohol in a Highland Maya Town: Water of Hope, Water of Sorrow.* Austin: University of Texas Press.

Eliade, Mircea. 1958. *Patterns in Comparative Religion.* New York: Meridian Books.

Fábrega, Horacio, and Daniel Silver. 1973. *Illness and Shamanistic Curing in Zinacantán: An Ethnomedical Analysis.* Stanford: Stanford University Press.

Farris, Nancy M. 1984. *Maya Society under Colonial Rule: The Collective Enterprise of Survival.* Princeton: Princeton University Press.

Fischer, Edward. 2002. *Cultural Logics and Global Economies: Maya Identity in Thought and Practice.* Austin: University of Texas Press.

Foster, George. 1944. "Nagualism in Mexico and Central America." *Acta Americana* 2: 85–103.

Foucault, Michel. 1984. *Las palabras y las cosas.* Barcelona: Planeta.

Frazer, James. 1980. *The Golden Bough: A Study in Magic and Religion.* London: Macmillan.

Gage, Thomas. 1987. *Viajes por la Nueva España y Guatemala*. Madrid: Historia 16.

Galinier, Jacques. 1990. *La mitad del mundo: Cuerpo y cosmos en los rituales otomíes*. Mexico City: Universidad Nacional Autónoma de México.

García de León, Antonio. 1985. *Resistencia y utopía*. 2 vols. Mexico City: Era.

Garza, Mercedes de la. 1990. *Sueño y alucinación en el mundo náhuatl y maya*. Mexico City: Universidad Nacional Autónoma de México.

Ginzburg, Carlo. 1989. "Indicios: Raíces de un paradigma de inferencias indiciales." In *Mitos, emblemas, indicios: Morfología e historia*, ed. Carlo Ginzburg, pp. 138–175. Barcelona: Gedisa.

———. 1991. *Historia nocturna*. Barcelona: Muchnik.

Gosner, Kevin. 1992. *Soldiers of the Virgin: The Moral Economy of a Colonial Maya Rebellion*. Tucson: University of Arizona Press.

Gossen, Gary H. 1974. *Chamulas in the World of the Sun: Time and Space in a Maya Oral Tradition*. Cambridge: Harvard University Press.

———. 1975. "Animal Souls and Human Destiny in Chamula." *Man* 10 (3): 448–461.

———. 1976. "Language as a Ritual Substance: Chamula View of Formal Language." In *Language in Religious Practice*, ed. William Samarin, pp. 40–60. Rowley, Mass.: Newbury House.

———. 1986. "The Chamula Festival of Games: Native Macroanalysis and Social Commentary in a Maya Carnival." In *Symbol and Meaning beyond the Closed Community: Essays in Mesoamerican Ideas*, ed. Gary H. Gossen, pp. 227–254. Albany, N.Y.: Institute for Mesoamerican Studies.

———. 1993. "Ser indio en una matríz euroafricana: Reflexiones personales sobre la identidad tzotzil Chamula." In *De palabra y obra en el Nuevo Mundo*, Vol. 3: *La formación del otro*, ed. Gary Gossen, Manuel Gutiérrez, Jorge Klor de Alva, and Miguel León-Portilla, pp. 37–74. Madrid: Siglo XXI.

———. 1994. "From Olmecs to Zapatistas: A Once and Future History of Souls." *American Anthropologist* 96: 553–570.

Guiteras, Calixta. 1946. *Informe de Cancúc*. Manuscripts on Middle American Cultural Anthropology 8. Chicago: University of Chicago Library.

———. 1947. "Clanes y sistema de parentesco de Cancúc (México)." *Acta Americana* 1–2: 155–178.

———. 1965. *Los peligros del alma: Visión del mundo de un tzotzil*. Mexico City: Fondo de Cultura Económica.

———. 1992. *Cancúc: Etnografía de un pueblo tzeltal de los Altos de Chiapas, 1944*. Mexico City: Instituto Chiapaneco de Cultura.

Gutiérrez Estévez, Manuel. 2002. "Interioridades." In *Según cuerpos: Ensayo de diccionario de uso etnográfico*, ed. Manuel Gutiérrez Estévez et al., pp. 27–45. Cáceres, Spain: Cycon.

Haehl, John H. 1980. "A Formal Analysis of Highland Maya Kinship: Tenejapa as a Special Case." Ph.D. diss., Dept. of Anthropology, University of California, Irvine.

Harman, Robert C. 1974. *Cambios médicos y sociales en una comunidad maya tzeltal*. Mexico City: Instituto Nacional Indigenista.

Haviland, John B. 1977. *Gossip, Reputation, and Knowledge in Zinacantán*. Chicago: University of Chicago Press.

———. 1989. "They Had a Very Great Many Photographs." In *Ethnographic Encounters in Southern Mesoamerica: Essays in Honor of Evon Zartman Vogt*, ed. Victoria Bricker and Gary H. Gossen, pp. 33–50. Albany, N.Y.: Institute for Mesoamerican Studies.

Héritier, Françoise. 1994. *Les deux soeurs et leur mère: Anthropologie de l'inceste*. Paris: Odile Jacob.

Hermitte, Esther. 1970. *Control social y poder sobrenatural en un pueblo maya contemporáneo*. Mexico City: Instituto Indigenista Interamericano.

Holland, William R. 1978. *Medicina maya en los Altos de Chiapas*. Mexico City: Instituto Nacional Indigenista.

Hopkins, Nicholas. 1988. "Classic Mayan Kinship Systems: Epigraphic and Ethnographic Evidence for Patrilineality." *Estudios de Cultura Maya* 17: 87–123.

Houston, Stephen, and David Stuart. 1989. *The Way Glyph: Evidence for Co-essences among the Classic Maya*. Washington, D.C.: Research Reports on Ancient Maya Writing 30, Center for Maya Research.

Hugh-Jones, Stephen. 1979. *The Palm and the Pleiades: Initiation and Cosmology in Northwestern Amazonia*. Cambridge: Cambridge University Press.

Hunn, Eugene S. 1977. *Tzeltal Folk Zoology: The Classification of Discontinuities in Nature*. New York: Academic Press.

Ichon, Alain. 1973. *La religión de los totonacas de la Sierra*. Mexico City: Instituto Nacional Indigenista.

Justeson, John, and Terrence Kaufman. 1993. "A Decipherment of Epi-Olmec Hieroglyphic Writing." *Science* 259: 1703–1711.

Klein, Herbert S. 1970. "Rebeliones de las comunidades campesinas: La república tzeltal de 1712." In *Ensayos de antropología en la zona central de Chiapas*, ed. Norman McQuown and Julian Pitt-Rivers, pp. 149–170. Mexico City: Instituto Nacional Indigenista.

Klor de Alva, Jorge. 1988. "Contar vidas: La autobiografía confesional y la reconstrucción del ser nahua." In *Biografías y confesiones de los indios de América*, ed. Manuel Gutiérrez Estévez. *Arbor* 515: 49–78.

Köhler, Ulrich. 1975. *Cambio cultural dirigido en los Altos de Chiapas*. Mexico City: Instituto Nacional Indigenista.

———. 1977. *Chonbilal ch'ulelal: Grundformen mesoamerikanischer Kosmologie und Religion in einem Gebetstext auf Maya-Tzotzil*. Geographica et Ethnographica Series 5. Wiesbaden: Acta Humboldtiana.

Laughlin, Robert M. 1966. "Oficio de tinieblas: Cómo el zinacanteco adivina sus sueños." In *Los zinacantecos: Un pueblo tzotzil de los Altos de Chiapas*, ed. Evon Z. Vogt, pp. 396–413. Mexico City: Instituto Nacional Indigenista.

———. 1975. *The Great Tzotzil Dictionary of San Lorenzo Zinacantán*. Smithsonian Contributions to Anthropology 19. Washington, D.C.: Smithsonian Institution.

———. 1988. *Of Wonders Wild and New: Dreams from Zinacantán*. Washington, D.C.: Smithsonian Institution Press.

Le Goff, Jacques. 1984. *The Birth of Purgatory*. Chicago: University of Chicago Press.

León-Portilla, Miguel. 1959. *La filosofía náhuatl estudiada en sus fuentes*. Mexico City: Universidad Nacional Autónoma de México.

———. 1978. "Testimonios nahuas sobre la conquista espiritual." *Estudios de Cultura Náhuatl* 11: 155–169.

Lévi-Strauss, Claude. 1969. *The Elementary Structures of Kinship*. Boston: Beacon Press.

Linn, Priscilla R. 1989. "Souls and Selves in Chamula: A Thought on Individuals, Fatalism, and Denial." In *Ethnographic Encounters in Southern Mesoamerica: Essays in Honor of Evon Zartman Vogt*, ed. Victoria Bricker and Gary H. Gossen, pp. 251–262. Albany, N.Y.: Institute for Mesoamerican Studies.

López Austin, Alfredo. 1973. *Hombre-Dios: Religión y política en el mundo náhuatl*. Mexico City: Universidad Nacional Autónoma de México.

———. 1980. *Cuerpo humano e ideología: Las concepciones de los antiguos nahuas*. 2 vols. Mexico City: Universidad Nacional Autónoma de México.

López García, Julián. 1994. "Restricciones culturales en la alimentación de mayas-chortís y ladinos del Oriente de Guatemala." Ph.D. diss., Universidad Complutense de Madrid.

Lupo, Alessandro. 1995. *La tierra nos escucha: La cosmología de los nahuas a través de las súplicas rituales*. Mexico City: Instituto Nacional Indigenista.

Martínez Peláez, Severo. n.d. *Motines de indios: La violencia colonial en Centroamérica y Chiapas*. Cuadernos de la Casa Presno 3. Puebla: Universidad Autónoma de Puebla.

Mason, Peter. 1990. *Deconstructing America*. London: Routledge.

———. 1993. "Escritura fragmentaria: Aproximaciones al Otro." In *De palabra y obra en el Nuevo Mundo*, Vol. 3: *La formación del Otro*, ed. Gary H. Gossen, Jorge Klor de Alva, Manuel Gutiérrez, and Miguel León-Portilla, pp. 395–430. Madrid: Siglo XXI.

Maurer, Eugenio. 1983. *Los tseltales: ¿Paganos o cristianos? Su religión: ¿Sincretismo o síntesis?* Mexico City: Centro de Estudios Educativos.

Metzger, Duane, and Gerald Williams. 1963. "Tenejapa Medicine I: The Curer." *Southwestern Journal of Anthropology* 19: 216–234.

Moliner, María. 1975. *Diccionario de uso del español*. Madrid: Gredos.

Montagu, Roberta. 1970. "Autoridad, control y sanción social en las fincas tzeltales." In *Ensayos de antropología en la zona central de Chiapas*, ed. Norman McQuown and Julian Pitt-Rivers, pp. 345–371. Mexico City: Instituto Nacional Indigenista.

Montaigne, Michel de. 1958. *The Complete Essays of Montaigne*. Trans. Donald M. Frame. Palo Alto, CA: Stanford University Press.

Nash, June. 1970. *In the Eyes of the Ancestors: Belief and Behavior in a Mayan Community*. Prospect Heights, Ill.: Waveland Press.

Núñez de la Vega, Francisco. 1988. *Constituciones diocesanas del obispado de Chiapas*, ed. María del Carmen León Cazares and Mario H. Ruz. Mexico City: Universidad Nacional Autónoma de México.

Ochiai, Kazuyasu. 1985. *Cuando los santos vienen marchando: Rituales públicos intercomunitarios tzotziles.* San Cristóbal de las Casas: Universidad Autónoma de Chiapas.

Pagden, Anthony. 1982. *The Fall of Natural Man.* Cambridge: Cambridge University Press.

Panofsky, Erwin. 1975. *Renacimiento y renacimientos en el arte occidental.* Madrid: Alianza Editorial.

Perezgrovas, Raúl. 1991. "La apropiación de la ovinicultura por los tzotziles de los Altos de Chiapas: Un pasaje de la historia, desde la perspectiva veterinaria." *Anuario del Centro de Estudios Indígenas* 3: 185–199.

Petrich, Perla. 1985. *La alimentación mochó: Acto y palabra.* San Cristóbal de Las Casas: Universidad Autónoma de Chiapas.

Pitarch, Pedro. 2000. "El mal del texto." In *Sustentos, aflicciones y postrimerías de los indios de América,* ed. Manuel Gutiérrez Estévez, pp. 137–157. Madrid: Casa de América.

———. 2004. "La conversión de los cuerpos: Singularidades de las identificaciones religiosas indígenas." *Liminar* 2 (2): 6–19.

———. 2008. "The Labyrinth of Translation: A Tzeltal Version of the Universal Declaration of Human Rights." In *Human Rights in the Maya Region: Global Politics, Cultural Contentions and Moral Engagements,* ed. Pedro Pitarch and Shannon Speed, pp. 91–123. Durham: Duke University Press.

———. 2009. "Los dos cuerpos mayas." In *Retóricas amerindias del cuerpo,* ed. Manuel Gutiérrez and Pedro Pitarch, pp. 98–133. Madrid: Universidad Complutense.

Pitt-Rivers, Julian. 1970. "Spiritual Power in Central America: The Naguals of Chiapas." In *Witchcraft Accusations and Confessions,* ed. Mary Douglas, pp. 183–206. A.S.A. Monographs 9. London: Tavistock.

———. 1971. "Thomas Gage parmi les Naguales." *L'Homme* 9: 64–85.

Platt, Tristan. 2001. "El feto agresivo: Parto, formación de la persona y mito-historia en los Andes." *Anuario de Estudios Hispanoamericanos* 58 (2): 152–194.

Pozas, Ricardo. 1977. *Chamula: Un pueblo indio en los altos de Chiapas.* Mexico City: Instituto Nacional Indigenista.

Remesal, Antonio de. 1988. *Historia general de las Indias Occidentales y particular de la gobernación de Chiapas y Guatemala.* 2 vols. Mexico City: Porrúa.

Ricoeur, Paul. 1979. "The Model of the Text: Meaningful Action Considered as a Text." In *Interpretive Social Science,* ed. Paul Rabinow and William M. Sullivan, pp. 73–101. Berkeley: University of California Press.

———. 1987. *Tiempo y narración.* Madrid: Editorial Cristiandad.

———. 1990. *Soi-même comme un autre.* Paris: Seuil.

Rus, Jan. 1995. "Local Adaptation to Global Change: The Reordering of Native Society in Highland Chiapas, 1974–1994." *European Review of Latin American and Caribbean Studies* 58: 71–89.

Ruz, Mario H. 1985. *Copanaguastla en un espejo: Un pueblo tzeltal en el virreinato.* San Cristóbal de Las Casas: Universidad Autónoma de Chiapas.

———. 1986. "Estudio preliminar." In *Vocabulario de lengua tzeldal según el orden de Copanabastla*, by Domingo de Ara, ed. Mario H. Ruz, pp. 15–45. Mexico City: Universidad Nacional Autónoma de México.

———. 1997. "Los rostros de la resistencia." In *Gestos cotidianos: Acercamientos etnológicos a los mayas de la época colonial*, ed. Mario H. Ruz, pp. 15–67. Campeche: Gobierno del Estado de Campeche.

Saignes, Thierry. 1993. "Borracheras andinas: ¿Por qué los indios ebrios hablan español?" In *Borrachera y memoria: La experiencia de los sagrados en los Andes*, ed. Thierry Saignes, pp. 43–73. La Paz: IFEA-Hisbol.

Sandstrom, Alan. 1991. *Corn Is Our Blood: Culture and Ethnic Identity in a Contemporary Aztec Indian Village.* Norman: University of Oklahoma Press.

Signorini, Italo, and Alessandro Lupo. 1989. *Los tres ejes de la vida: Almas, cuerpo, enfermedad entre los nahuas de la Sierra de Puebla.* Xalapa: Universidad Veracruzana.

Silver, Daniel B. 1966. "Enfermedad y curación en Zinacantán: Esquema provisional." In *Los zinacantecos: Un pueblo tzotzil en los Altos de Chiapas*, ed. Evon Z. Vogt, pp. 455–473. Mexico City: Instituto Nacional Indigenista.

Siverts, Henning. 1965. "The 'cacique' of K'ankujk'." *Estudios de Cultura Maya* 5: 339–360.

———. 1969. *Oxchuc: Una tribu maya de México.* Mexico City: Instituto Indigenista Interamericano.

Slocum, Mariana, and Florencia Gerdel. 1981. *Vocabulario tzeltal de Bachajón.* Serie de Vocabularios Indígenas 13. Mexico City: Instituto Lingüístico de Verano.

Stross, Brian. 1973. "El contexto sociocultural en la adquisición de la lengua tzeltal." *Estudios de Cultura Maya* 9: 257–301.

———. 1974. "Speaking of Speaking: Tenejapa Tzeltal Metalinguistics." In *Explorations in the Ethnographics of Speaking*, ed. Richard Bauman and Joel Sherzer, pp. 213–239. Cambridge: Cambridge University Press.

Taussig, Michael. 1987. *Shamanism, Colonialism and the Wild Man: A Study in Terror and Healing.* Chicago: University of Chicago Press.

———. 1993. *Mimesis and Alterity: A Particular History of the Senses.* New York: Routledge.

Tedlock, Barbara. 1981. "Quiché Maya Dream Interpretation." *Ethos* 4: 48–72.

———. 1982. *Time and the Highland Maya.* Albuquerque: University of New Mexico Press.

Villa Rojas, Alfonso. 1947. "Kinship and Nagualism in a Tzeltal Community, Southeastern Mexico." *American Anthropologist* 49: 578–587.

———. 1963. "El nagualismo como recurso de control social entre los grupos mayances de Chiapas, México." *Estudios de Cultura Maya* 3: 243–260.

Viqueira, Juan Pedro. 1997. "¿Qué había detrás del petate de la ermita de Cancúc?" In *Indios rebeldes e idólatras: Dos ensayos históricos sobre la rebelión india de Cancúc, Chiapas, acaecida en el año 1712*, ed. Juan Pedro Viqueira, pp. 95–165. Mexico City: CIESAS.

Viveiros de Castro, Eduardo. 1998. "Cosmological Deixis and Amerindian Perspectivism." *Journal of the Royal Anthropological Institute* 4: 469–488.

———. 2002a. *A inconstância da alma selvagem.* São Paulo: Cosac & Naify.

————. 2002b. "Perspectivismo e multinaturalismo na América indígena." In *A inconstância da alma selvagem*, ed. Eduardo Viveiros de Castro, pp. 345–400. São Paulo: Cosac & Naify.

Vogt, Evon Z. 1969. *Zinacantán: A Maya Community in the Highlands of Chiapas*. Cambridge: Harvard University Press.

————. 1970. "Human Souls and Animal Spirits in Zinacantán." In *Échanges et communications: Mèlanges offerts á Claude Lévi-Strauss á l'occasion de son 60ème anniversaire*, ed. Pierre Maranda and Jean Pouillon, pp. 1148–1167. The Hague: Mouton.

————. 1976. *Tortillas for the Gods: A Symbolic Analysis of Zinacanteco Rituals*. Cambridge: Harvard University Press.

Vos, Jan de. 1980. *La Paz de Dios y del Rey: La conquista de la selva lacandona por los españoles*. Mexico City: FONAPAS.

Wagner, Roy. 1978. *Lethal Speech: Daribi Myth as Symbolic Obviation*. Ithaca, N.Y.: Cornell University Press.

————. 1981. *The Invention of Culture*. Chicago: University of Chicago Press.

————. 2001. *An Anthropology of the Subject*. Berkeley: University of California Press.

Wasserstrom, Robert. 1983. *Class and Society in Central Chiapas*. Berkeley: University of California Press.

Watanabe, John. 1989. "Elusive Essences: Souls and Social Identity in Two Highland Communities." In *Ethnographic Encounters in Southern Mesoamerica: Essays in Honor of Evon Zartman Vogt*, ed. Victoria Bricker and Gary H. Gossen, pp. 263–274. Albany, N.Y.: Institute for Mesoamerican Studies.

————. 1992. *Maya Saints and Souls in a Changing World*. Austin: University of Texas Press.

White, Hayden. 1987. *The Content of the Form: Narrative Discourse and Historical Representation*. Baltimore: Johns Hopkins University Press.

Williams García, Roberto. 1963. *Los tepehuas*. Xalapa: Universidad Veracruzana.

Wittgenstein, Ludwig. 1985. *Comentarios sobre La Rama Dorada*. Ed. Rush Rhees. Mexico City: Universidad Nacional Autónoma de México.

Ximénez, Francisco. 1931. *Historia de la Provincia de San Vicente de Chiapas y Guatemala de la Orden de Predicadores*. 6 vols. Guatemala City: Biblioteca "Goathemala" de la Sociedad de Geografía e Historia.

Index

Acosta, José de, 141
agriculture: coffee cultivation, 16–17, 19, 50, 66, 120–121, 171; cycle of, 10; and dreams, 19, 65; and economy of Cancuc, 16–17; and *lab*, 45, 52
ajawetik. *See* Mountain Lords (*ajawetik*)
ak'chamel (illness-giver): appearance of, 46–47, 48, 49, 50; evolution of, 98–99; execution of, 225n12; historical souls as, 98; internal *lab* as, 54; signs of, 47–48, 56; and words as vehicle of illness, 49, 72, 98–99, 171, 193–194, 195, 196. See also *pále*
alterity: correlation with illness, 9; effects of, 96–97; maintaining sameness through, 208; souls representing, 3, 224n5; and writing, 113
Alvarado, Pedro de, 225–226n2
Amerindians: culture of, 6, 8, 90, 168, 207, 208; and innate/artificial relationship, 3–4, 5; multinaturalist cosmology of, 4. *See also* Chol-speaking people; Tzeltal people; Tzotzil-speaking people
anejme'jtatik (our mother-father angels), 53–54
animals: as *lab*, 40–43, 135, 219n10; and Mountain Lords, 219n10, 226n4

ants, as *lab*, 40, 87–88
Ara, Domingo de, 63, 67–69, 222n8, 223n2

Bakhtin, Mikhail, 198
baptism: baptismal records, 112, 118, 217n3; cooking of Bird of the Heart as simulacrum of, 47, 99, 154, 168; and description of *pále*, 219n12; and evangelism, 106, 145; and leaders of Indian Rebellion of 1712, 107; and pastors' claims of *lab* expelled during, 153; Tetón on, 226n3
Barthes, Roland, 142, 221–222n6
Basso, Keith, 146
bats'il winik (genuine people), 204
Becquelin-Monod, Aurore, 194
Berlin, Brent, 219n14
Bird of the Heart (*mutil o'tan*): Castilian character of, 99; and death, 22, 35, 213, 216n1; and identity, 60; as indispensable life spirit, 22–23; and *lab*, 34–35, 37, 213, 214; and liturgical chants, 7, 99, 123, 168; madcap character of, 89; and *pále*, 22–23, 47–48, 168; recovery of, 23–24, 35, 193; and religious beliefs, 153, 154; types of birds as, 99–100, 216n1
birds, as *lab*, 40, 51, 86. *See also* Bird of the Heart (*mutil o'tan*)
bishop *lab*, 102

domestic sphere (*continued*)
protection ceremonies for, 69–70,
74–75, 136, 154; public domain
contrasted with, 103–105, 139–
140, 142, 208, 227n7; secrecy of,
152; shamanic rituals in, 153, 168
Dominicans: collective identity imposed on Indians, 207; and converts' objection to wine, 152; enforced departure from Cancuc,
112; founding of Cancuc, 16, 112;
and Indian Rebellion of 1712, 107–
108; and indigenous subordination
to colonial power, 103–107, 116; liturgical chants of, 7; narratives of,
132; and public rituals, 141, 142,
145, 146; and shamanic ritual, 194;
strict doctrines of, 145, 146; sugar
mills owned by, 108, 114; vestments of, 102
dreams and dream interpretation: and
ch'iibal, 81, 83–84, 85; and fiestas,
83, 84; and genuine *ch'ulel*, 36–37,
65, 67; and knowledge of souls, 8;
lab associated with dreams, 36, 40,
47, 49, 67; and P'in Xun, 36–37,
66–67, 172; and *principales*, 19, 46;
signs in dreams, 65–67, 73
drunkenness: and Castilian stereotype, 93; and *ch'iibal*, 83–85; and
emotion, 92; and European behavior, 8; and inner luminescence, 167; and *lab*, 41; and limping dance, 94; and loss of body
consciousness, 8, 36, 91–97; and
references to soul principles, 76;
and religion, 152; in San Cristóbal
de Las Casas, 224n9; and showing the heart, 94–95, 160, 203,
209; and Spanish language, 92–93,
123, 225n11; and Stewards of the
Saints, 160; studies of, 224–225n10

eating customs, 88, 100–101, 204,
224n7
Eber, Christine, 224–225n10
education, 116, 122

emotion: concealment of, 90; and
drunkenness, 92; and genuine
ch'ulel, 24, 62, 91; and heart, 62,
89–90
Europeans: and body/soul relationship, 3; concept of identity, 97,
206, 207; illness as consequence of
European past, 7, 99, 125; and *lab*,
86; multiculturalist cosmology of,
4; as other, 6, 97; and power relations, 6–7, 8, 9; and self, 5–8
evangelical music and songs, as *lab*,
49–50, 118–120, 123
evangelical religion, 151–154, 209
Extul, Rominko, 39, 50, 218n5

feline family, as *lab*, 40, 47, 51, 52, 63
fetus: aggressive fetus, 216n4; and
fold, 2–3, 164, 167, 202, 203
fiestas: and Cancuc's public rituals,
9, 10, 11, 20, 88, 135–137, 138; and
ch'iibal, 83–88, 203; and evangelical musicians, 119–120; and reli-
gious-political office holders, 88,
224n7; and saints, 84, 135, 136, 137
Fischer, Edward, 215–216n2
fold and folding: and fetus, 2–3, 164,
167, 202, 203; and heart, 2, 78; and
human beings, 163; internalization
of sacred state, 6–7; and "other"
world, 3, 122, 202, 203; permitting
individual life, 210; and saints, 9,
166, 196
Foucault, Michel, 68–69, 123
Frazer, James, 88

Gage, Thomas, 102
García, Feliciano, 109–111
García, Juan, 164
genuine *ch'ulel* (*bats'il ch'ulel*): absence
of, 32–33; in *ch'iibal*, 1, 24–32, 36,
59, 79, 83, 203, 204, 218n8, 225n12;
and crosses, 149; and death, 30,
38–39, 214; and dream interpretation, 36–37, 65, 67; and emotion,
24, 62, 91; and Europeanness, 97;
and form of human body, 1, 24, 25;

in heart, 1, 24, 27, 30, 32–35, 36, 37, 62, 64, 78, 197, 203, 213; kidnapping of, 34, 87, 149, 171, 173, 214; and *lab*, 59; and memory, 24, 36, 91; and Mountain Lords, 34, 35, 214; plane of, 96; recovery of, 33, 172, 173, 174–175; and religious beliefs, 153, 154; and shadows, 37, 213; and sleep, 32, 36, 37, 93, 197, 203, 213, 225n12

gestures: limitations on, 90, 204; signs in, 60–62

Ginzburg, Carlo, 222n7, 225n13

goats: Christian devil compared with, 101; as *lab*, 49, 86, 100

Gossen, Gary, 2, 196, 220n18

gossip: and beliefs, 222n9; and domestic sphere, 75–76; hidden agenda of, 127; and knowledge of souls, 8; and meaning, 77; and public rituals, 142

grackles, 100

Great Mother, and *ch'iibal*, 28–29, 80

greetings, appropriateness of, 17, 140, 218n5

Greimas, Algirdas Julius, 222n6

Guatemala, 128, 132–133, 145, 156, 164, 225–226n2

Guiteras, Calixta, 21, 95–96, 116, 126, 216n1, 217n3, 219n12

Haviland, John, 222n9, 223n4

head: and body, 96; heart distinguished from, 89–91, 153; as Indian, 90; and reasoning, 89; and sensory perception, 89

healing chants: addressed to *me'tiktatik*, 174–175; addressed to words, 193–194, 195; and *ch'iibal*, 25–27; and death of a child, 29; European objects and qualities in, 200, 206; form of, 197–198; and historical experience, 200; and knowledge of souls, 8, 9; and *lab* with Castilian features, 87; and movement of illness, 194–195; and offerings, 175; polyphony of, 198–

199; *poxil*-genre songs, 169, 170, 171, 172, 176, 196–197. *See also* prayers

heart: Castilian character of, 90, 124, 208, 211; and Catholic priests, 105–106; and character, 89; and drinking liquor, 153; and emotions, 62, 89–90; European qualities of, 6, 8; genuine *ch'ulel* in, 1, 24, 27, 30, 32–35, 36, 37, 62, 64, 78, 203, 213; head distinguished from, 89–91, 153; heterogeneity of, 205; historical distinctions deposited in, 102; identity of, 64; *lab* in, 1, 40, 54–56, 63, 64, 214; legacy within, 91; as mirror of past, 98; past contained in, 6–7, 206, 210; public domain compared to, 139, 140, 156; and saints, 159, 166; showing of, 75, 94–95, 160, 203, 209; souls within, 1, 2, 6, 9, 22, 60, 203, 205; symbols of domination in, 123. *See also* Bird of the Heart (*mutil o'tan*)

Héritier, François, 86

Hermitte, Esther, 70, 217–218n4

He state, and Amazonian people, 2

historical memory: narrative of, 126–135, 207; and shamanic rituals, 7, 9

history: narrative history of Tzeltal people, 126–135, 143, 144, 145, 206; soul history, 121–125; and subjectivization of the past, 7–8

Holland, William, 119, 220n19

Holy Spirit, pigeon and dove representing, 101

Houston, Stephen, 224n6

Hugh-Jones, Stephen, 2

identity: acquisition of, 90; and body, 5, 60–62, 208; ethnographic interpretation of, 207; European concept of, 97, 206, 207; illusion of, 211; of *lab*, 63, 64–65, 73, 91, 204, 214; personal identity in body, 5, 60–62, 208; poles of personal and ethnic identification, 210;

identity (*continued*)
and souls, 5, 60–61, 64, 199–200, 206–207

idolatry, 106, 158–159

illness: and Bird of the Heart, 23, 34; and *ch'iibal*, 30, 31, 32, 84–85; as consequence of European past, 7, 99, 125; correlation with alterity, 9; defined as Castilian, 200; and dreams, 65; and evangelical religion, 153; and exploration of ethnic difference, 201; and *k'exlal*, 62; and *lab*, 42, 46–50, 54, 56, 98; movement of, 194–195, 197; obsession with, 168–169, 201; and public rituals, 142; "word of God" as protection against, 153–154; words as vehicle of, 49, 72, 98, 122, 171, 193–194, 195, 196, 198. *See also ak'chamel* (illness-giver)

incestuous relationships, 85–86

Indian Rebellion of 1712: and changes in priests' attitudes, 108–109; Indian leaders in role of Europeans, 107, 160; and metal tools, 101; narrative of, 128, 132–133, 144–145, 164; and religious practices, 226n7; suppression of, 108, 146, 156, 160; "witches" carried on shoulders during, 161

inebriation. *See* drunkenness

Instituto Nacional Indigenista (INI), 20, 113, 115–116, 124

jamalal state: *ch'ul* state compared to, 78, 202–203; as everyday plane of existence, 1–2, 33; and genuine *ch'ulel*, 32–35

Jesuit *lab*, 47, 55, 103

Jesuits, 7, 102–103, 141

Jesus Christ, 228n9

jtaleltik, as group of souls, 4, 207

jun te kuil-mamil, 17–18

K'aal, Alonso: background of, 14; and Bird of the Heart, 23–24; and *ch'iibal*, 31; on fiestas, 141; and *lab*,

48–49; on souls, 13, 14, 15; on vertically ordered space, 147

K'aal, Sebastian, 90, 162

Kaqchikel people, 215–216n2

kaxlan ech' (orchids of Castile), 45, 88–89

kaxlanetik: in dreams, 66; as *lab*, 49, 86; as non-Indian, 6; and public rituals, 11. *See also* Castilian scribes

Kaxtil, Marian, 154

k'exlal, 62

kinship: and Cancuc, 17–18; and *ch'iibal*, 24–25, 28, 29–31, 86, 217n3, 218n7; and domestic sphere, 75; and *lab*, 44, 56–57, 58

Klor de Alva, Jorge, 229n13

Köhler, Ulrich, 194

k'op, meaning of, 85

K'oy, Antonio, 153

kun, as numerical classifier for *lab*, 51–52

kuxlejal prayers, and *lab*, 42

kuyuyil, 63, 73

lab: animals as, 40–43, 135, 219n10; ants as, 40, 87–88; birds as, 40, 51, 86; Castilian features in, 86–89, 97; and complete human beings, 53–54, 133, 155, 225n12; and crosses, 149; dreams associated with, 36, 40, 47, 49, 67; euphemisms for, 51; evangelical music and songs as, 49–50, 118–120, 123; feline family as, 40, 47, 51, 52, 63; and function of person, 70; and genuine *ch'ulel*, 59; hidden plane of, 96; identity of, 63, 64–65, 73, 91, 204, 214; internal, 54–56, 197, 214, 220n16; kidnapping Bird of the Heart, 34–35, 37, 213, 214; kidnapping of *ch'ulel*, 34, 87, 149, 214; and lack of restraint, 88; and metallic instruments, 43, 86, 87, 101, 162; meteor *lab*, 44–46, 47, 52, 87; nonhuman form of, 1; as personal power, 50–53, 55, 214, 220n15; and